BLACK HAMMER

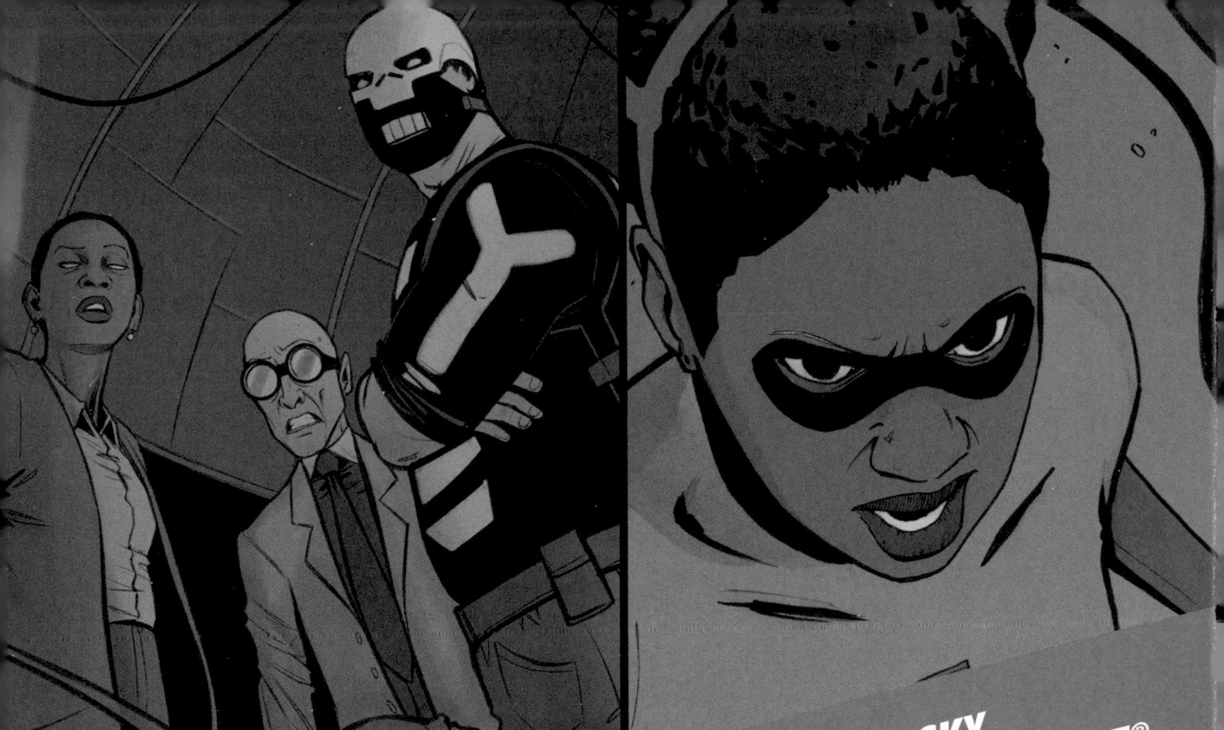

WRITER **JEFF LEMIRE** ARTIST **CAITLIN YARSKY**

COLORIST **DAVE STEWART** LETTERER **NATE PIEKOS OF BLAMBOT®**

CHAPTER BREAKS BY CAITLIN YARSKY

CHAPTER DESIGN PAGES BY AARON CONLEY, ANDREA MUTTI, STEFANO SIMEONE, RAÚL ALLEN

BLACK HAMMER CREATED BY JEFF LEMIRE AND DEAN ORMSTON

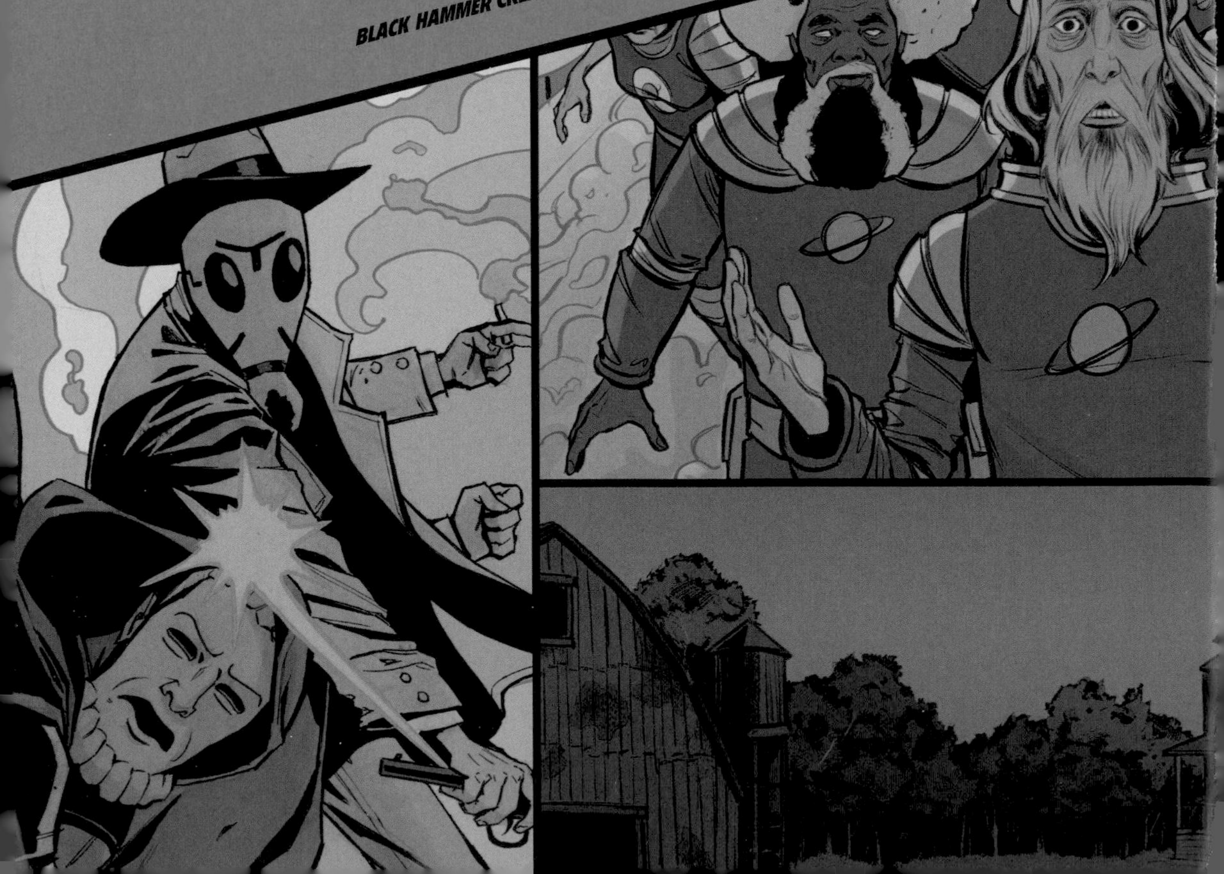

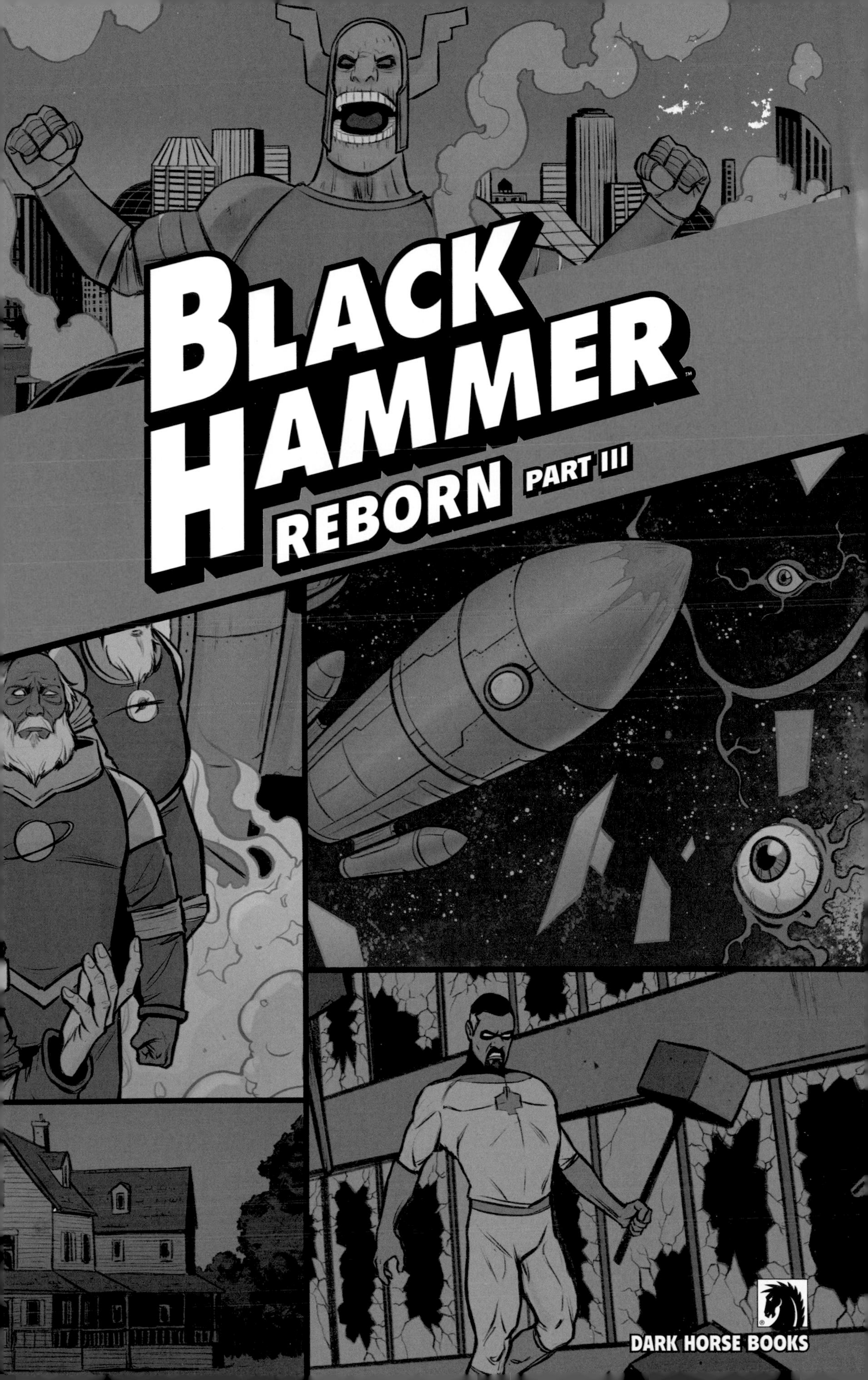
BLACK HAMMER™
REBORN PART III
DARK HORSE BOOKS

PRESIDENT & PUBLISHER
MIKE RICHARDSON

EDITOR
DANIEL CHABON

ASSISTANT EDITORS
CHUCK HOWITT-LEASE
AND MISHA GEHR

DESIGNER
ETHAN KIMBERLING

DIGITAL ART TECHNICIAN
JOSIE CHRISTENSEN

BLACK HAMMER VOLUME 7: REBORN PART III

Collects issues #9–#12 of the Dark Horse Comics series *Black Hammer Reborn.*

Published by
Dark Horse Books
A division of Dark Horse Comics LLC
10956 SE Main Street
Milwaukie, OR 97222

DarkHorse.com

To find a comics shop in your area, visit comicshoplocator.com

First edition: September 2022
Ebook ISBN   978-1-50672-016-6
Trade Paperback ISBN 978-1-50672-015-9

10 9 8 7 6 5 4 3 2 1
Printed in China

NEIL HANKERSON Executive Vice President TOM WEDDLE Chief Financial Officer DALE LAFOUNTAIN Chief Information Officer TIM WIESCH Vice President of Licensing MATT PARKINSON Vice President of Marketing VANESSA TODD-HOLMES Vice President of Production and Scheduling MARK BERNARDI Vice President of Book Trade and Digital Sales RANDY LAHRMAN Vice President of Product Development KEN LIZZI General Counsel DAVE MARSHALL Editor in Chief DAVEY ESTRADA Editorial Director CHRIS WARNER Senior Books Editor CARY GRAZZINI Director of Specialty Projects LIA RIBACCHI Art Director MATT DRYER Director of Digital Art and Prepress MICHAEL GOMBOS Senior Director of Licensed Publications KARI YADRO Director of Custom Programs KARI TORSON Director of International Licensing

Library of Congress Cataloging-in-Publication Data

Names: Lemire, Jeff, writer. | Yarsky, Caitlin, artist. | Stewart, Dave,
  colourist. | Piekos, Nate, letterer.
Title: Reborn. Part III / writer, Jeff Lemire ; artist, Caitlin Yarsky ;
  colorist, Dave Stewart ; letterer, Nate Piekos of Blambot.
Description: First edition. | Milwaukie, OR : Dark Horse Books, 2022. |
  Series: Black hammer ; vol 7 | "Black Hammer Created by Jeff Lemire and
  Dean Ormston" | Summary: "Things have gotten crazy in Black Hammer!
  First a parallel Spiral City collided with the actual one spawning a
  multiverse nightmare of heroes and villains from both worlds going to
  war, and now Lucy Weber picks back up the mantle of Black Hammer and
  teams up with Skulldigger for answers on how to end the madness.
  Collects issues #9-#12 of Black Hammer: Reborn. "Jeff Lemire's story is
  leading to something major as Black Hammer: Reborn nears the final issue
  [...] I am really eager to see where this all is leading."-DC Comic
  News "Black Hammer: Reborn #9 is the biggest proof of the idea this
  series will always have your back."-ComicBook.com"-- Provided by
  publisher.
Identifiers: LCCN 2022015748 (print) | LCCN 2022015749 (ebook) | ISBN
  9781506720159 (trade paperback) | ISBN 9781506720166 (ebook)
Subjects: LCGFT: Paranormal comics. | Superhero comics. | Fantasy comics. |
  Graphic novels.
Classification: LCC PN6728.B51926 L454 2022 (print) | LCC PN6728.B51926
  (ebook) | DDC 741.5/973--dc23/eng/20220503
LC record available at https://lccn.loc.gov/2022015748
LC ebook record available at https://lccn.loc.gov/2022015749

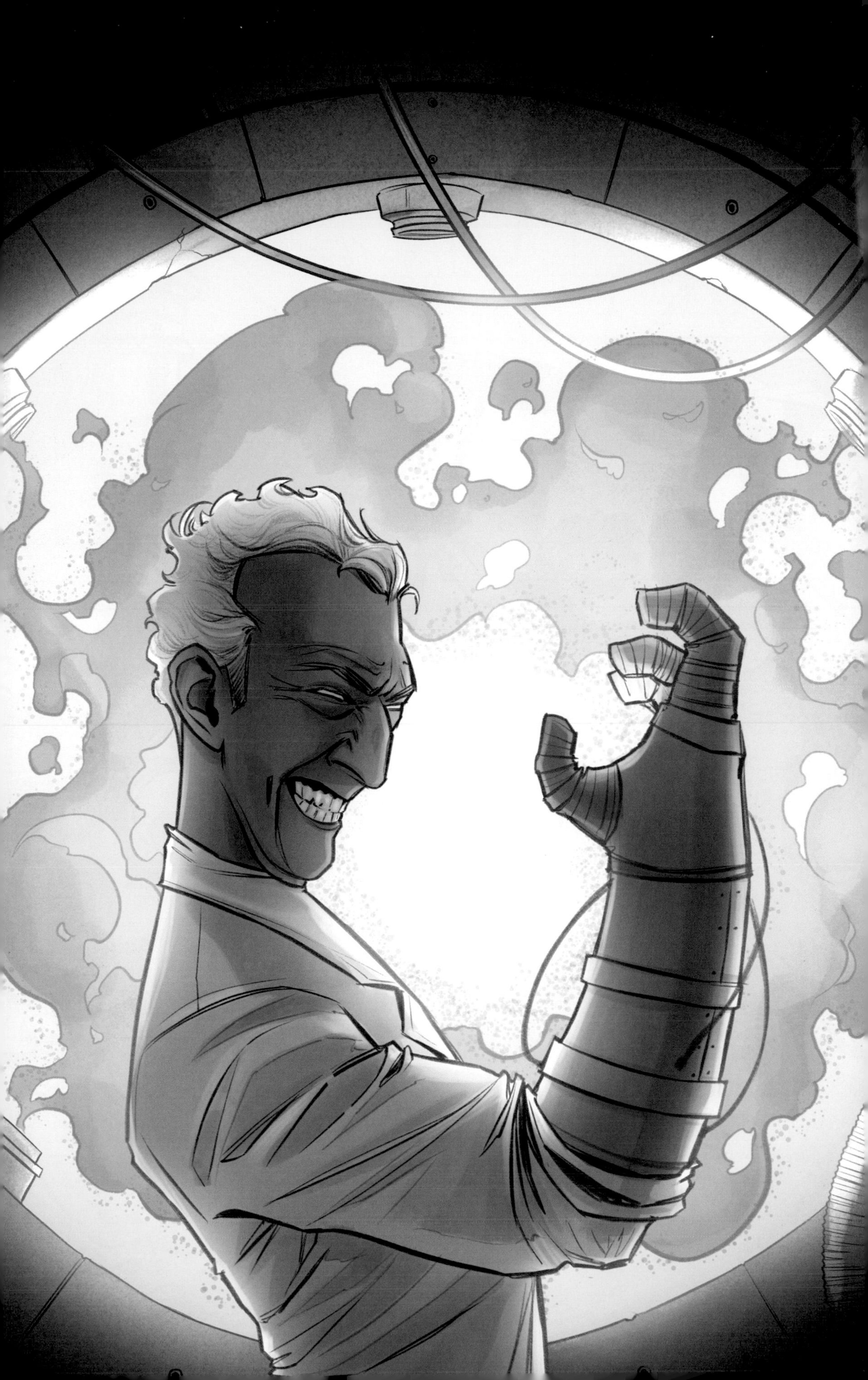

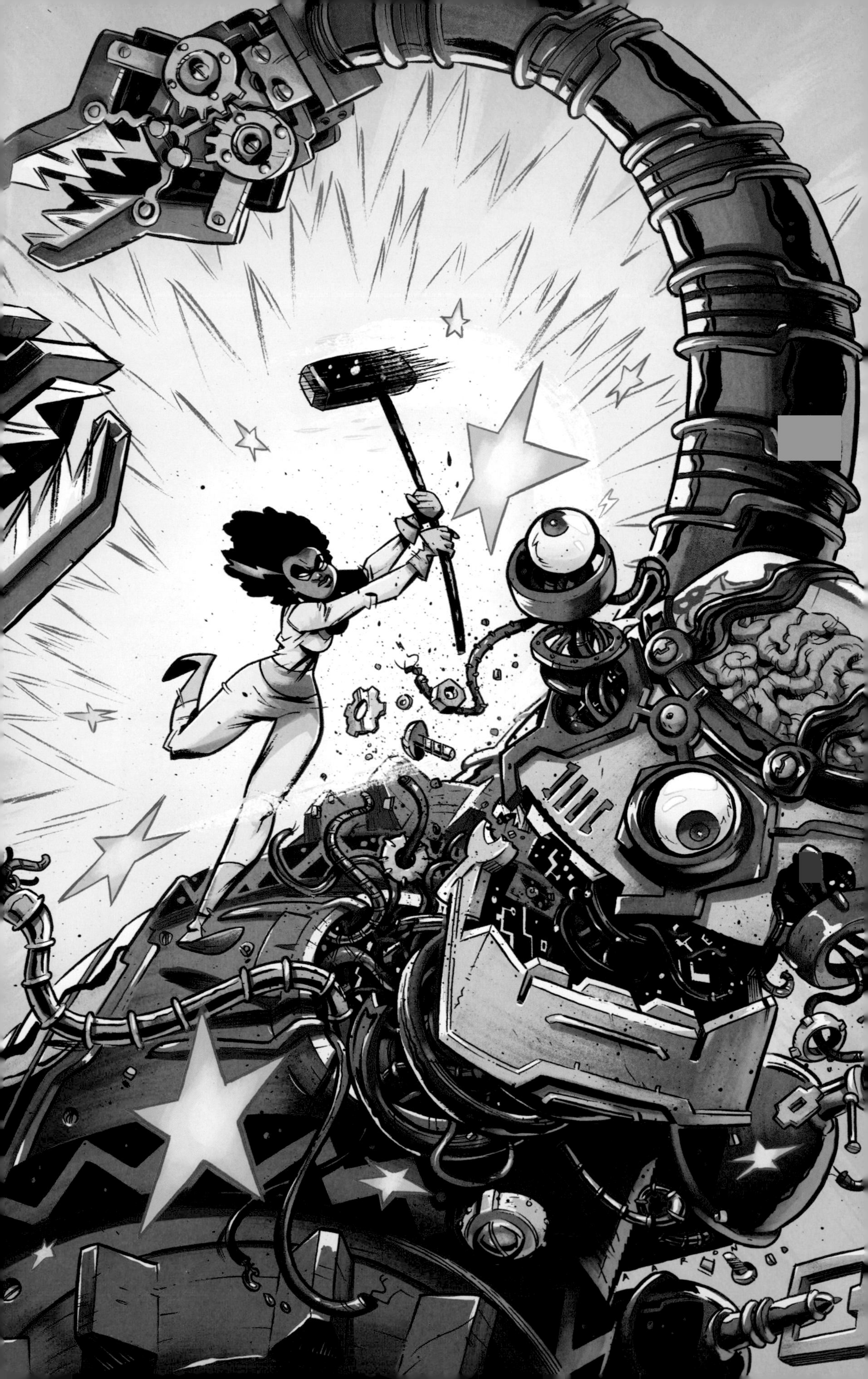

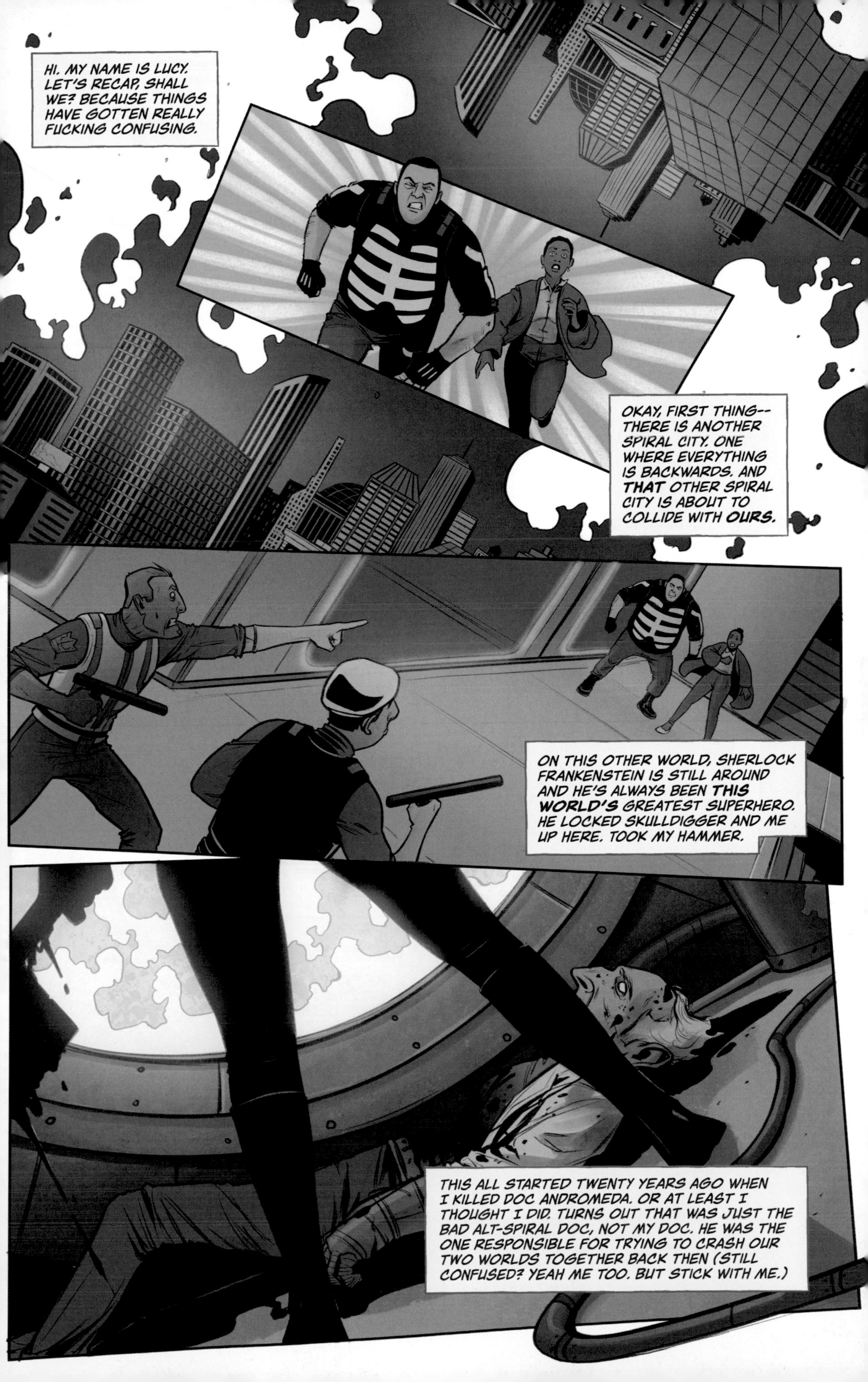
HI. MY NAME IS LUCY. LET'S RECAP, SHALL WE? BECAUSE THINGS HAVE GOTTEN REALLY FUCKING CONFUSING.
OKAY, FIRST THING-- THERE IS ANOTHER SPIRAL CITY. ONE WHERE EVERYTHING IS BACKWARDS. AND THAT OTHER SPIRAL CITY IS ABOUT TO COLLIDE WITH OURS.
ON THIS OTHER WORLD, SHERLOCK FRANKENSTEIN IS STILL AROUND AND HE'S ALWAYS BEEN THIS WORLD'S GREATEST SUPERHERO. HE LOCKED SKULLDIGGER AND ME UP HERE. TOOK MY HAMMER.
THIS ALL STARTED TWENTY YEARS AGO WHEN I KILLED DOC ANDROMEDA. OR AT LEAST I THOUGHT I DID. TURNS OUT THAT WAS JUST THE BAD ALT-SPIRAL DOC, NOT MY DOC. HE WAS THE ONE RESPONSIBLE FOR TRYING TO CRASH OUR TWO WORLDS TOGETHER BACK THEN (STILL CONFUSED? YEAH ME TOO. BUT STICK WITH ME.)

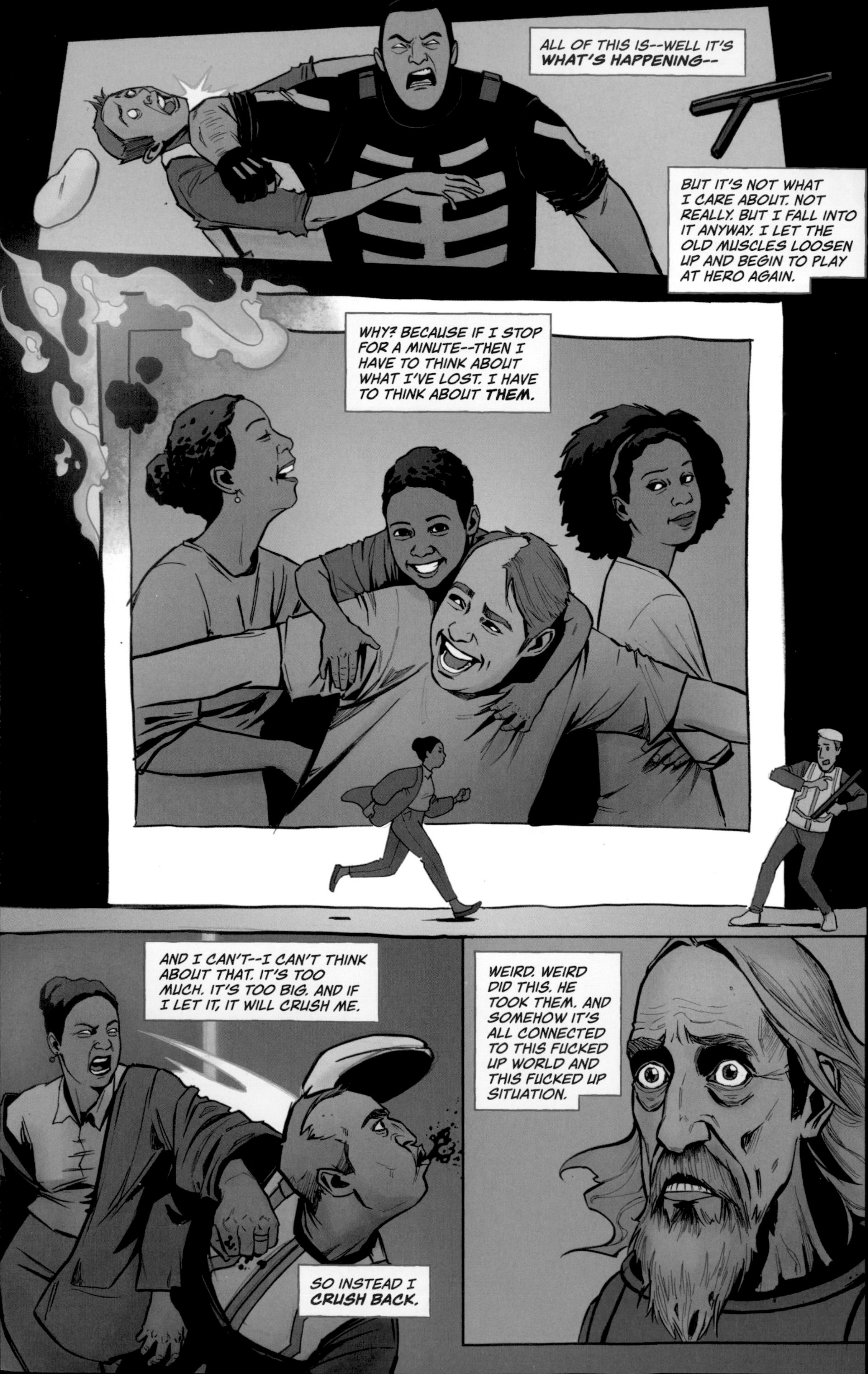
ALL OF THIS IS--WELL IT'S WHAT'S HAPPENING--
BUT IT'S NOT WHAT I CARE ABOUT. NOT REALLY. BUT I FALL INTO IT ANYWAY. I LET THE OLD MUSCLES LOOSEN UP AND BEGIN TO PLAY AT HERO AGAIN.
WHY? BECAUSE IF I STOP FOR A MINUTE--THEN I HAVE TO THINK ABOUT WHAT I'VE LOST. I HAVE TO THINK ABOUT THEM.
AND I CAN'T--I CAN'T THINK ABOUT THAT. IT'S TOO MUCH. IT'S TOO BIG. AND IF I LET IT, IT WILL CRUSH ME.
SO INSTEAD I CRUSH BACK.
WEIRD. WEIRD DID THIS. HE TOOK THEM. AND SOMEHOW IT'S ALL CONNECTED TO THIS FUCKED UP WORLD AND THIS FUCKED UP SITUATION.

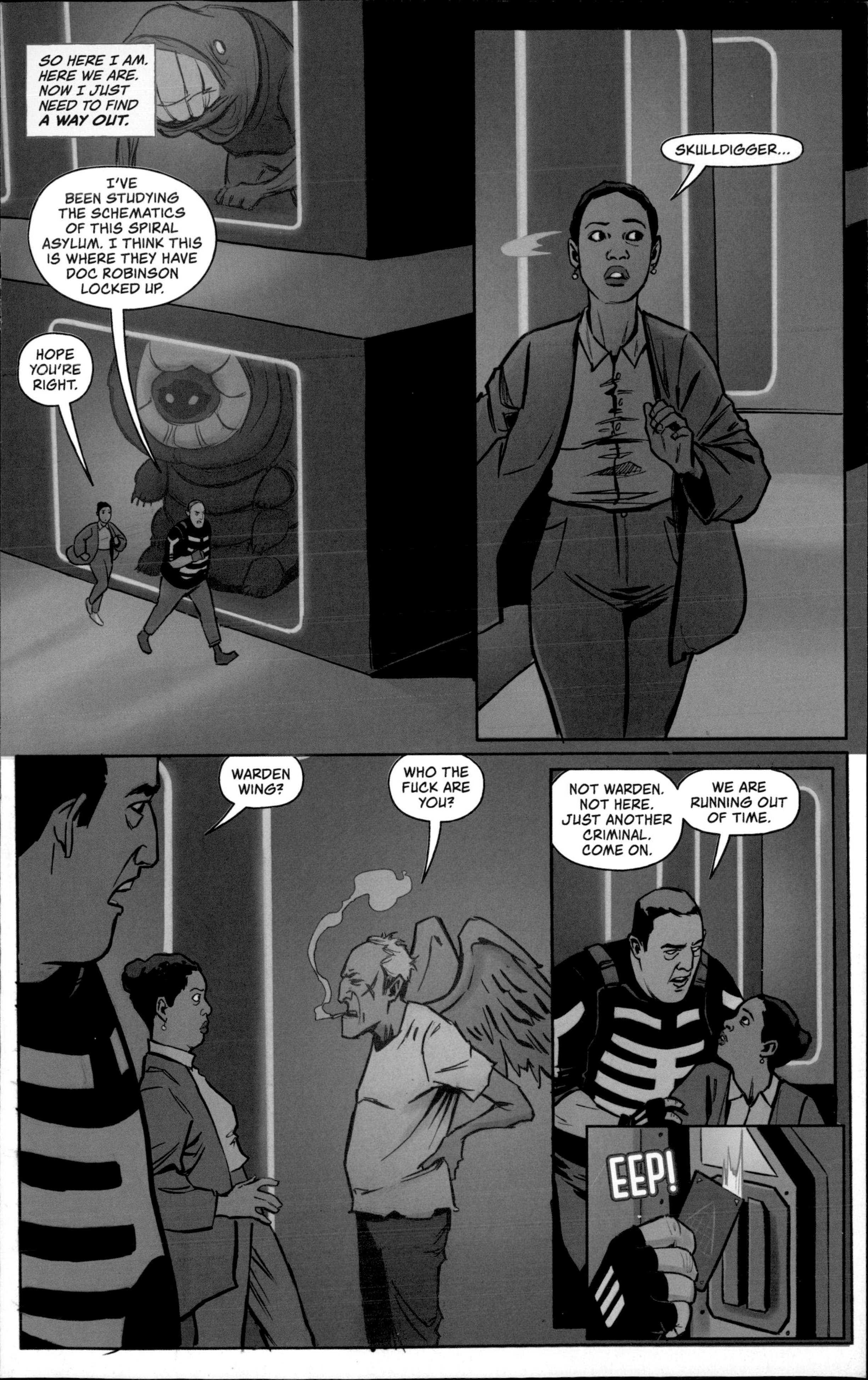
SO HERE I AM. HERE WE ARE. NOW I JUST NEED TO FIND **A WAY OUT.**
I'VE BEEN STUDYING THE SCHEMATICS OF THIS SPIRAL ASYLUM. I THINK THIS IS WHERE THEY HAVE DOC ROBINSON LOCKED UP.
HOPE YOU'RE RIGHT.
SKULLDIGGER...
WARDEN WING?
WHO THE FUCK ARE YOU?
NOT WARDEN. NOT HERE. JUST ANOTHER CRIMINAL. COME ON.
WE ARE RUNNING OUT OF TIME.
EEP!

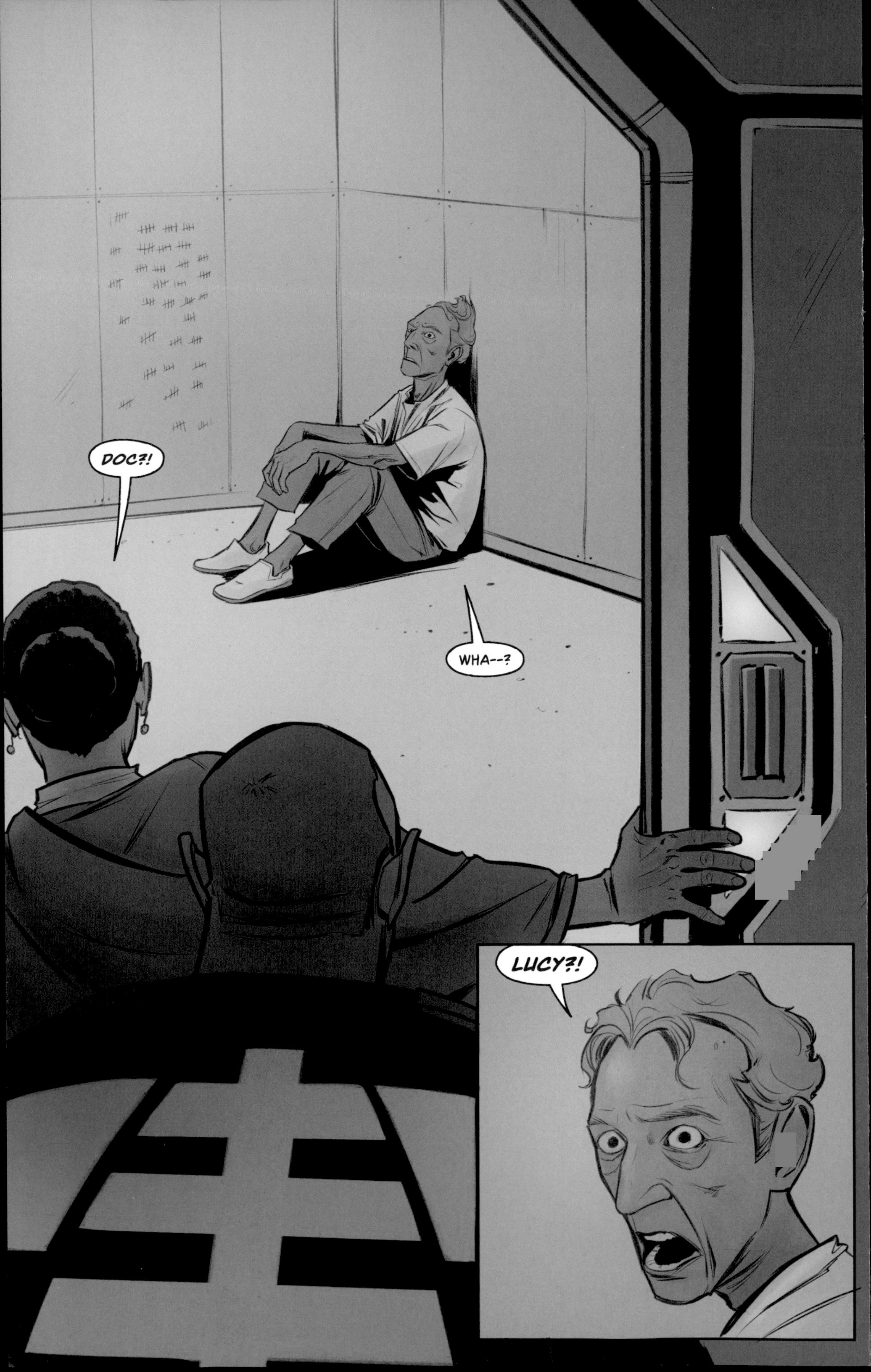
DOC?!
WHA--?
LUCY?!

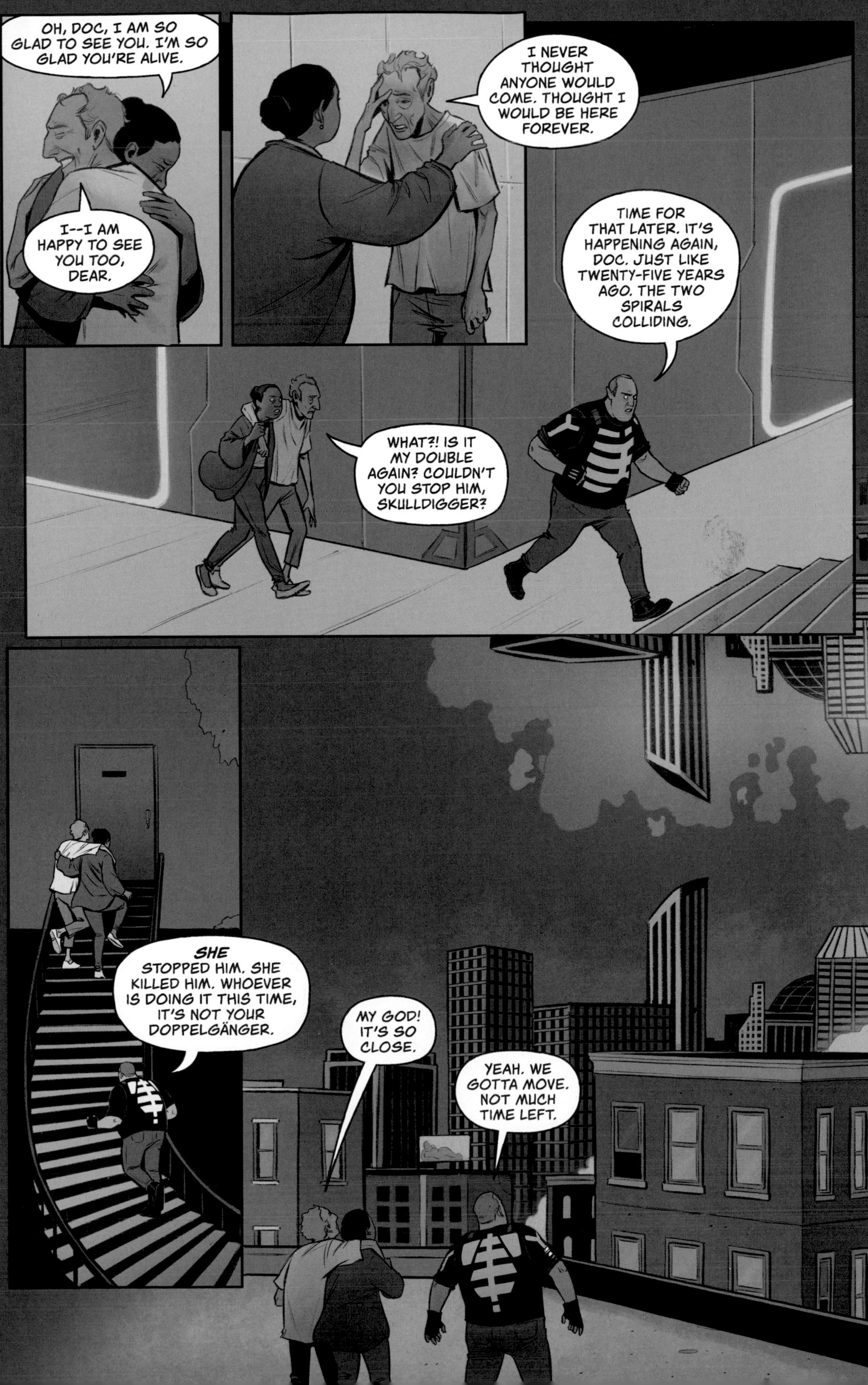
OH, DOC, I AM SO GLAD TO SEE YOU. I'M SO GLAD YOU'RE ALIVE.
I--I AM HAPPY TO SEE YOU TOO, DEAR.
I NEVER THOUGHT ANYONE WOULD COME. THOUGHT I WOULD BE HERE FOREVER.
TIME FOR THAT LATER. IT'S HAPPENING AGAIN, DOC. JUST LIKE TWENTY-FIVE YEARS AGO. THE TWO SPIRALS COLLIDING.
WHAT?! IS IT MY DOUBLE AGAIN? COULDN'T YOU STOP HIM, SKULLDIGGER?
SHE STOPPED HIM. SHE KILLED HIM. WHOEVER IS DOING IT THIS TIME, IT'S NOT YOUR DOPPELGÄNGER.
MY GOD! IT'S SO CLOSE.
YEAH. WE GOTTA MOVE. NOT MUCH TIME LEFT.

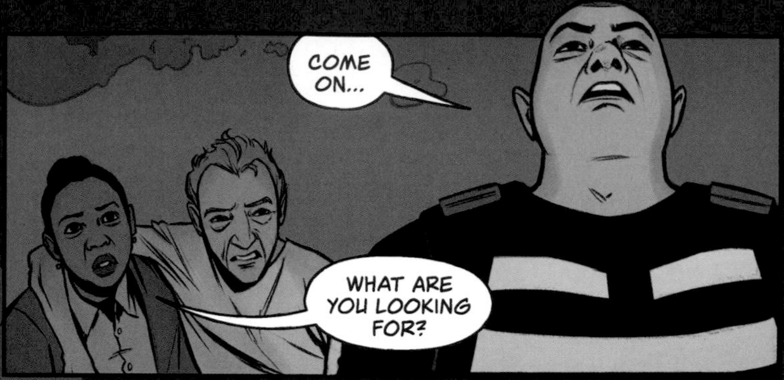
COME ON...
WHAT ARE YOU LOOKING FOR?

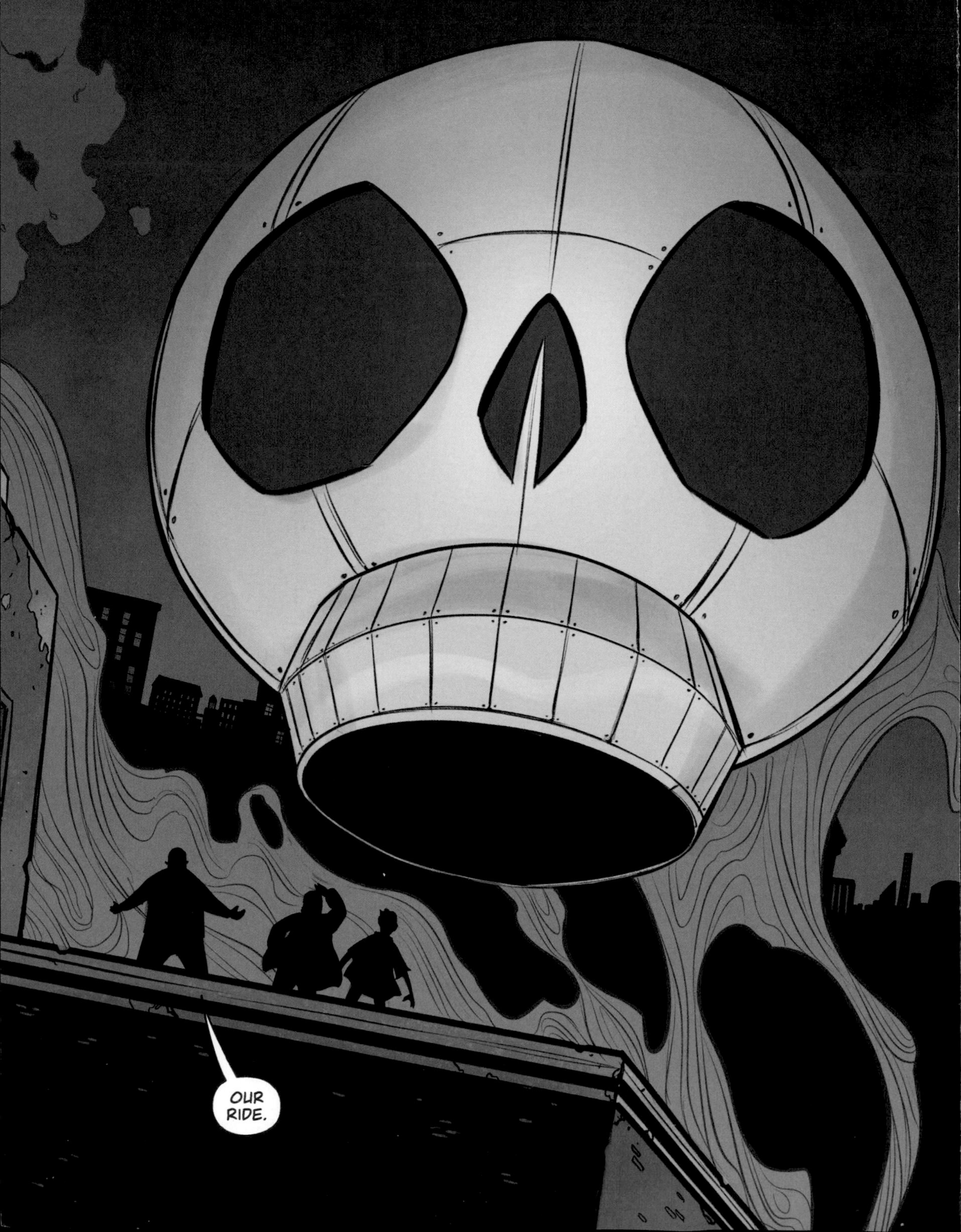
OUR RIDE.

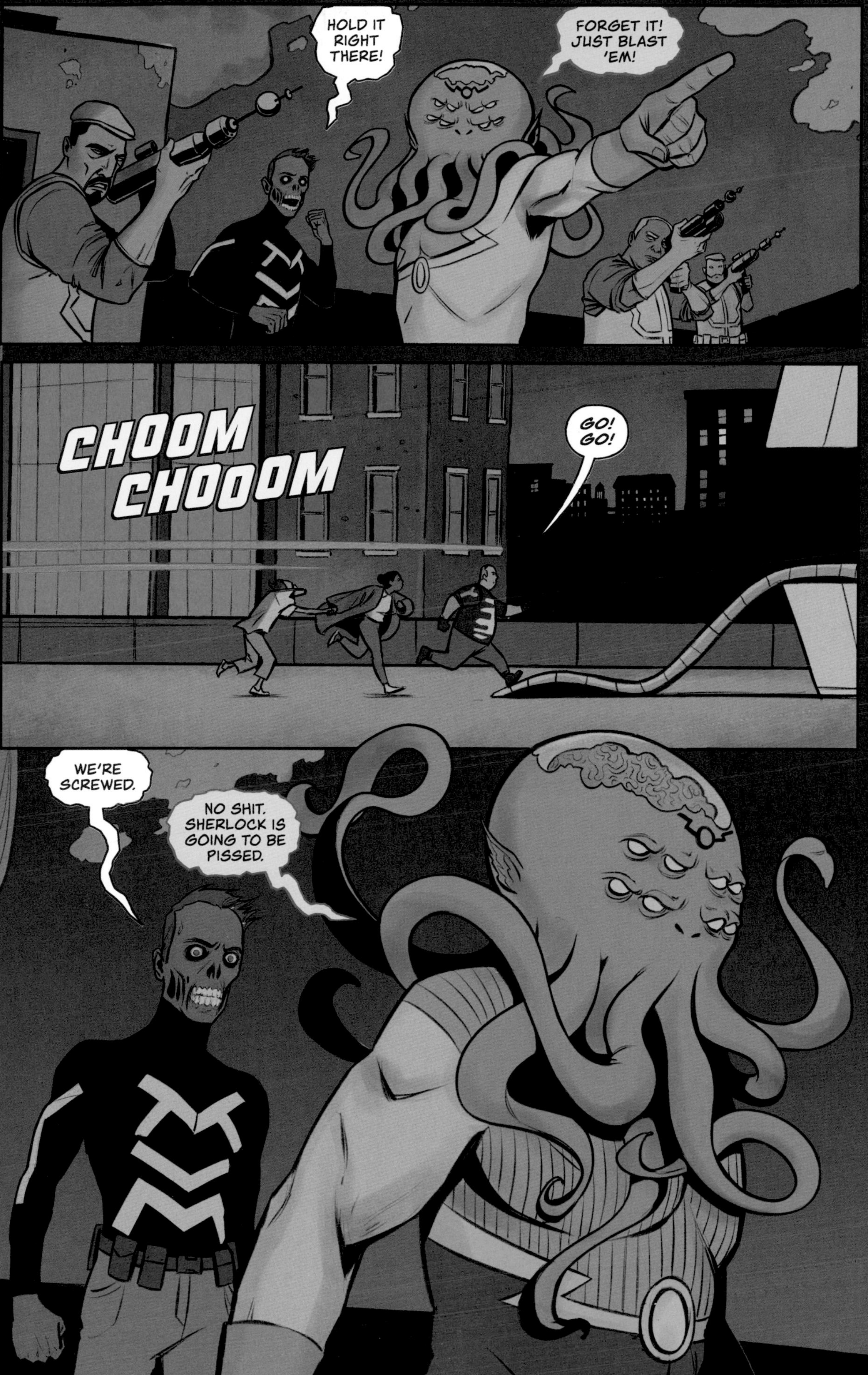

HOLD IT RIGHT THERE!
FORGET IT! JUST BLAST 'EM!
CHOOM CHOOOM
GO! GO!
WE'RE SCREWED.
NO SHIT. SHERLOCK IS GOING TO BE PISSED.

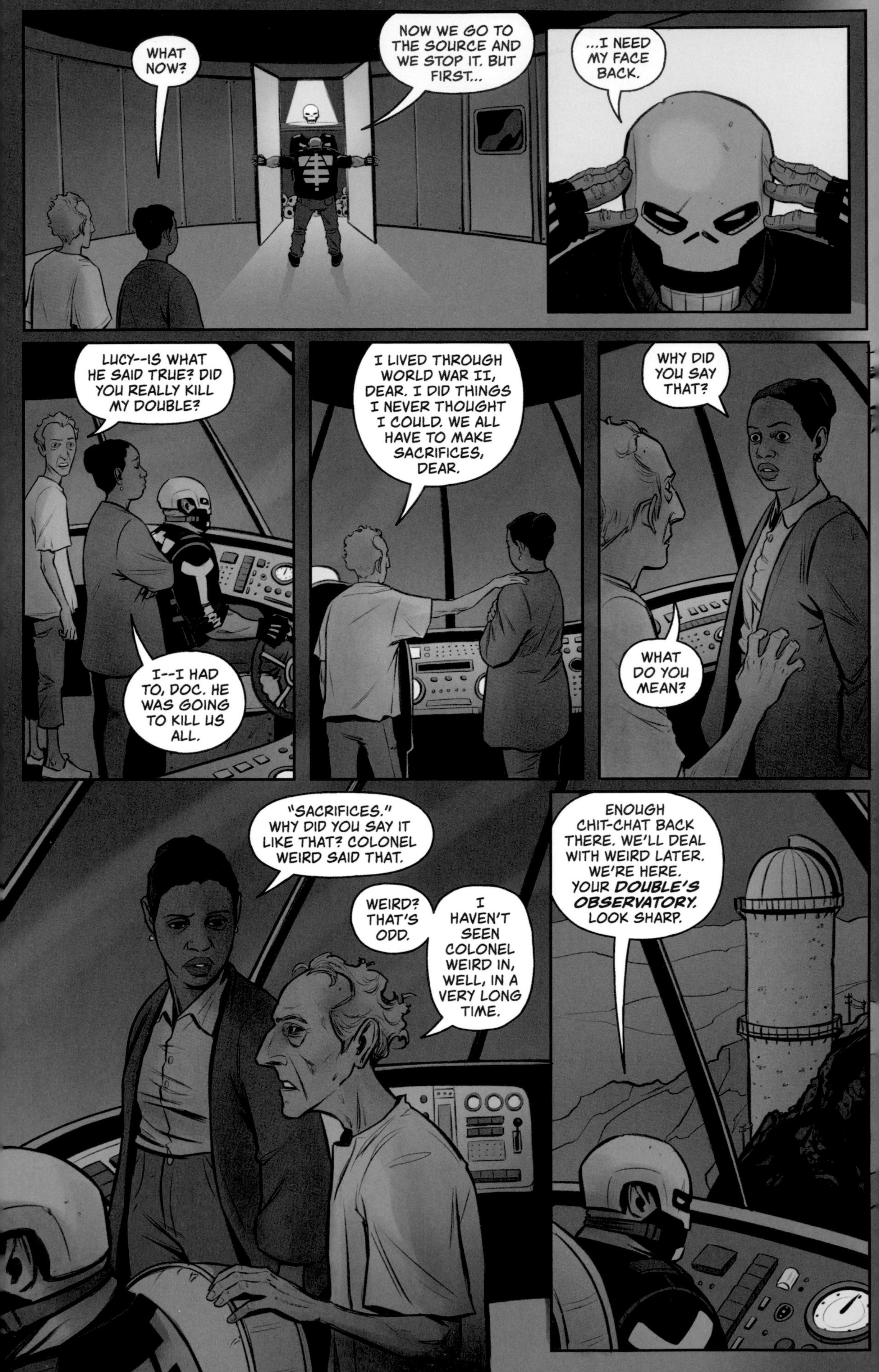
WHAT NOW?
NOW WE GO TO THE SOURCE AND WE STOP IT. BUT FIRST...
...I NEED MY FACE BACK.
LUCY--IS WHAT HE SAID TRUE? DID YOU REALLY KILL MY DOUBLE?
I--I HAD TO, DOC. HE WAS GOING TO KILL US ALL.
I LIVED THROUGH WORLD WAR II, DEAR. I DID THINGS I NEVER THOUGHT I COULD. WE ALL HAVE TO MAKE SACRIFICES, DEAR.
WHY DID YOU SAY THAT?
WHAT DO YOU MEAN?
"SACRIFICES." WHY DID YOU SAY IT LIKE THAT? COLONEL WEIRD SAID THAT.
WEIRD? THAT'S ODD.
I HAVEN'T SEEN COLONEL WEIRD IN, WELL, IN A VERY LONG TIME.
ENOUGH CHIT-CHAT BACK THERE. WE'LL DEAL WITH WEIRD LATER. WE'RE HERE. YOUR **DOUBLE'S OBSERVATORY.** LOOK SHARP.

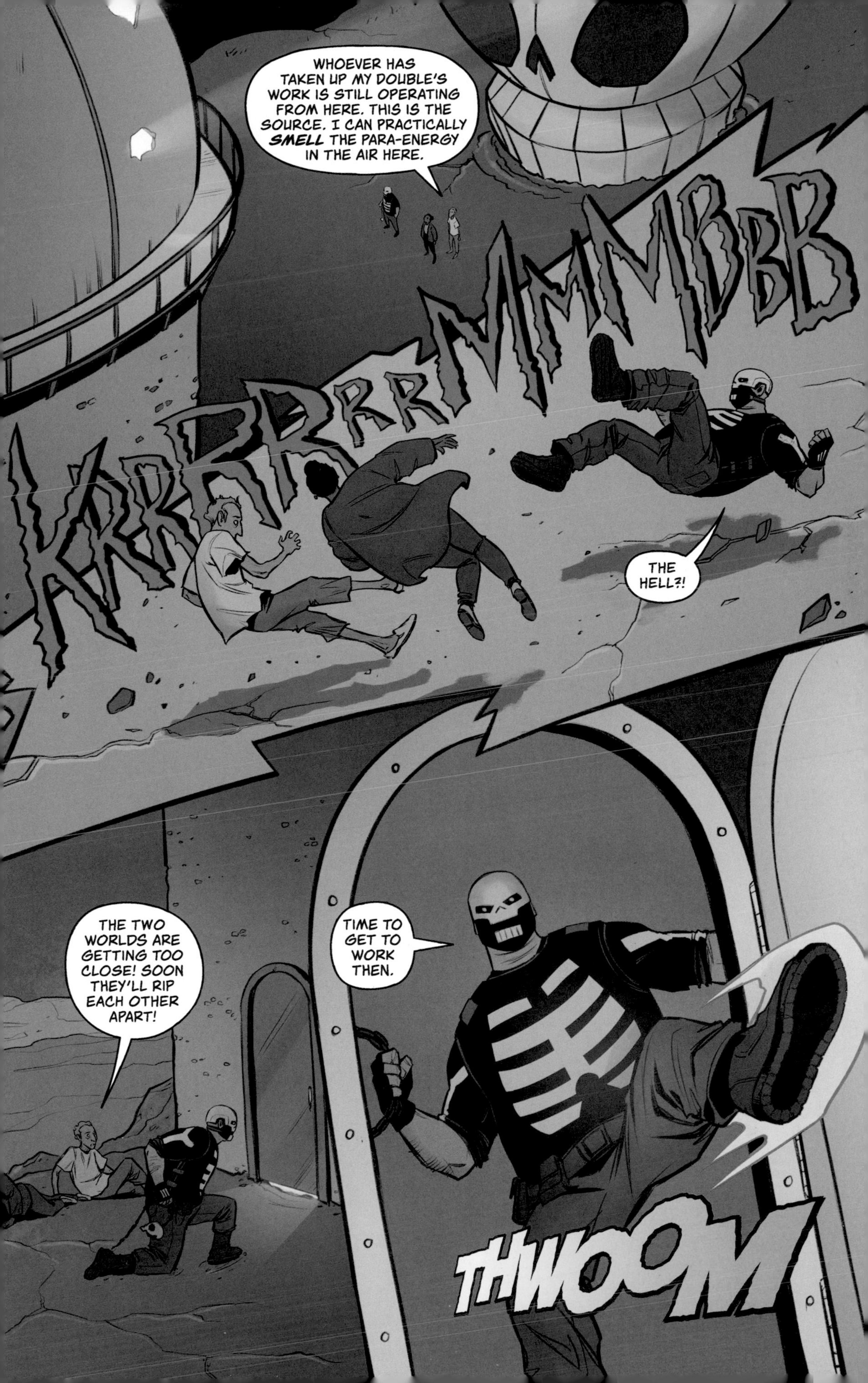
WHOEVER HAS TAKEN UP MY DOUBLE'S WORK IS STILL OPERATING FROM HERE. THIS IS THE SOURCE. I CAN PRACTICALLY **SMELL** THE PARA-ENERGY IN THE AIR HERE.
KRRRRRRRMMMBBB
THE HELL?!
THE TWO WORLDS ARE GETTING TOO CLOSE! SOON THEY'LL RIP EACH OTHER APART!
TIME TO GET TO WORK THEN.
THWOOM

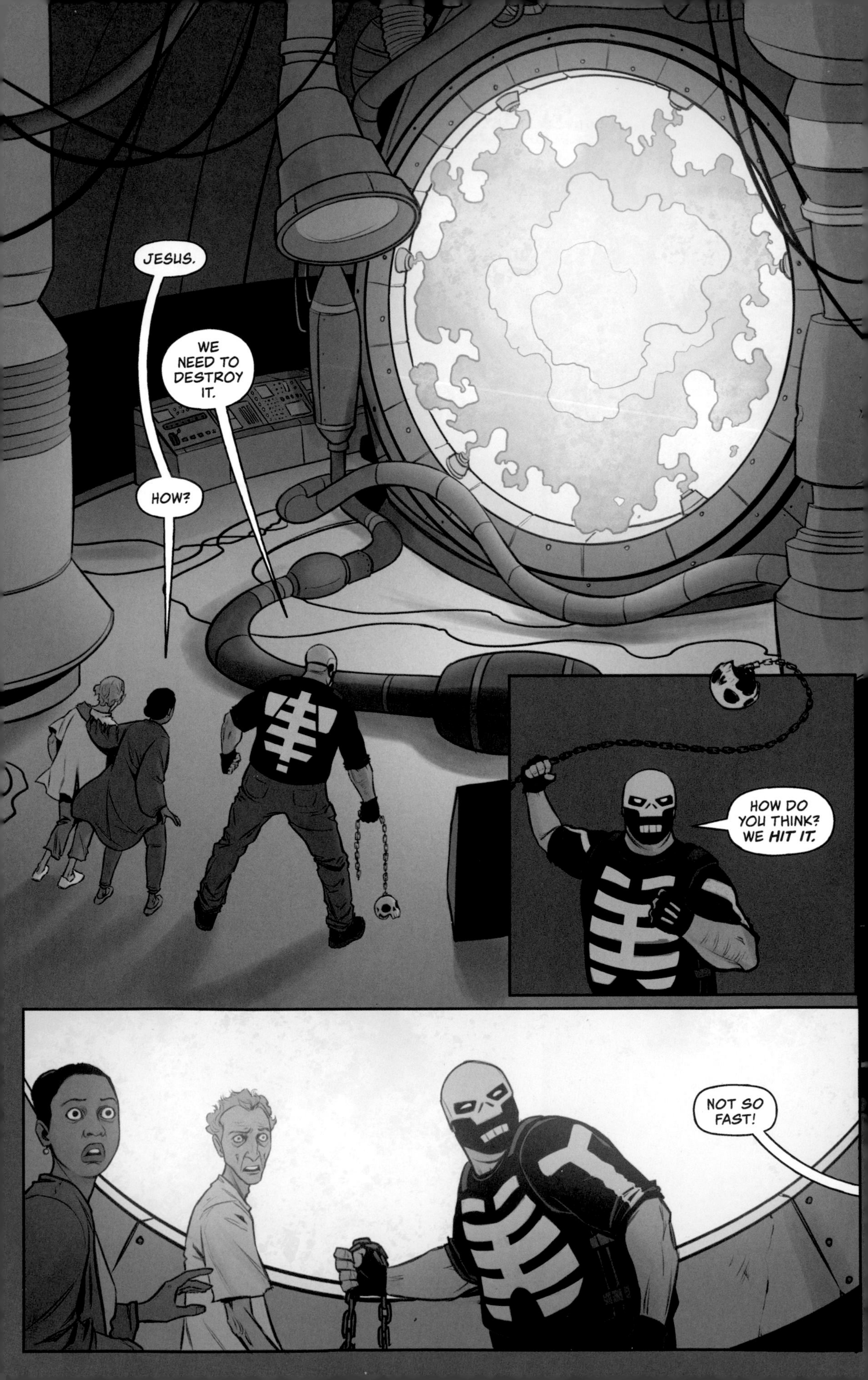
JESUS.
WE NEED TO DESTROY IT.
HOW?
HOW DO YOU THINK? WE *HIT IT.*
NOT SO FAST!

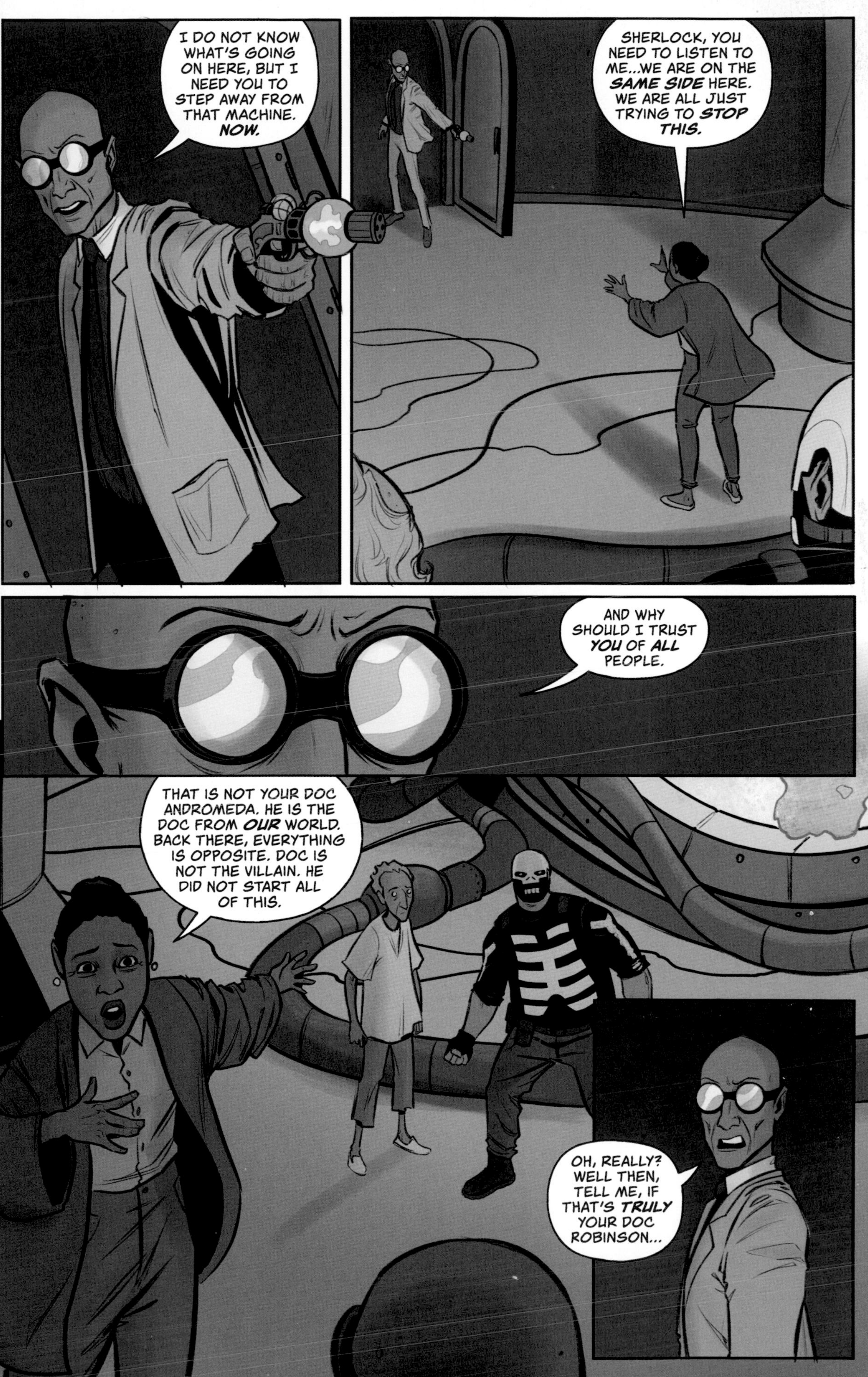
I DO NOT KNOW WHAT'S GOING ON HERE, BUT I NEED YOU TO STEP AWAY FROM THAT MACHINE. NOW.
SHERLOCK, YOU NEED TO LISTEN TO ME...WE ARE ON THE SAME SIDE HERE. WE ARE ALL JUST TRYING TO STOP THIS.
AND WHY SHOULD I TRUST YOU OF ALL PEOPLE.
THAT IS NOT YOUR DOC ANDROMEDA. HE IS THE DOC FROM OUR WORLD. BACK THERE, EVERYTHING IS OPPOSITE. DOC IS NOT THE VILLAIN. HE DID NOT START ALL OF THIS.
OH, REALLY? WELL THEN, TELL ME, IF THAT'S TRULY YOUR DOC ROBINSON...

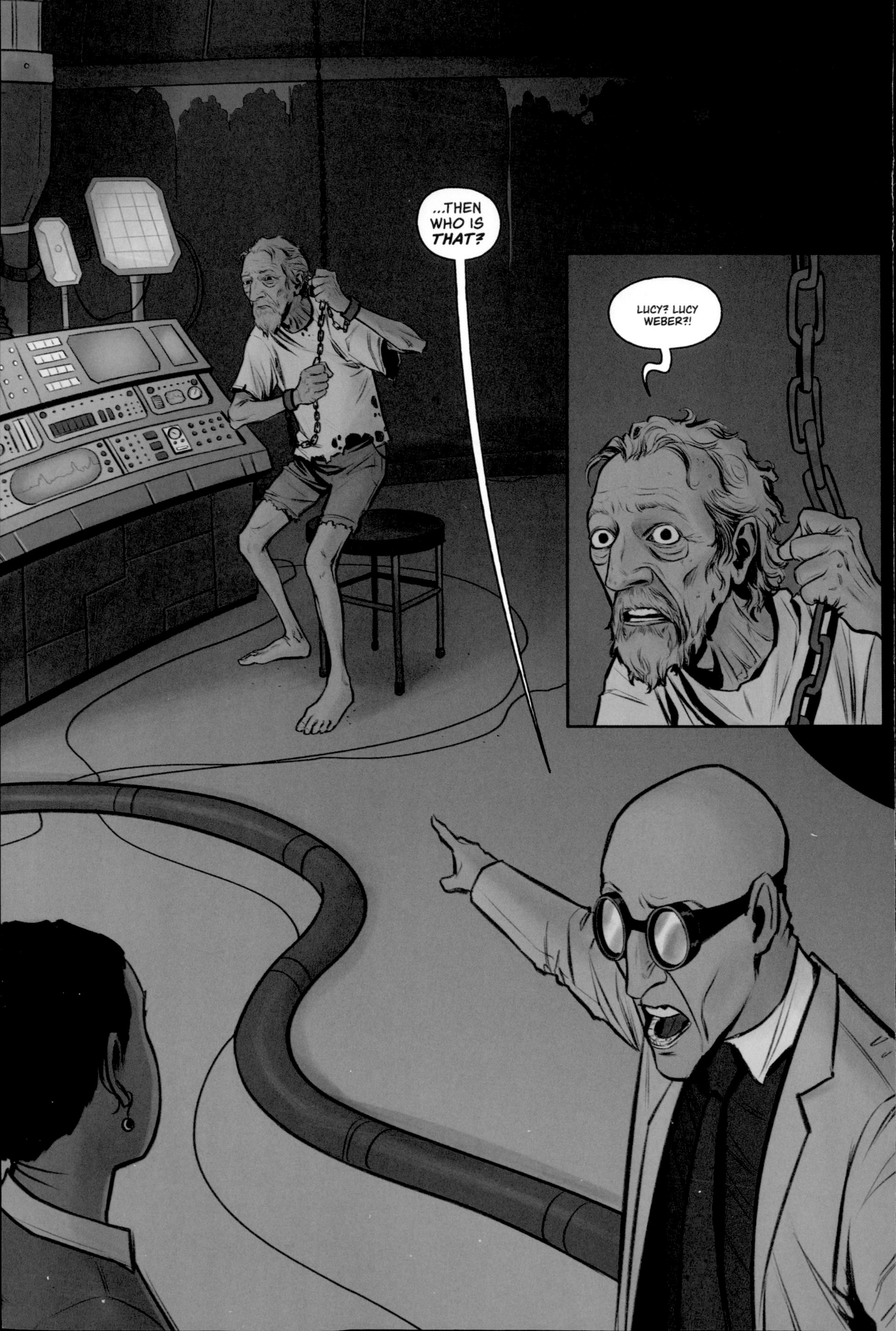
...THEN WHO IS THAT?
LUCY? LUCY WEBER?!

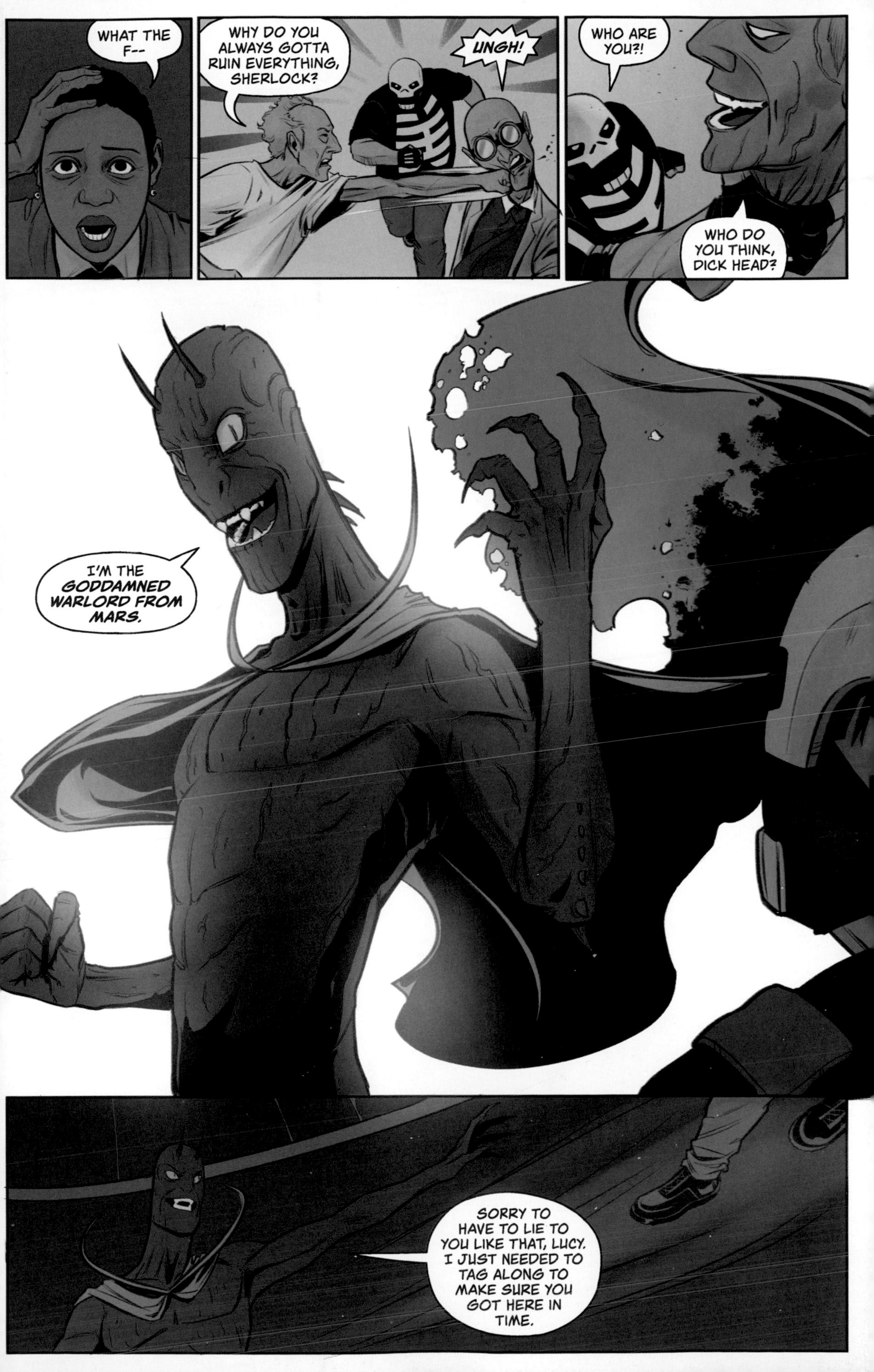
WHAT THE F--
WHY DO YOU ALWAYS GOTTA RUIN EVERYTHING, SHERLOCK?
UNGH!
WHO ARE YOU?!
WHO DO YOU THINK, DICK HEAD?
I'M THE GODDAMNED WARLORD FROM MARS.
SORRY TO HAVE TO LIE TO YOU LIKE THAT, LUCY. I JUST NEEDED TO TAG ALONG TO MAKE SURE YOU GOT HERE IN TIME.

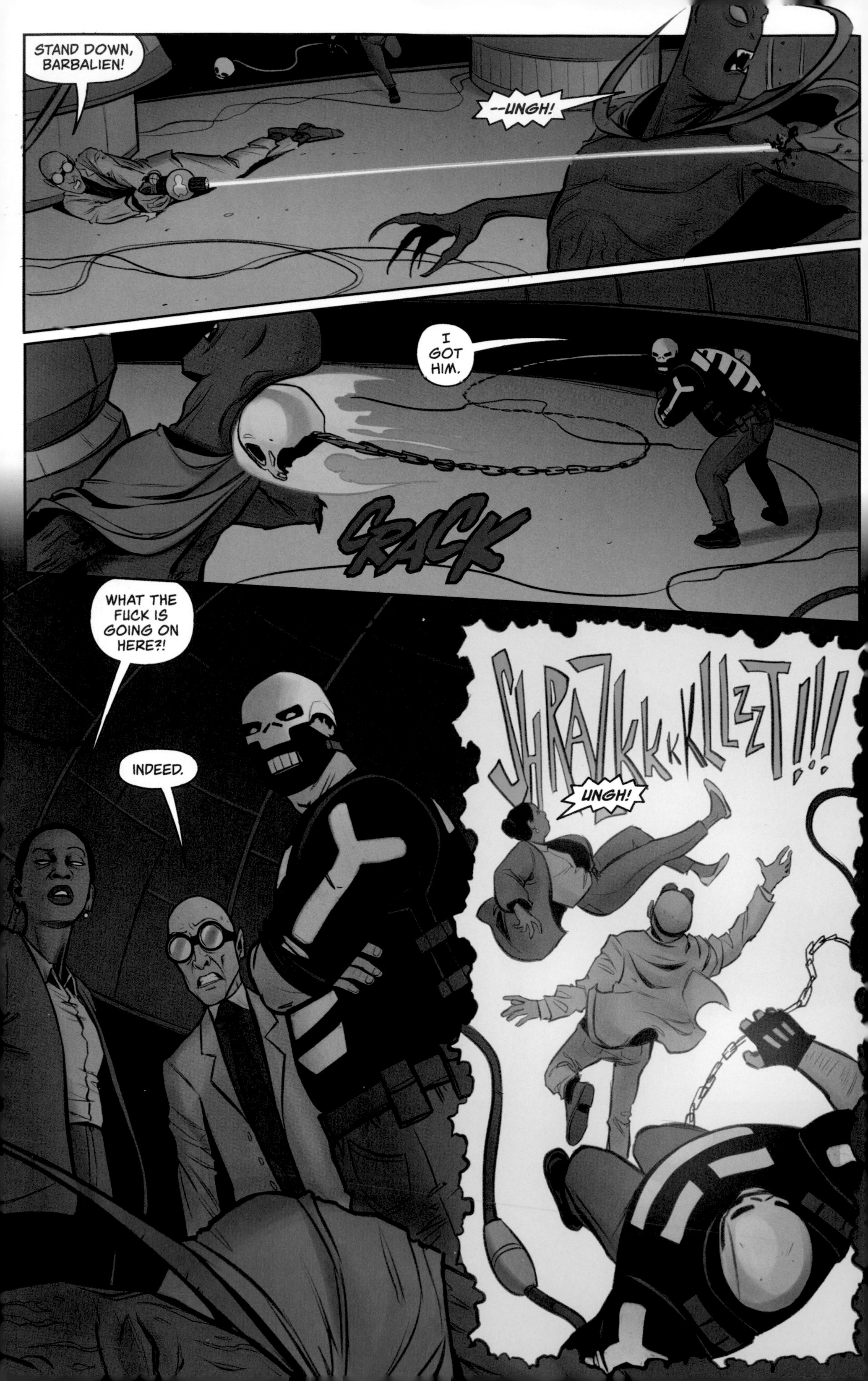
STAND DOWN, BARBALIEN!
--UNGH!
I GOT HIM.
CRACK
WHAT THE FUCK IS GOING ON HERE?!
INDEED.
SHRAZKKKKLLZZT!!!
UNGH!

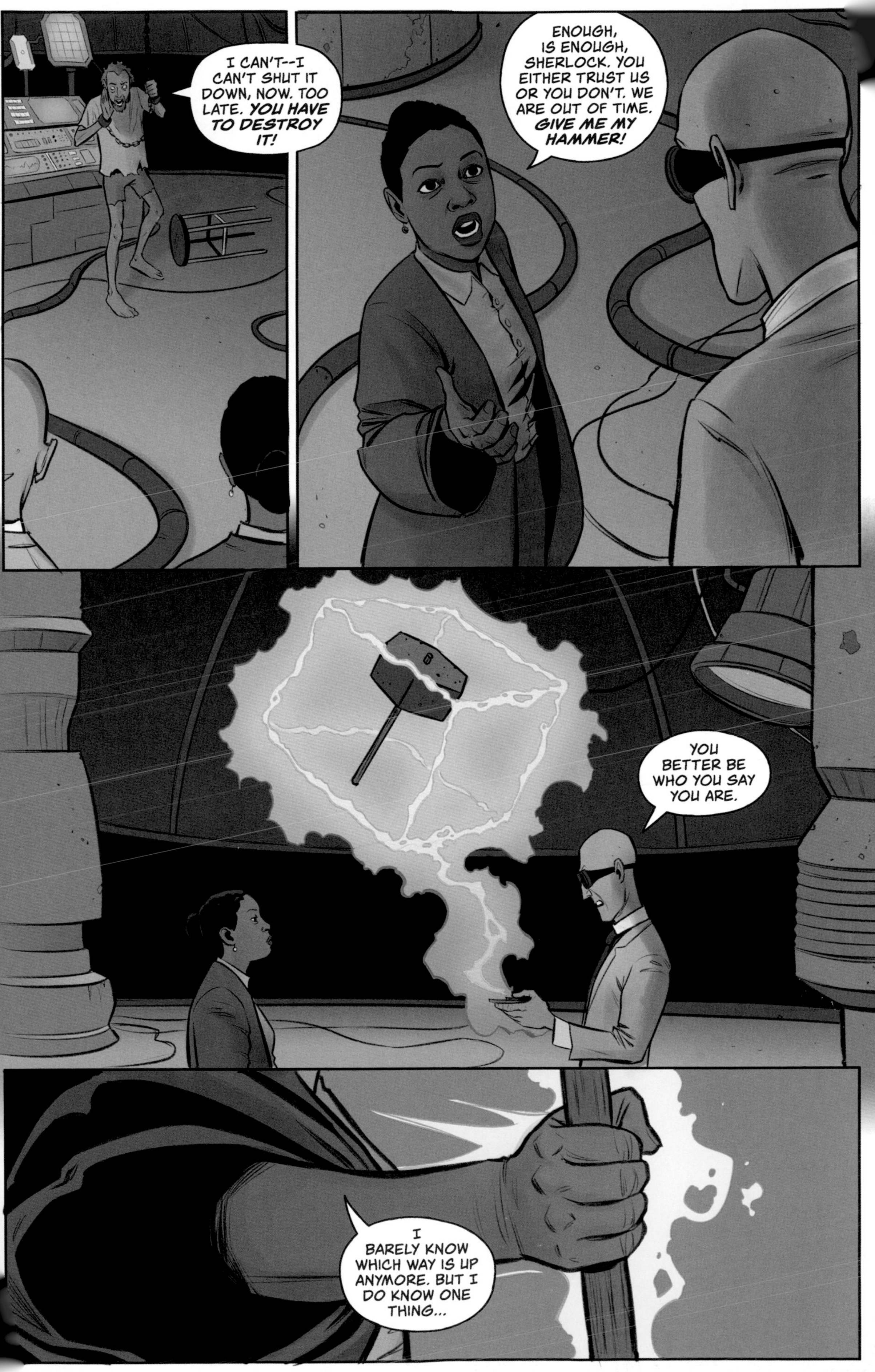
I CAN'T--I CAN'T SHUT IT DOWN, NOW. TOO LATE. *YOU HAVE TO DESTROY IT!*
ENOUGH, IS ENOUGH, SHERLOCK. YOU EITHER TRUST US OR YOU DON'T. WE ARE OUT OF TIME. *GIVE ME MY HAMMER!*
YOU BETTER BE WHO YOU SAY YOU ARE.
I BARELY KNOW WHICH WAY IS UP ANYMORE. BUT I DO KNOW ONE THING...

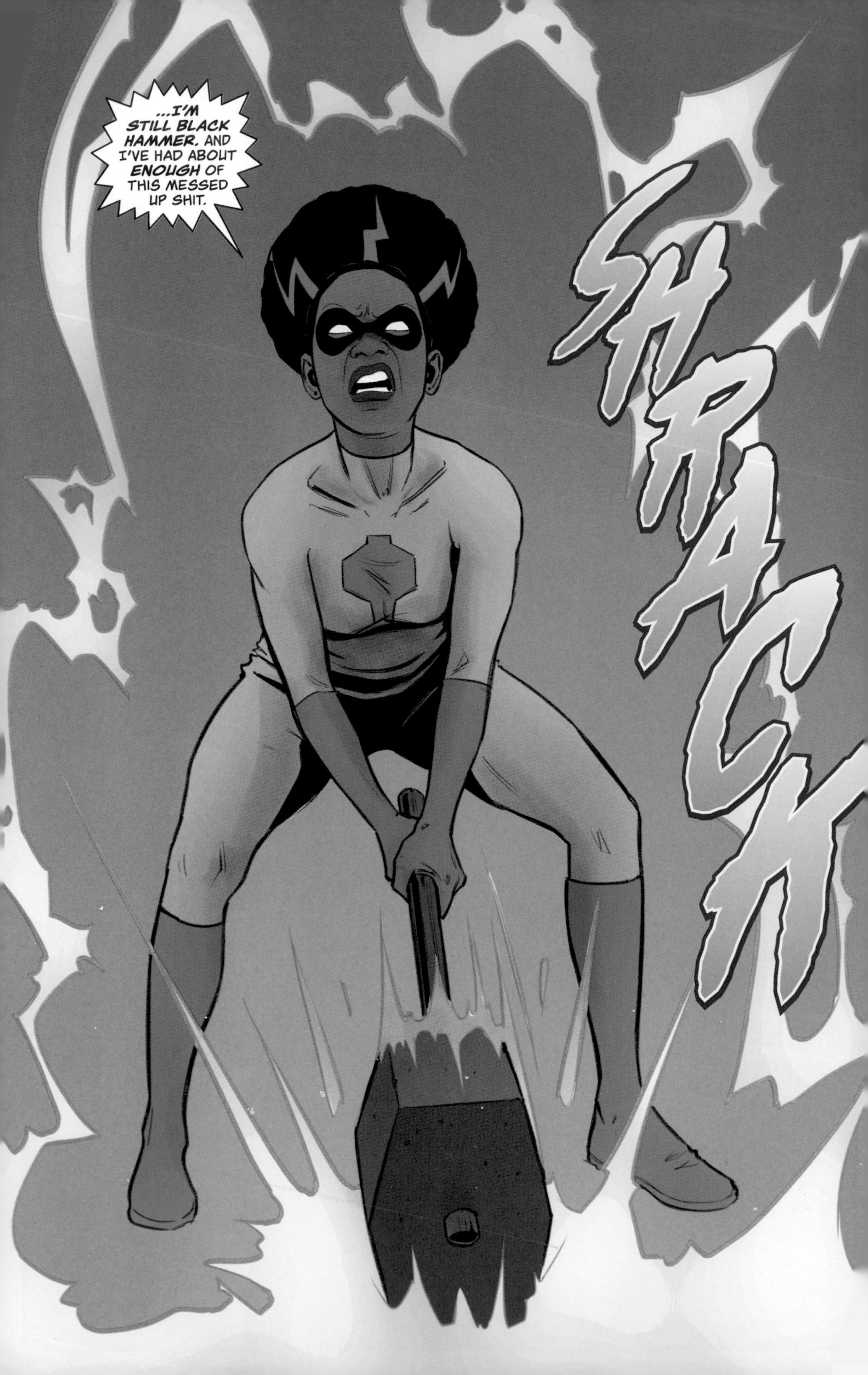
...I'M STILL BLACK HAMMER. AND I'VE HAD ABOUT ENOUGH OF THIS MESSED UP SHIT.
SHRACK

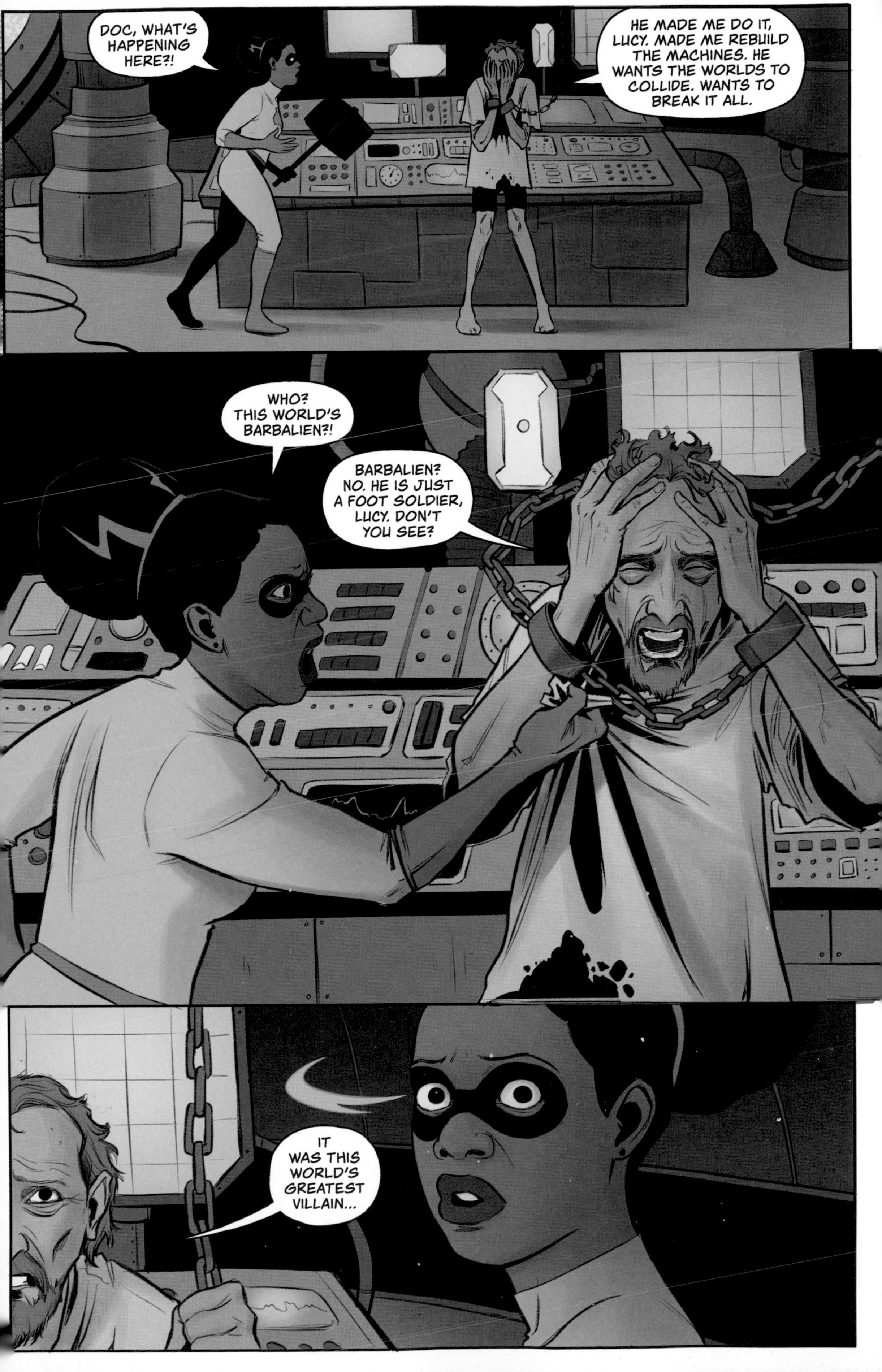
DOC, WHAT'S HAPPENING HERE?!
HE MADE ME DO IT, LUCY. MADE ME REBUILD THE MACHINES. HE WANTS THE WORLDS TO COLLIDE. WANTS TO BREAK IT ALL.
WHO? THIS WORLD'S BARBALIEN?!
BARBALIEN? NO. HE IS JUST A FOOT SOLDIER, LUCY. DON'T YOU SEE?
IT WAS THIS WORLD'S GREATEST VILLAIN...

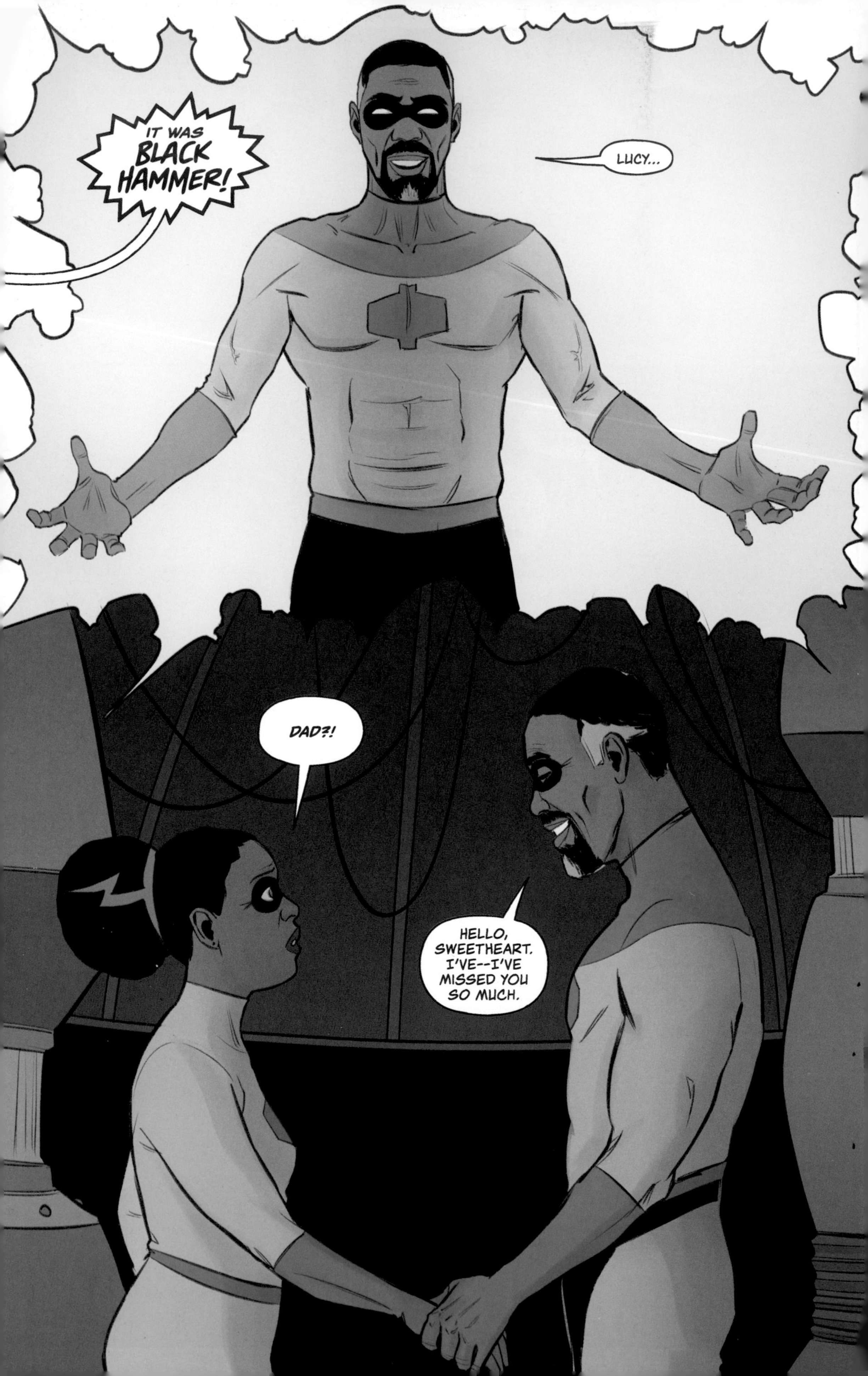
IT WAS BLACK HAMMER!
LUCY...
DAD?!
HELLO, SWEETHEART. I'VE--I'VE MISSED YOU SO MUCH.

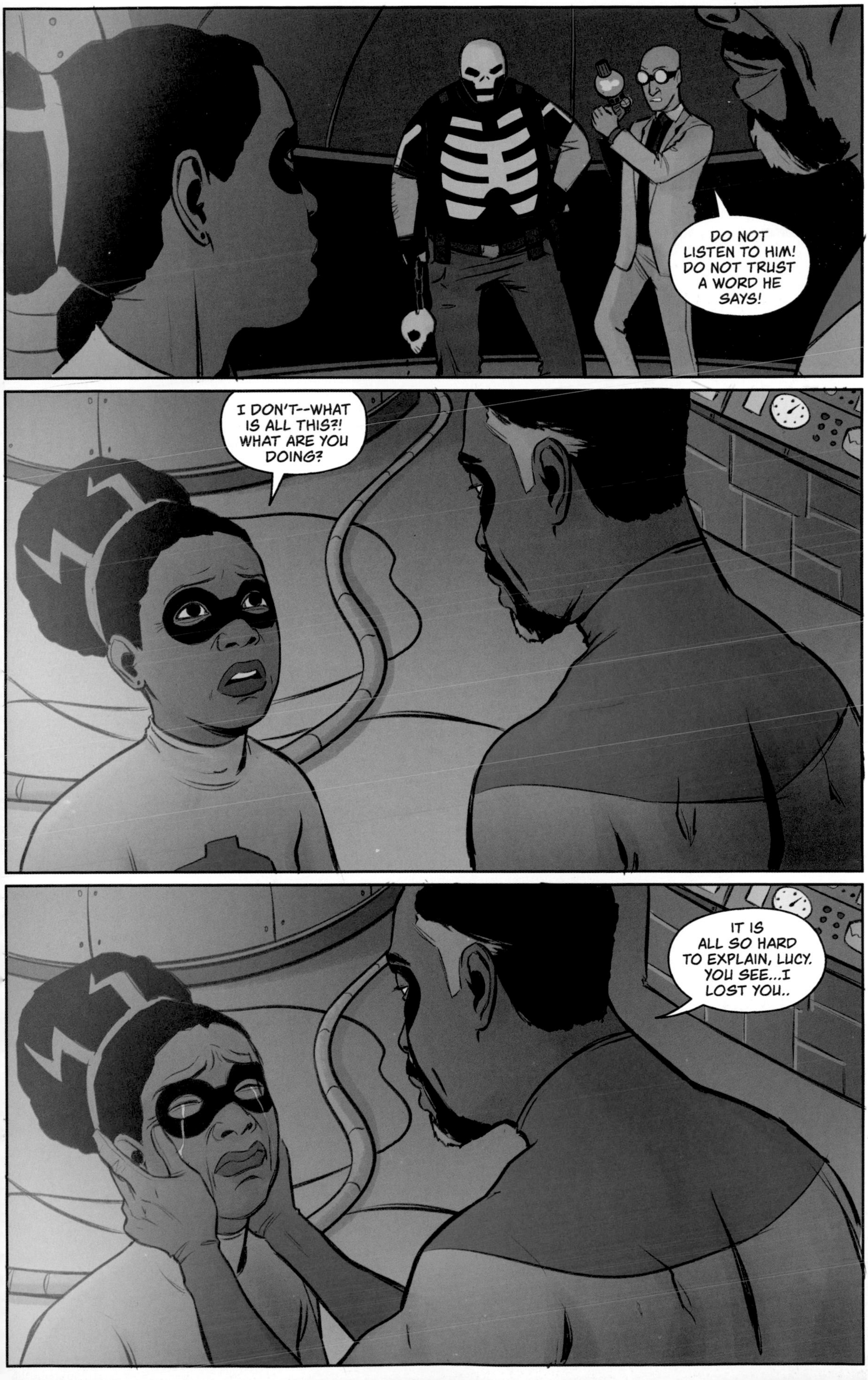
DO NOT LISTEN TO HIM! DO NOT TRUST A WORD HE SAYS!
I DON'T--WHAT IS ALL THIS?! WHAT ARE YOU DOING?
IT IS ALL SO HARD TO EXPLAIN, LUCY. YOU SEE...I LOST YOU..

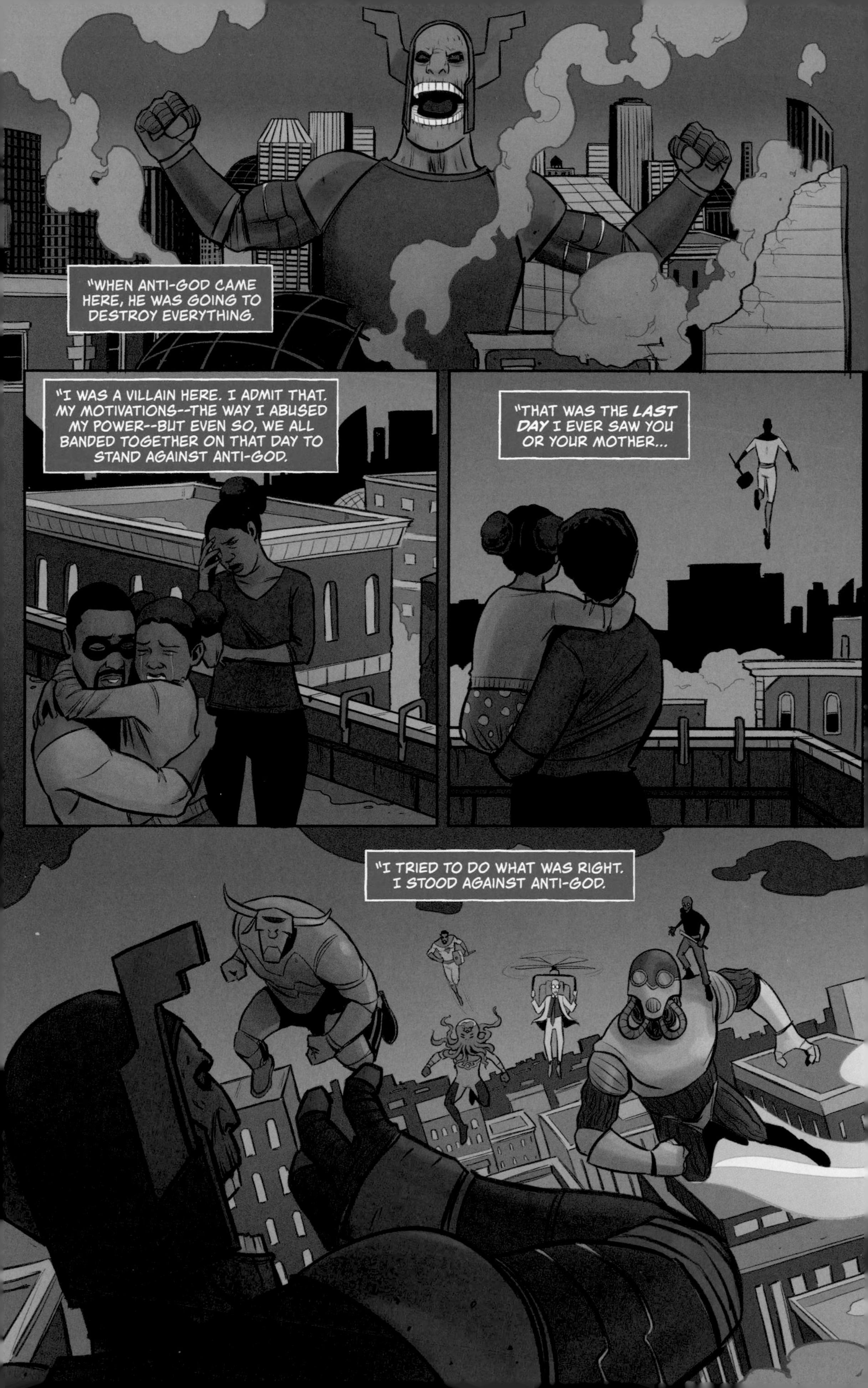
"WHEN ANTI-GOD CAME HERE, HE WAS GOING TO DESTROY EVERYTHING.
"I WAS A VILLAIN HERE. I ADMIT THAT. MY MOTIVATIONS--THE WAY I ABUSED MY POWER--BUT EVEN SO, WE ALL BANDED TOGETHER ON THAT DAY TO STAND AGAINST ANTI-GOD.
"THAT WAS THE *LAST DAY* I EVER SAW YOU OR YOUR MOTHER...
"I TRIED TO DO WHAT WAS RIGHT. I STOOD AGAINST ANTI-GOD.

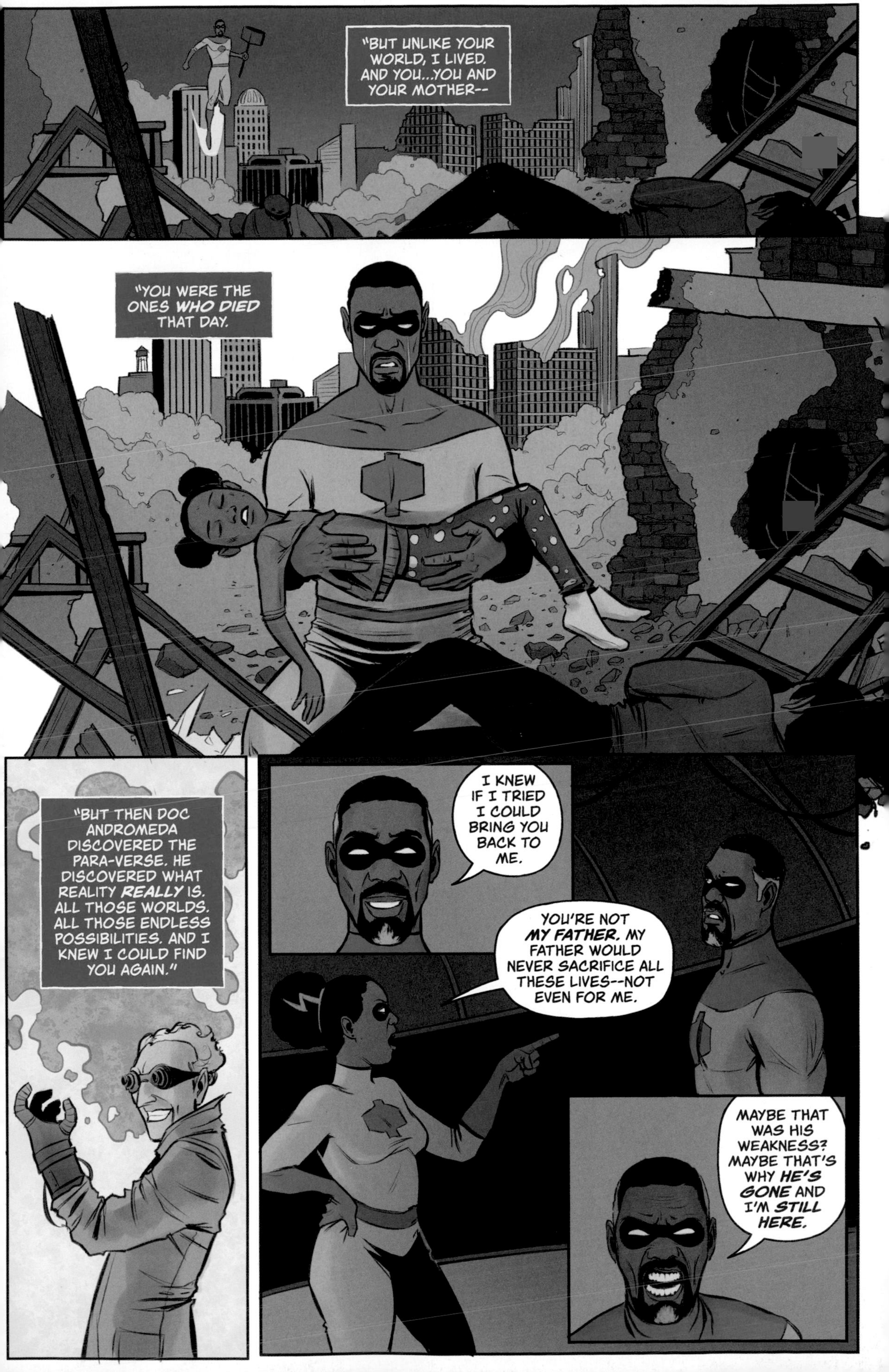
"BUT UNLIKE YOUR WORLD, I LIVED. AND YOU...YOU AND YOUR MOTHER--
"YOU WERE THE ONES WHO DIED THAT DAY.
"BUT THEN DOC ANDROMEDA DISCOVERED THE PARA-VERSE. HE DISCOVERED WHAT REALITY REALLY IS. ALL THOSE WORLDS. ALL THOSE ENDLESS POSSIBILITIES. AND I KNEW I COULD FIND YOU AGAIN."
I KNEW IF I TRIED I COULD BRING YOU BACK TO ME.
YOU'RE NOT MY FATHER. MY FATHER WOULD NEVER SACRIFICE ALL THESE LIVES--NOT EVEN FOR ME.
MAYBE THAT WAS HIS WEAKNESS? MAYBE THAT'S WHY HE'S GONE AND I'M STILL HERE.

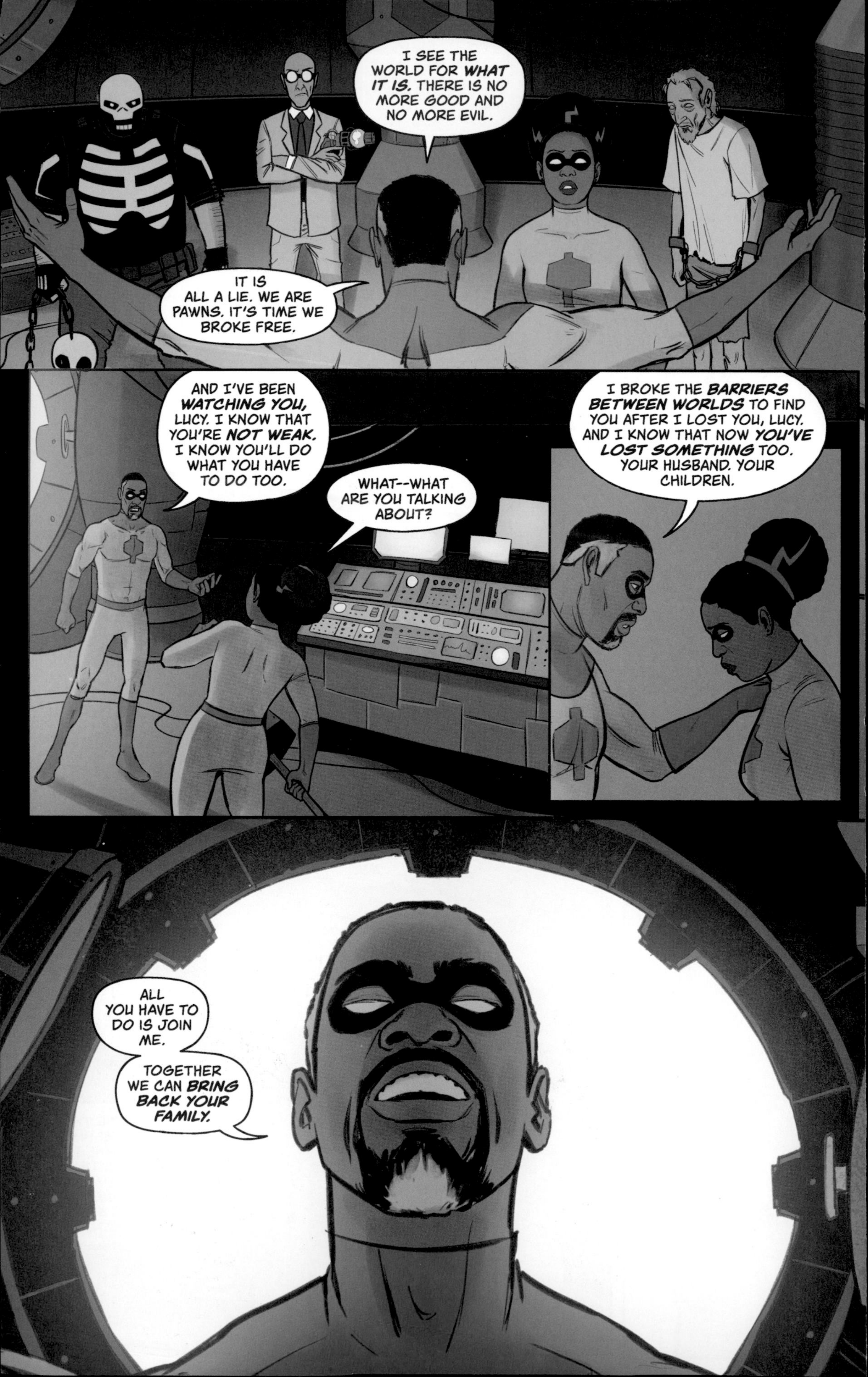
I SEE THE WORLD FOR WHAT IT IS. THERE IS NO MORE GOOD AND NO MORE EVIL.
IT IS ALL A LIE. WE ARE PAWNS. IT'S TIME WE BROKE FREE.
AND I'VE BEEN WATCHING YOU, LUCY. I KNOW THAT YOU'RE NOT WEAK. I KNOW YOU'LL DO WHAT YOU HAVE TO DO TOO.
WHAT--WHAT ARE YOU TALKING ABOUT?
I BROKE THE BARRIERS BETWEEN WORLDS TO FIND YOU AFTER I LOST YOU, LUCY. AND I KNOW THAT NOW YOU'VE LOST SOMETHING TOO. YOUR HUSBAND. YOUR CHILDREN.
ALL YOU HAVE TO DO IS JOIN ME.
TOGETHER WE CAN BRING BACK YOUR FAMILY.

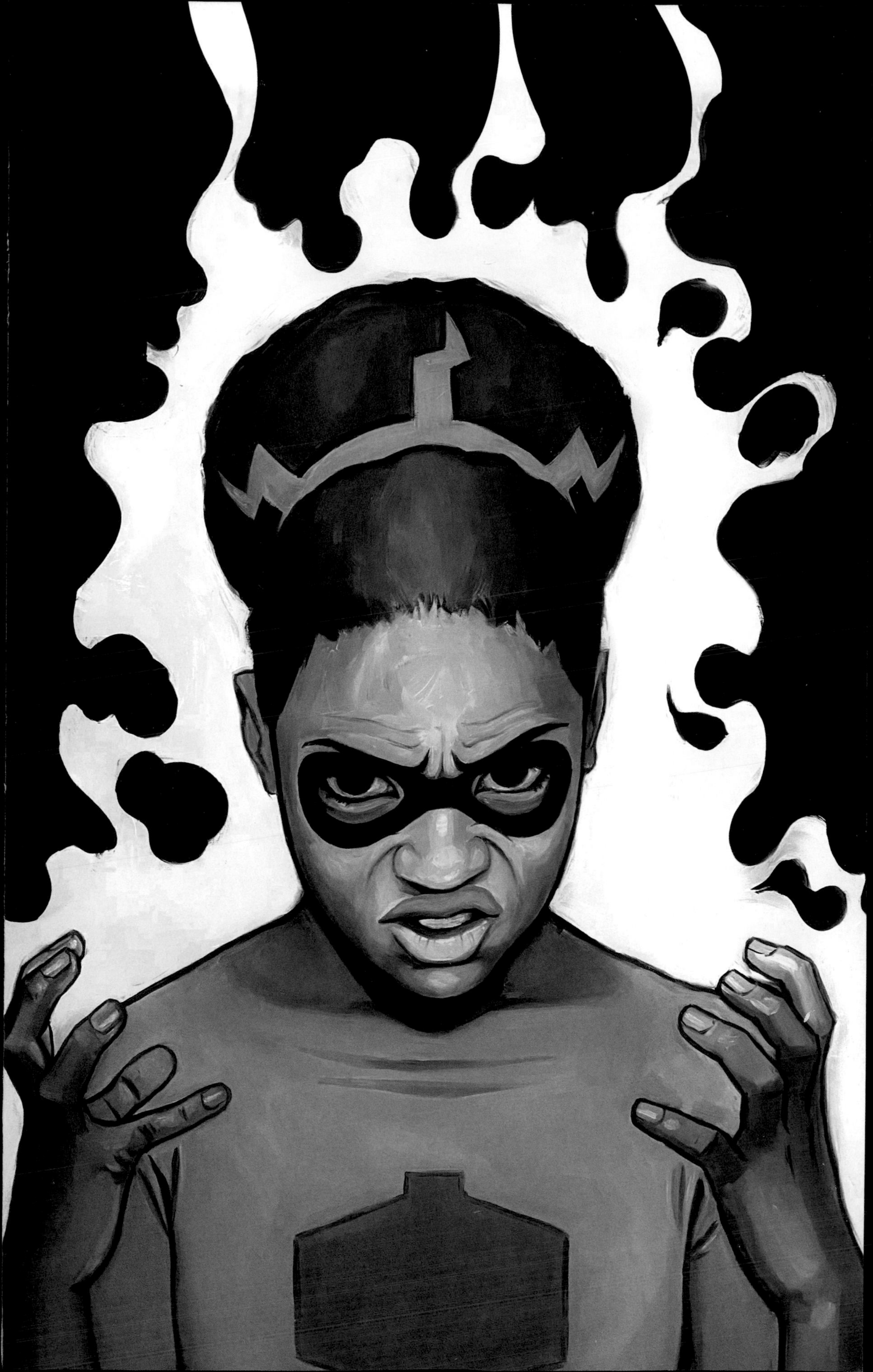

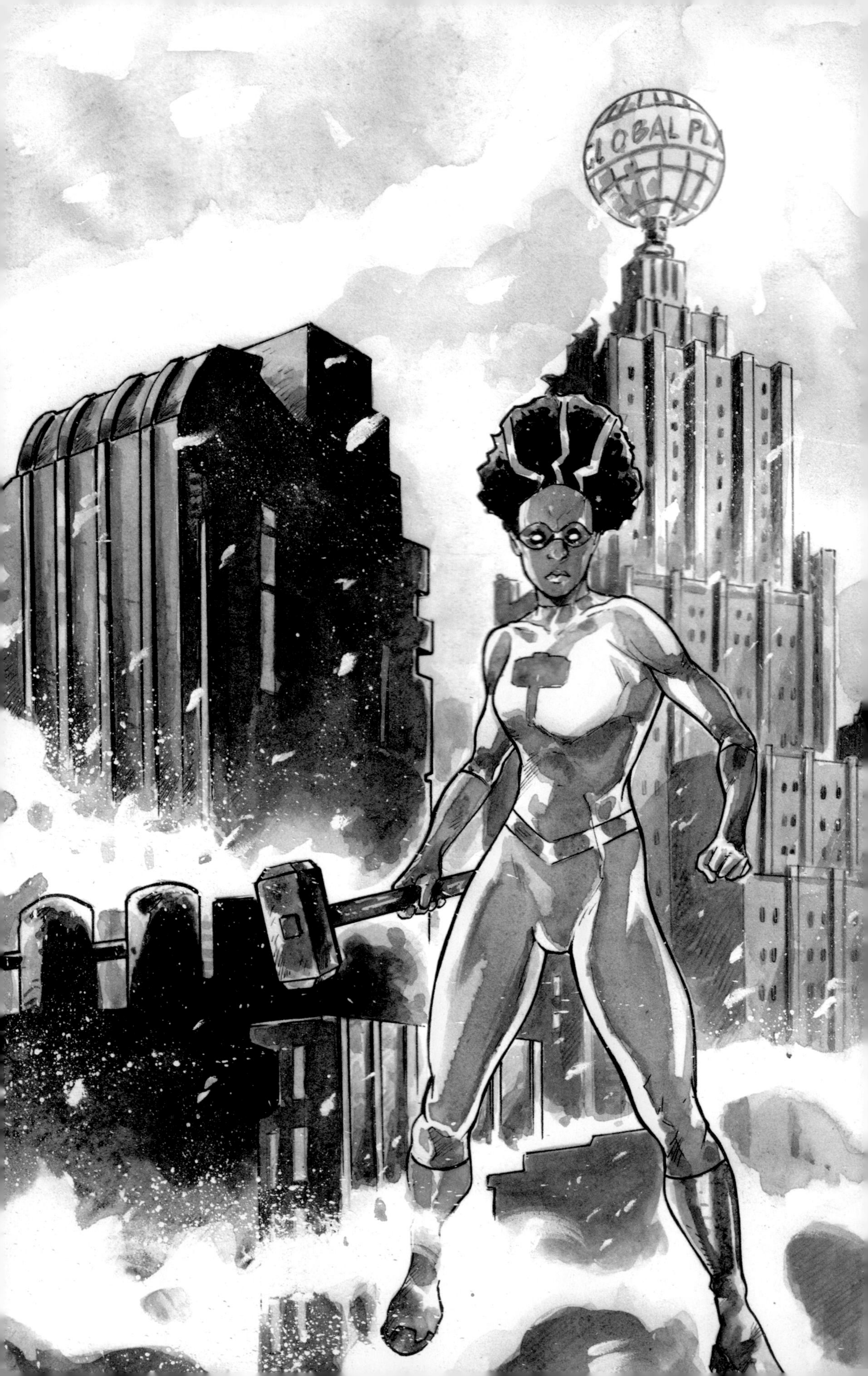
GLOBAL PL

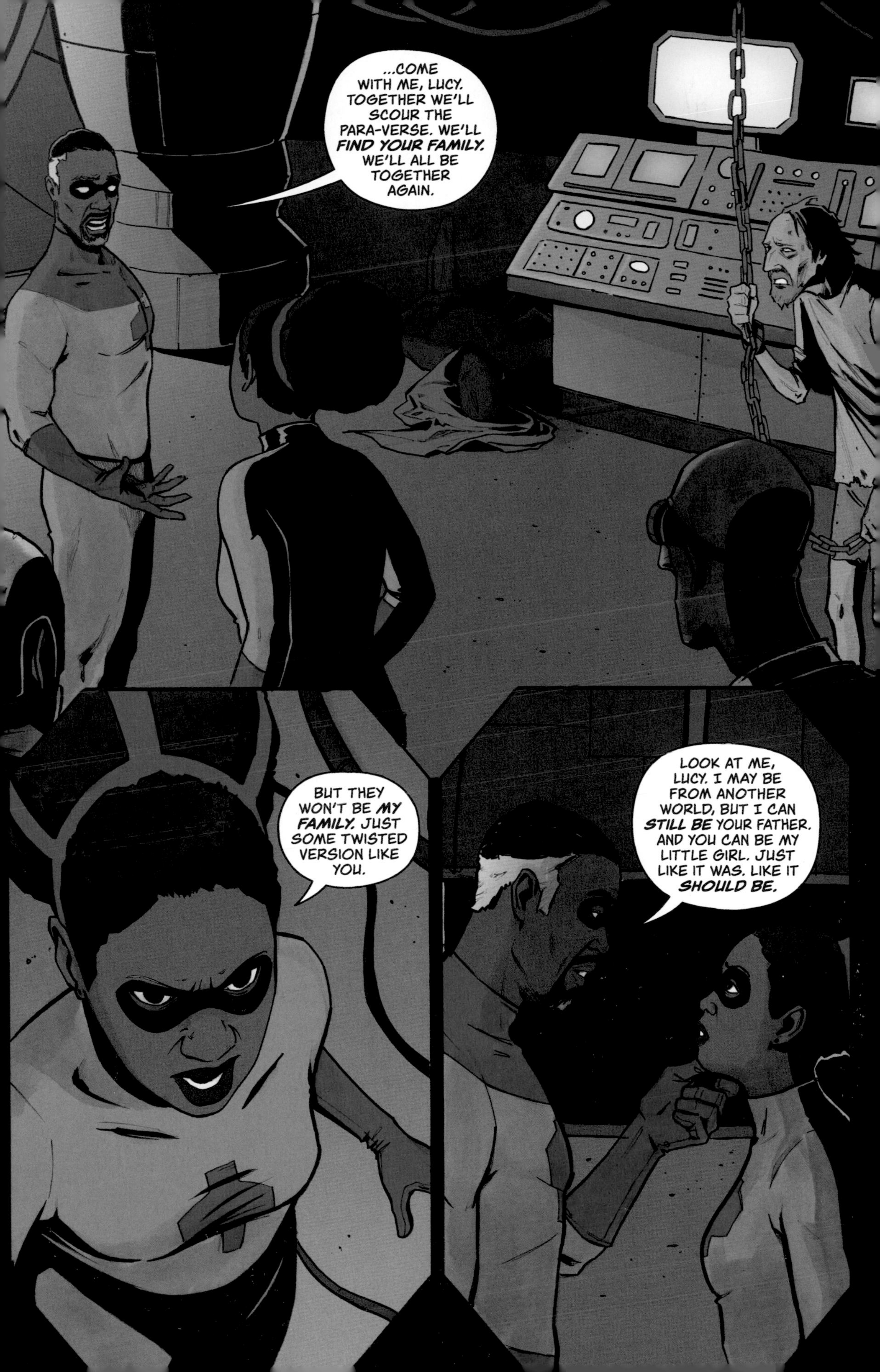
...COME WITH ME, LUCY. TOGETHER WE'LL SCOUR THE PARA-VERSE. WE'LL FIND YOUR FAMILY. WE'LL ALL BE TOGETHER AGAIN.
BUT THEY WON'T BE MY FAMILY. JUST SOME TWISTED VERSION LIKE YOU.
LOOK AT ME, LUCY. I MAY BE FROM ANOTHER WORLD, BUT I CAN STILL BE YOUR FATHER. AND YOU CAN BE MY LITTLE GIRL. JUST LIKE IT WAS. LIKE IT SHOULD BE.

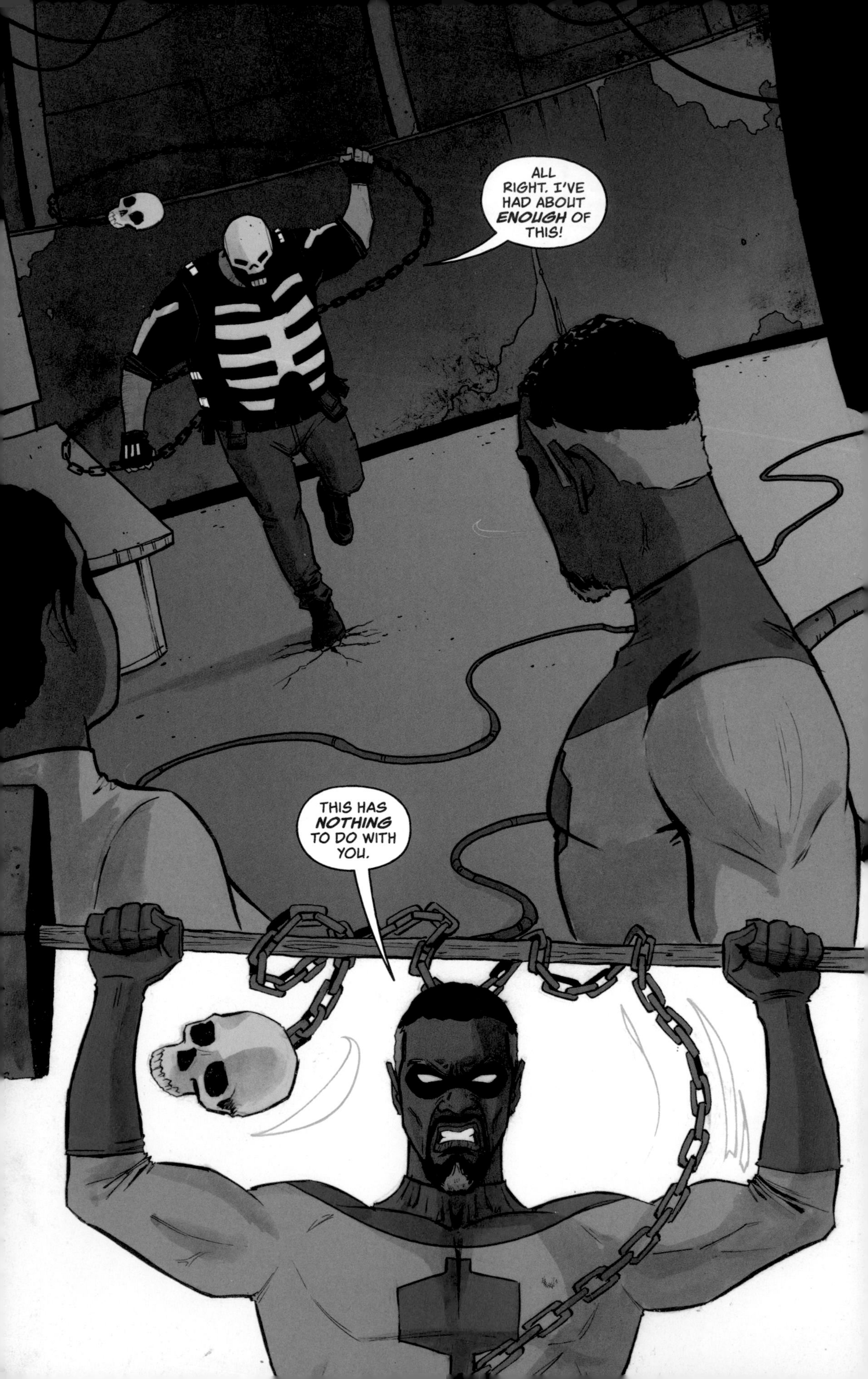
ALL RIGHT. I'VE HAD ABOUT ENOUGH OF THIS!
THIS HAS NOTHING TO DO WITH YOU.

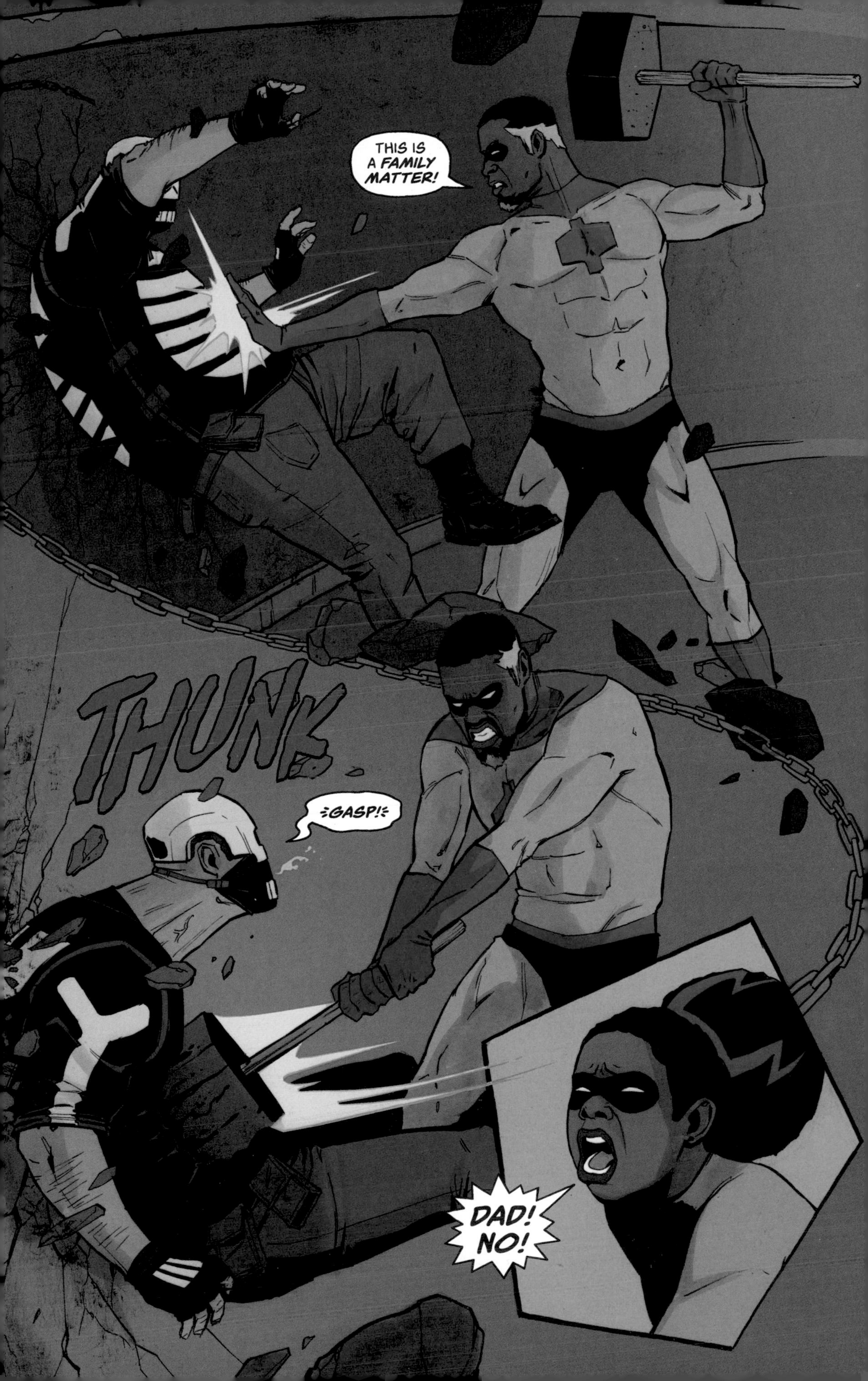
THIS IS A *FAMILY MATTER!*
THUNK
GASP!
DAD! NO!

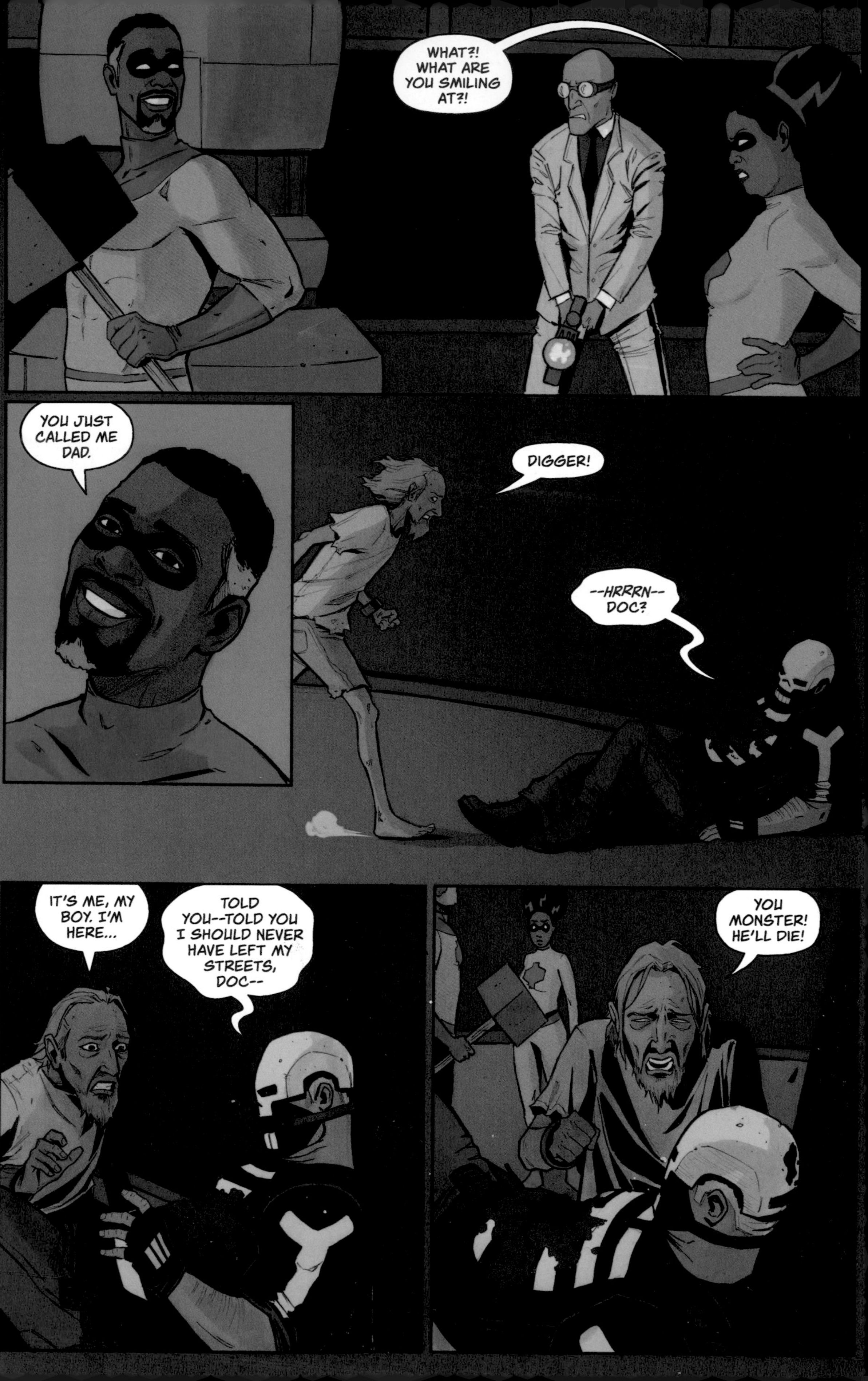
WHAT?! WHAT ARE YOU SMILING AT?!
YOU JUST CALLED ME DAD.
DIGGER!
--HRRRN-- DOC?
IT'S ME, MY BOY. I'M HERE...
TOLD YOU--TOLD YOU I SHOULD NEVER HAVE LEFT MY STREETS, DOC--
YOU MONSTER! HE'LL DIE!

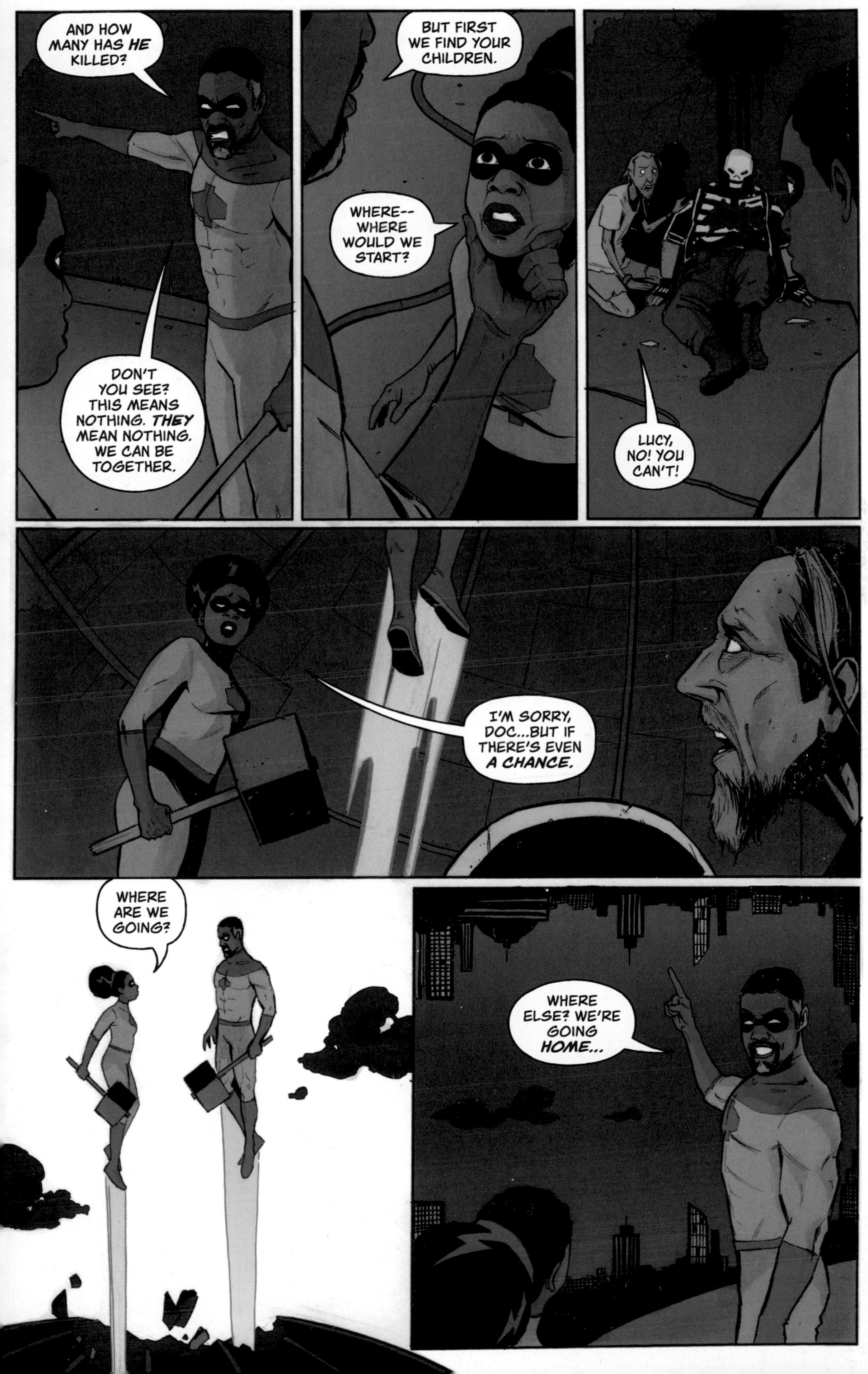
AND HOW MANY HAS *HE* KILLED?
DON'T YOU SEE? THIS MEANS NOTHING. *THEY* MEAN NOTHING. WE CAN BE TOGETHER.
BUT FIRST WE FIND YOUR CHILDREN.
WHERE-- WHERE WOULD WE START?
LUCY, NO! YOU CAN'T!
I'M SORRY, DOC...BUT IF THERE'S EVEN *A CHANCE.*
WHERE ARE WE GOING?
WHERE ELSE? WE'RE GOING *HOME...*

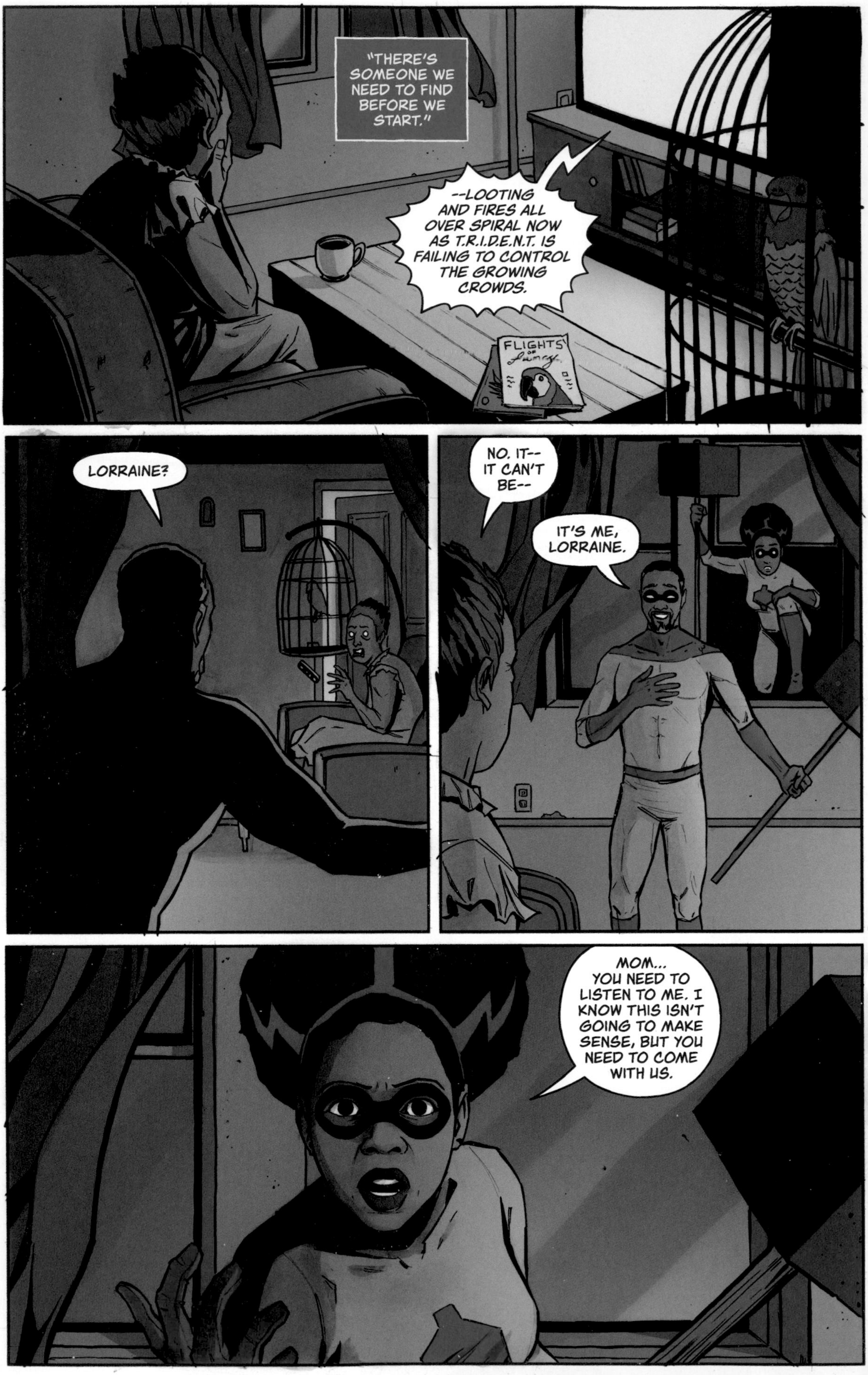
"THERE'S SOMEONE WE NEED TO FIND BEFORE WE START."
--LOOTING AND FIRES ALL OVER SPIRAL NOW AS T.R.I.D.E.N.T. IS FAILING TO CONTROL THE GROWING CROWDS.
FLIGHTS
LORRAINE?
NO. IT-- IT CAN'T BE--
IT'S ME, LORRAINE.
MOM... YOU NEED TO LISTEN TO ME. I KNOW THIS ISN'T GOING TO MAKE SENSE, BUT YOU NEED TO COME WITH US.

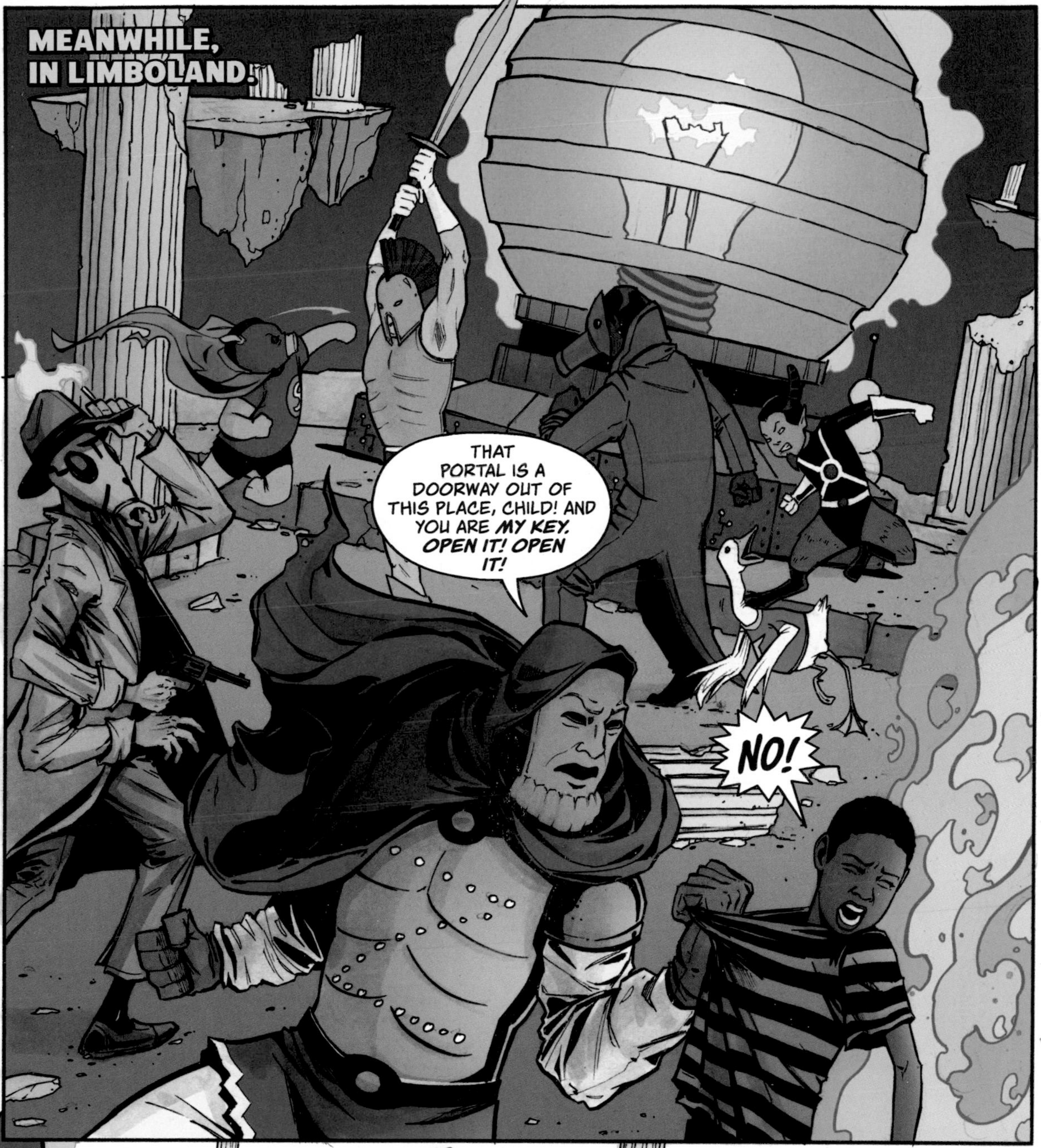
MEANWHILE, IN LIMBOLAND.
THAT PORTAL IS A DOORWAY OUT OF THIS PLACE, CHILD! AND YOU ARE MY KEY. OPEN IT! OPEN IT!
NO!

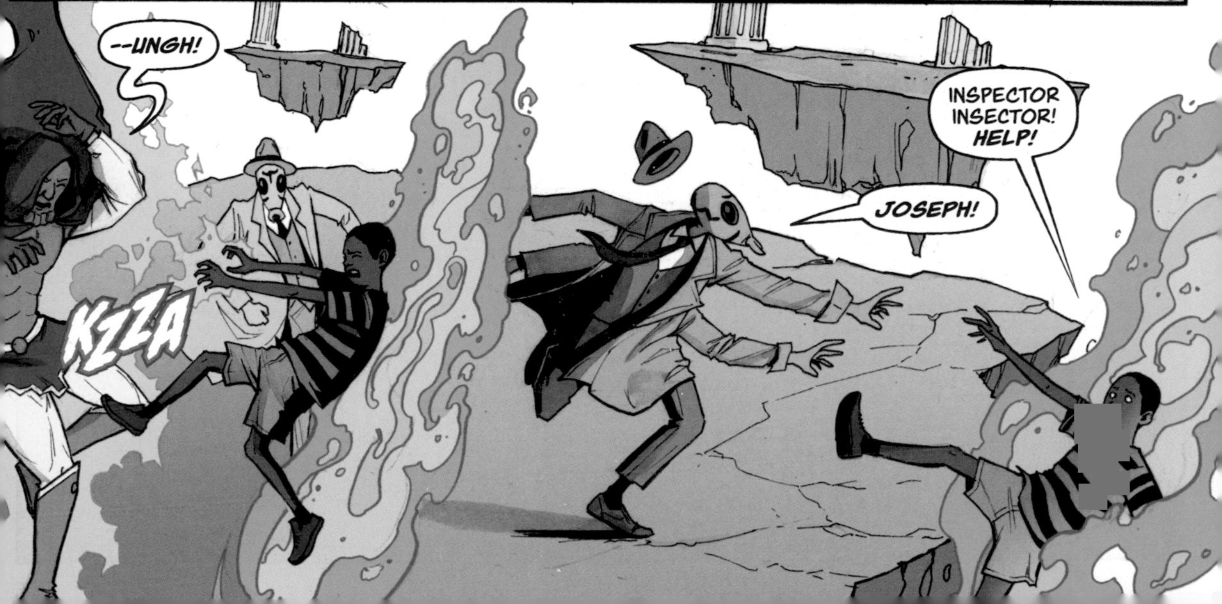
--UNGH!
KZZA
INSPECTOR INSECTOR! HELP!
JOSEPH!

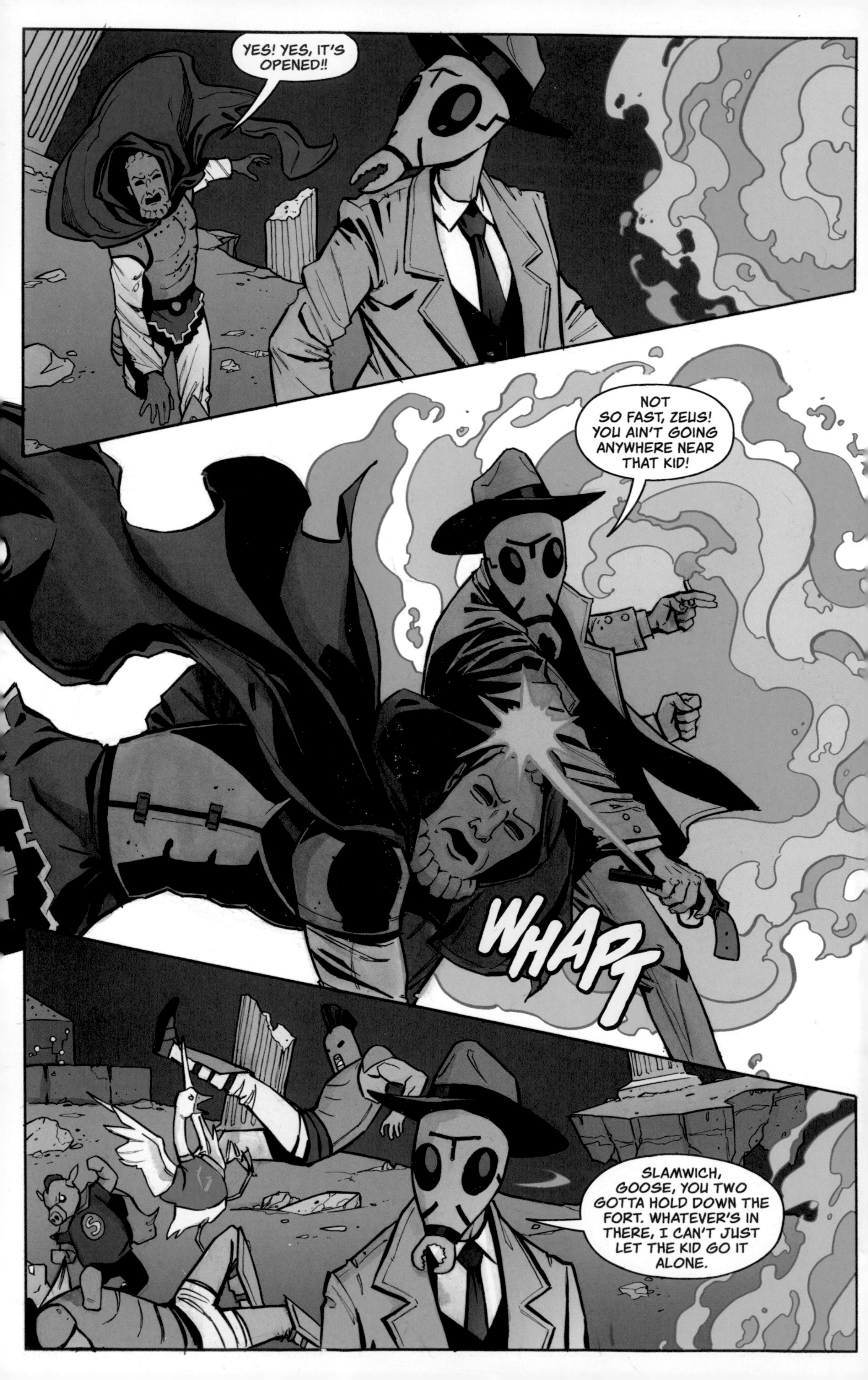
YES! YES, IT'S OPENED!!
NOT SO FAST, ZEUS! YOU AIN'T GOING ANYWHERE NEAR THAT KID!
WHAPT
SLAMWICH, GOOSE, YOU TWO GOTTA HOLD DOWN THE FORT. WHATEVER'S IN THERE, I CAN'T JUST LET THE KID GO IT ALONE.

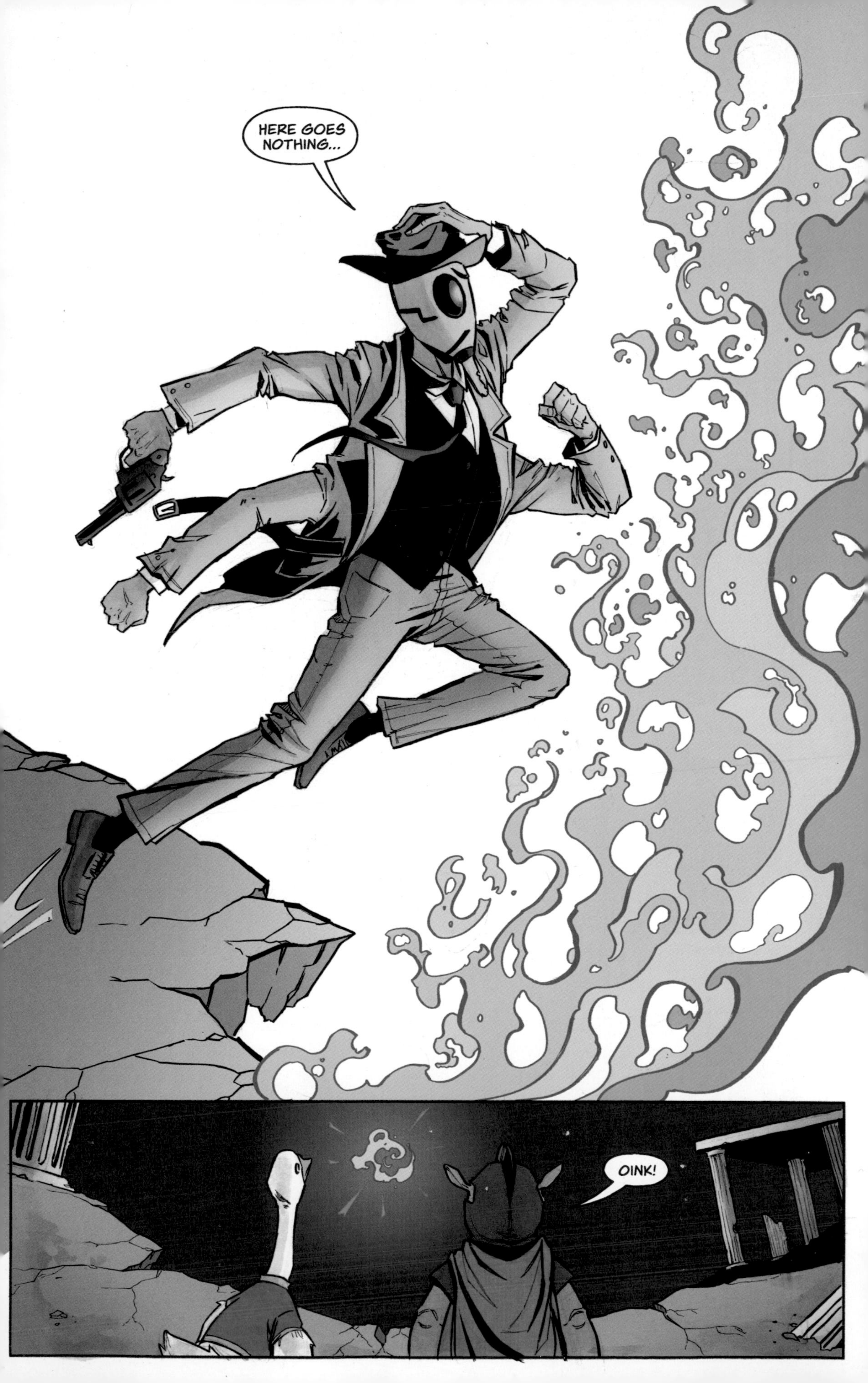
HERE GOES NOTHING...
OINK!

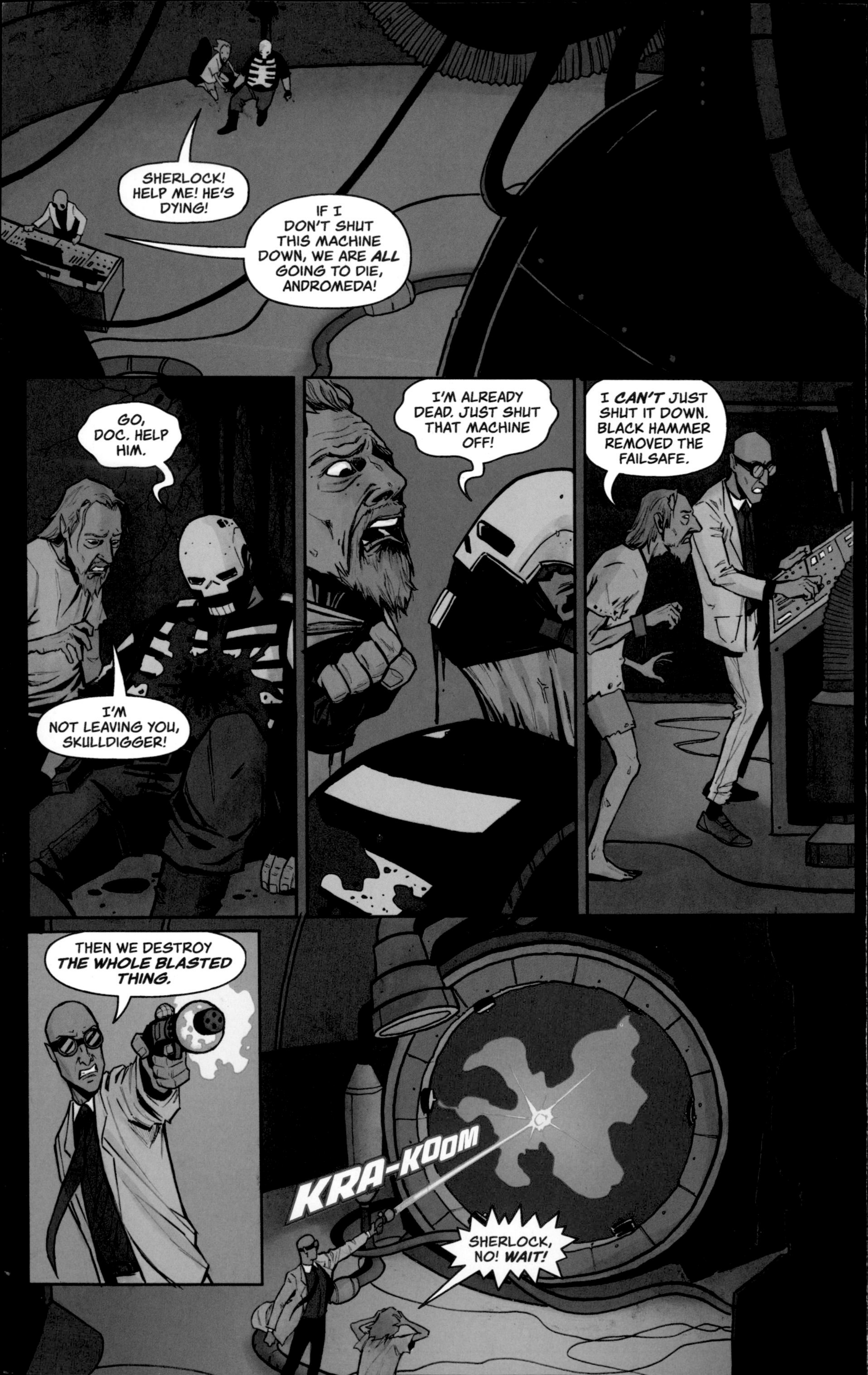
SHERLOCK! HELP ME! HE'S DYING!
IF I DON'T SHUT THIS MACHINE DOWN, WE ARE ALL GOING TO DIE, ANDROMEDA!
GO, DOC. HELP HIM.
I'M NOT LEAVING YOU, SKULLDIGGER!
I'M ALREADY DEAD. JUST SHUT THAT MACHINE OFF!
I CAN'T JUST SHUT IT DOWN. BLACK HAMMER REMOVED THE FAILSAFE.
THEN WE DESTROY THE WHOLE BLASTED THING.
KRA-KOOM
SHERLOCK, NO! WAIT!

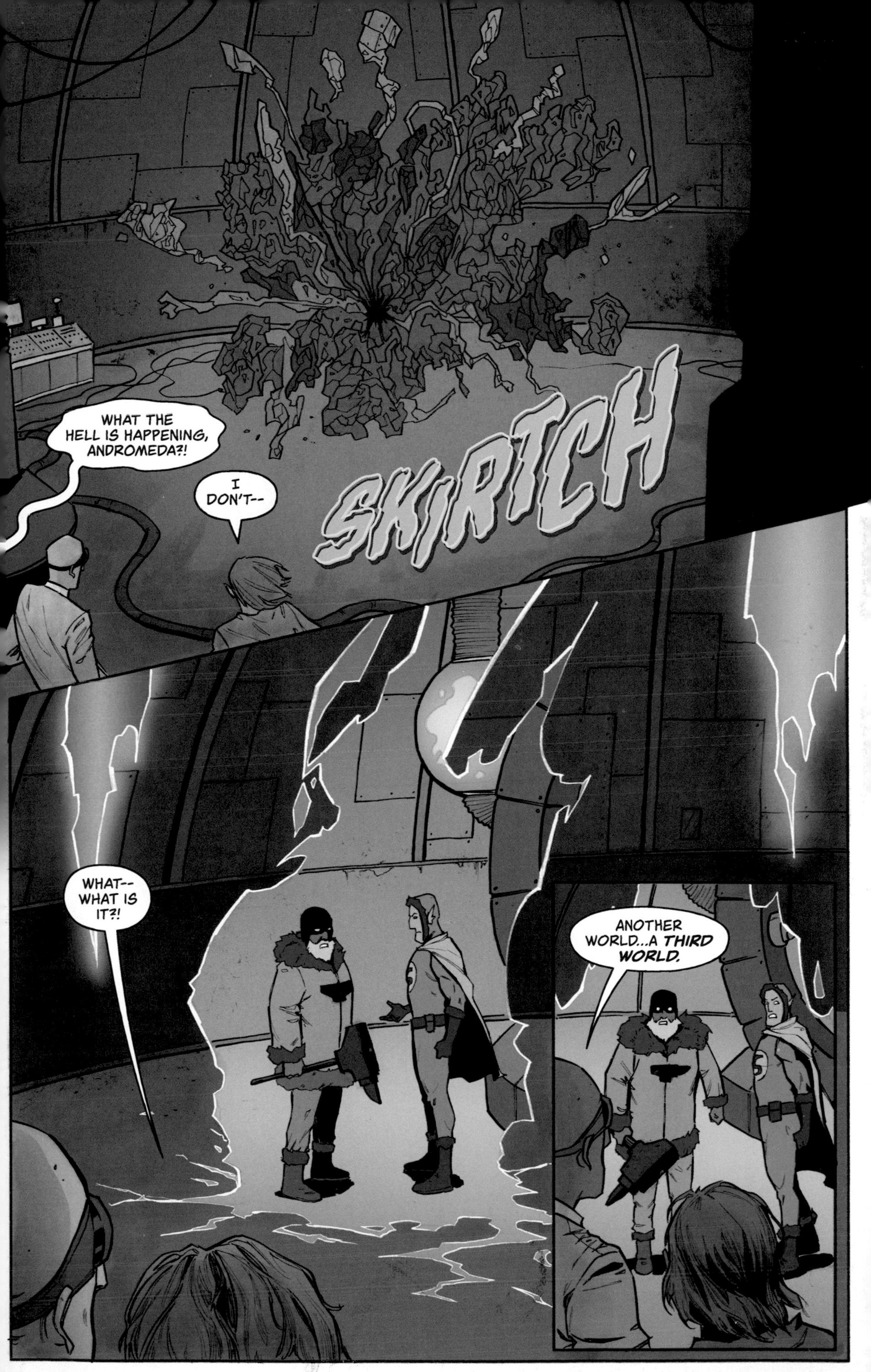
WHAT THE HELL IS HAPPENING, ANDROMEDA?!
I DON'T--
SKIRTCH
WHAT-- WHAT IS IT?!
ANOTHER WORLD...A *THIRD WORLD.*

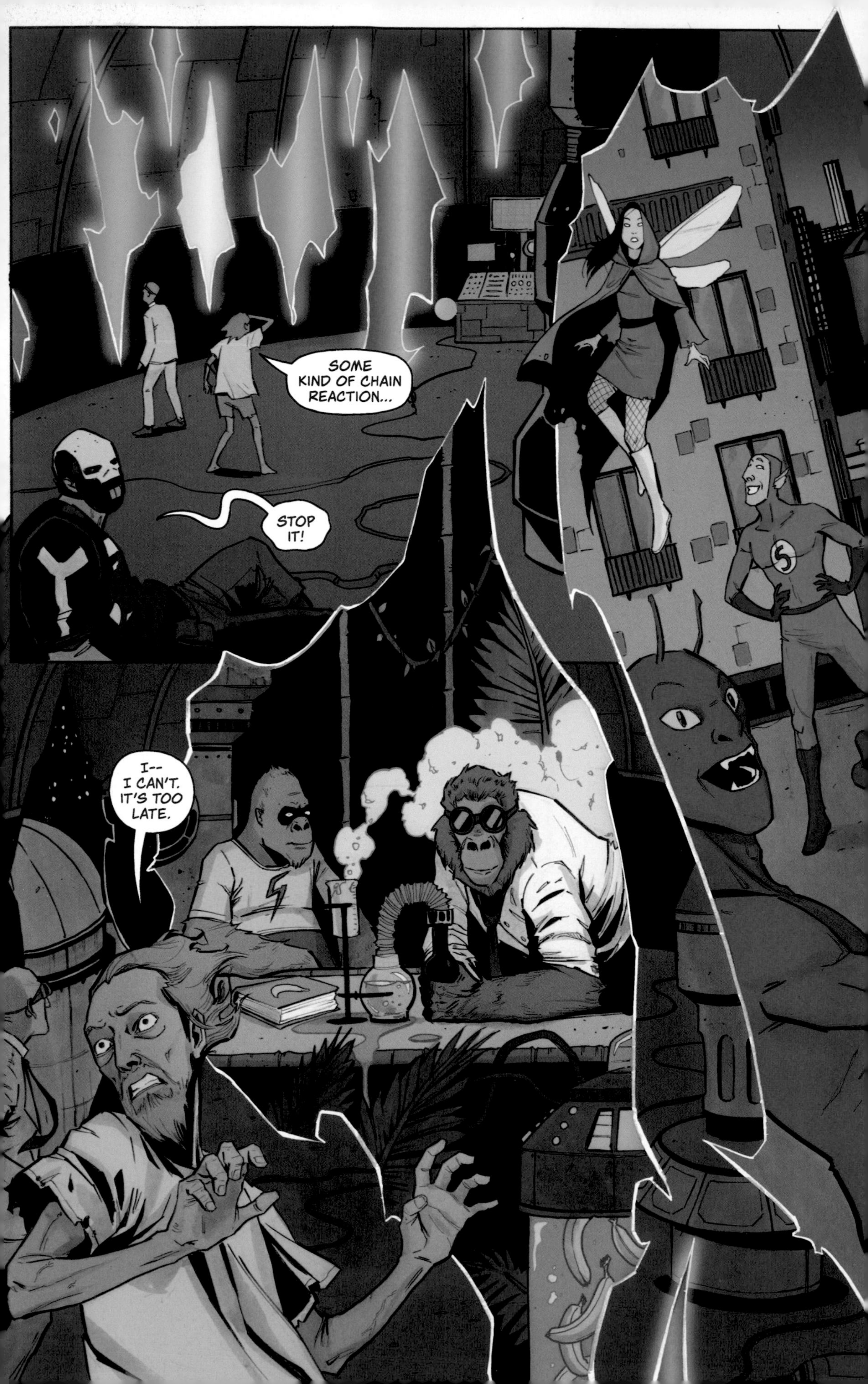
SOME KIND OF CHAIN REACTION...
STOP IT!
I-- I CAN'T. IT'S TOO LATE.

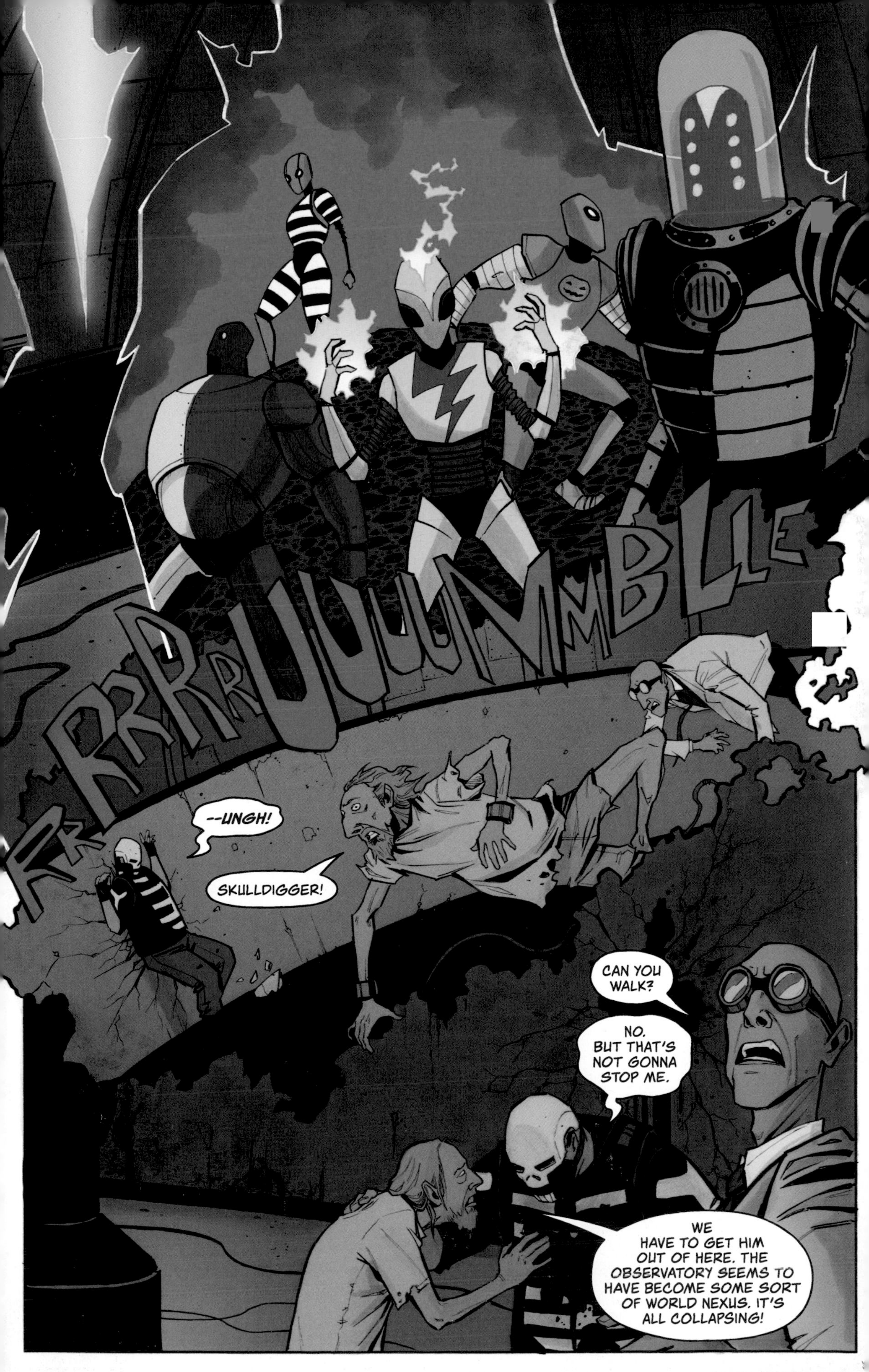
RRRRRUUUUMMMBLLE
--UNGH!
SKULLDIGGER!
CAN YOU WALK?
NO. BUT THAT'S NOT GONNA STOP ME.
WE HAVE TO GET HIM OUT OF HERE. THE OBSERVATORY SEEMS TO HAVE BECOME SOME SORT OF WORLD NEXUS. IT'S ALL COLLAPSING!

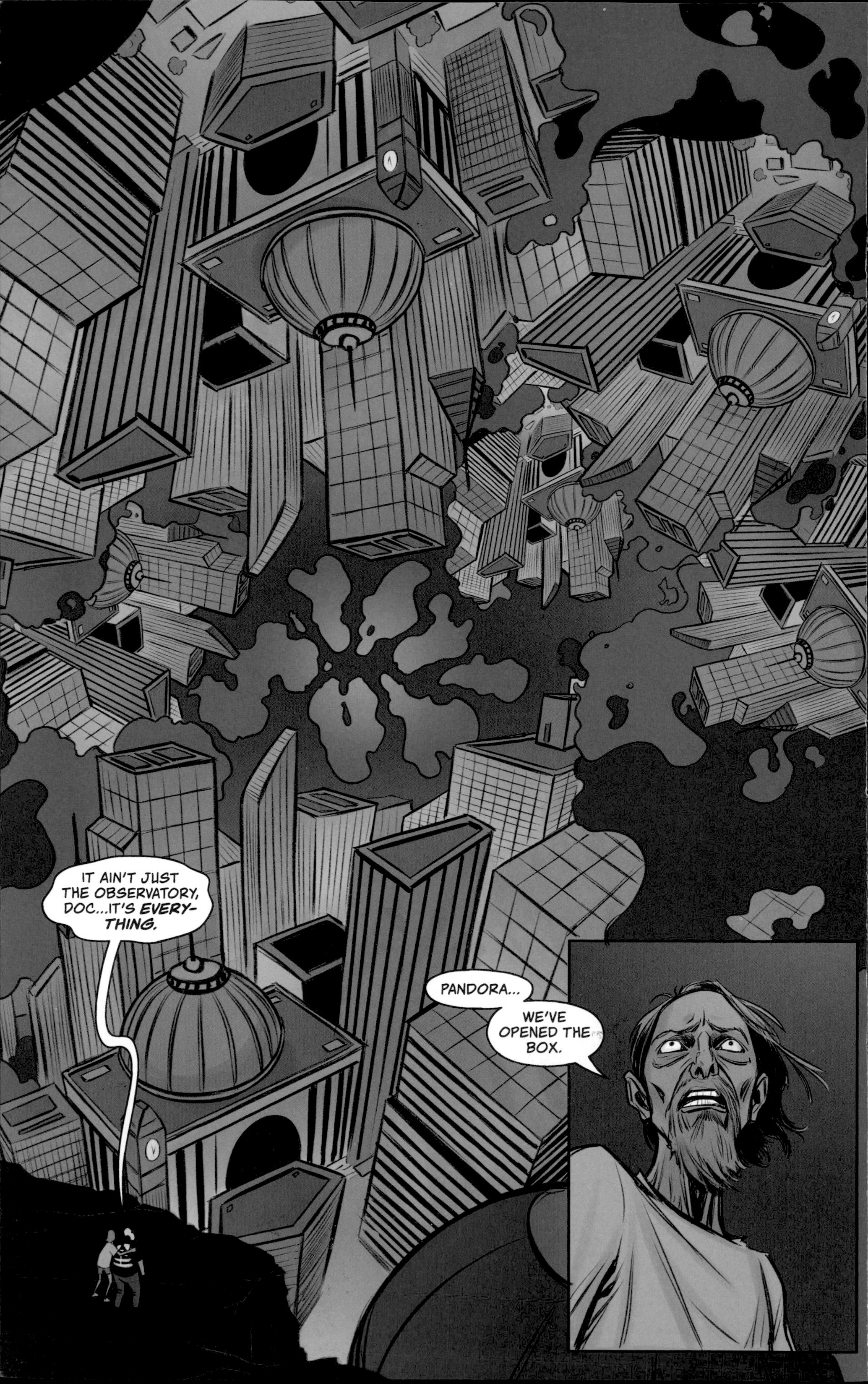
IT AIN'T JUST THE OBSERVATORY, DOC...IT'S *EVERYTHING.*
PANDORA...
WE'VE OPENED THE BOX.

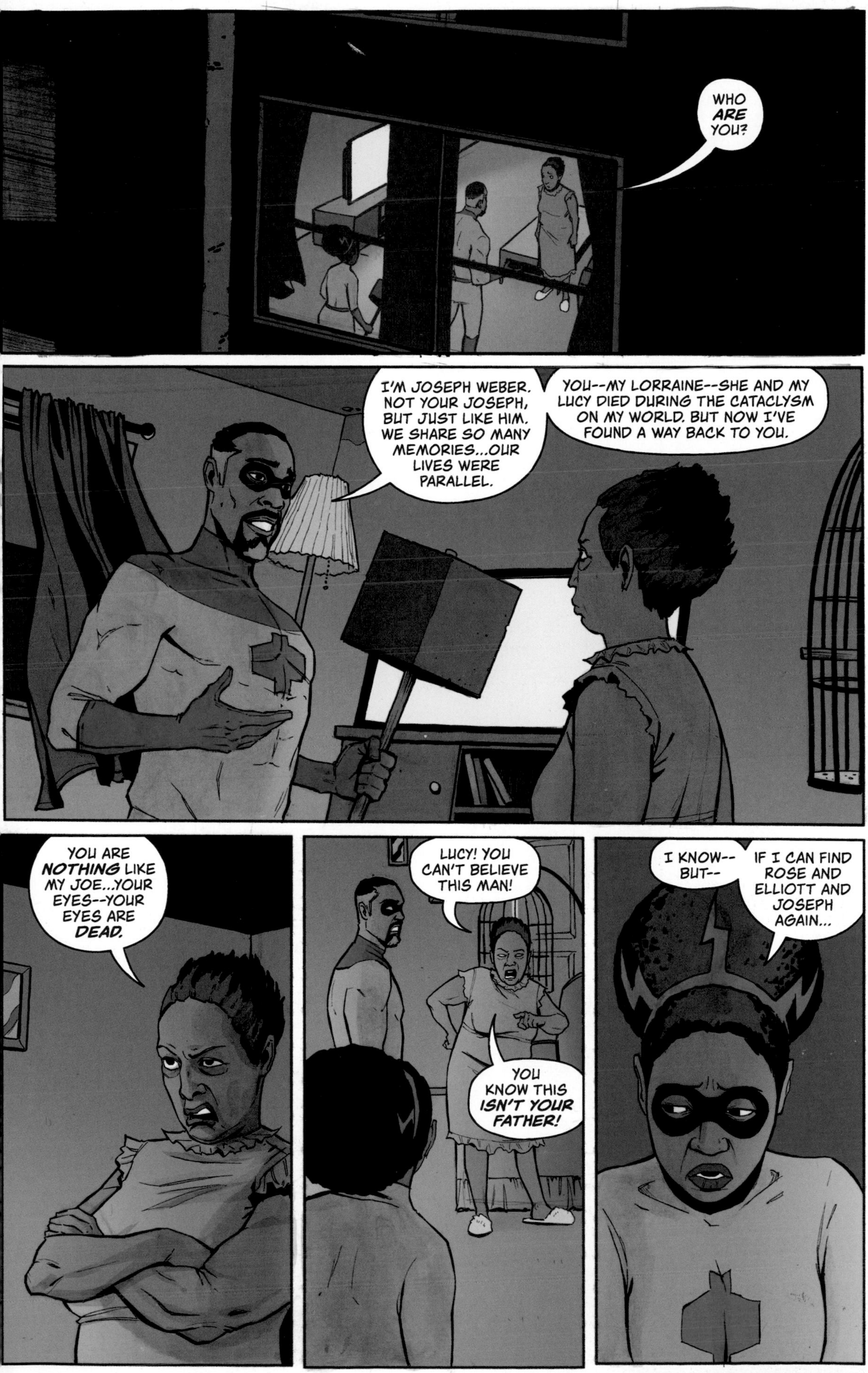
WHO ARE YOU?
I'M JOSEPH WEBER. NOT YOUR JOSEPH, BUT JUST LIKE HIM. WE SHARE SO MANY MEMORIES...OUR LIVES WERE PARALLEL.
YOU--MY LORRAINE--SHE AND MY LUCY DIED DURING THE CATACLYSM ON MY WORLD. BUT NOW I'VE FOUND A WAY BACK TO YOU.
YOU ARE NOTHING LIKE MY JOE...YOUR EYES--YOUR EYES ARE DEAD.
LUCY! YOU CAN'T BELIEVE THIS MAN!
YOU KNOW THIS ISN'T YOUR FATHER!
I KNOW-- BUT--
IF I CAN FIND ROSE AND ELLIOTT AND JOSEPH AGAIN...

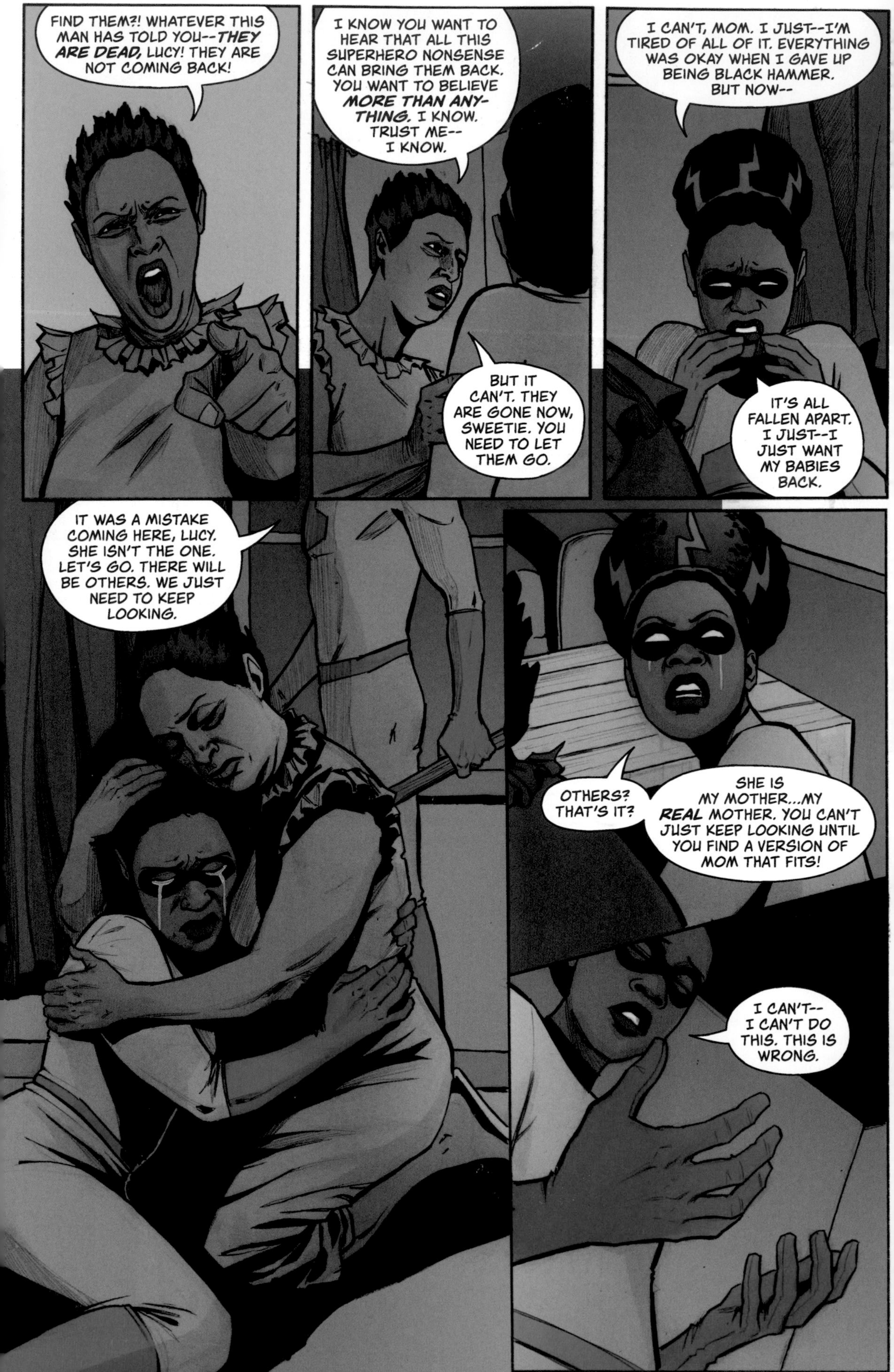
FIND THEM?! WHATEVER THIS MAN HAS TOLD YOU--THEY ARE DEAD, LUCY! THEY ARE NOT COMING BACK!
I KNOW YOU WANT TO HEAR THAT ALL THIS SUPERHERO NONSENSE CAN BRING THEM BACK. YOU WANT TO BELIEVE MORE THAN ANY-THING. I KNOW. TRUST ME-- I KNOW.
BUT IT CAN'T. THEY ARE GONE NOW, SWEETIE. YOU NEED TO LET THEM GO.
I CAN'T, MOM. I JUST--I'M TIRED OF ALL OF IT. EVERYTHING WAS OKAY WHEN I GAVE UP BEING BLACK HAMMER. BUT NOW--
IT'S ALL FALLEN APART. I JUST--I JUST WANT MY BABIES BACK.
IT WAS A MISTAKE COMING HERE, LUCY. SHE ISN'T THE ONE. LET'S GO. THERE WILL BE OTHERS. WE JUST NEED TO KEEP LOOKING.
OTHERS? THAT'S IT?
SHE IS MY MOTHER...MY REAL MOTHER. YOU CAN'T JUST KEEP LOOKING UNTIL YOU FIND A VERSION OF MOM THAT FITS!
I CAN'T-- I CAN'T DO THIS. THIS IS WRONG.

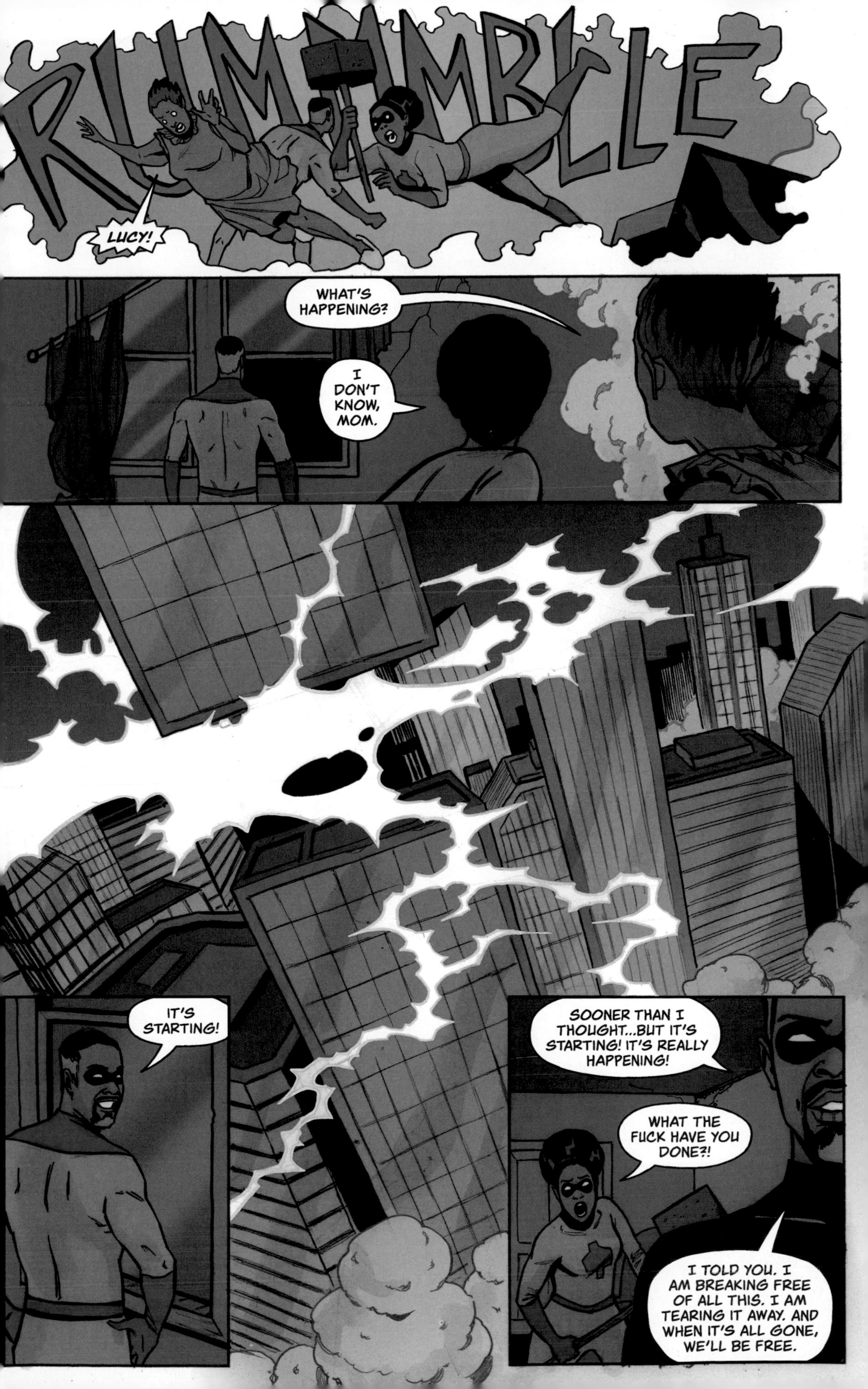
RUMMMBLE
LUCY!
WHAT'S HAPPENING?
I DON'T KNOW, MOM.
IT'S STARTING!
SOONER THAN I THOUGHT...BUT IT'S STARTING! IT'S REALLY HAPPENING!
WHAT THE FUCK HAVE YOU DONE?!
I TOLD YOU. I AM BREAKING FREE OF ALL THIS. I AM TEARING IT AWAY. AND WHEN IT'S ALL GONE, WE'LL BE FREE.

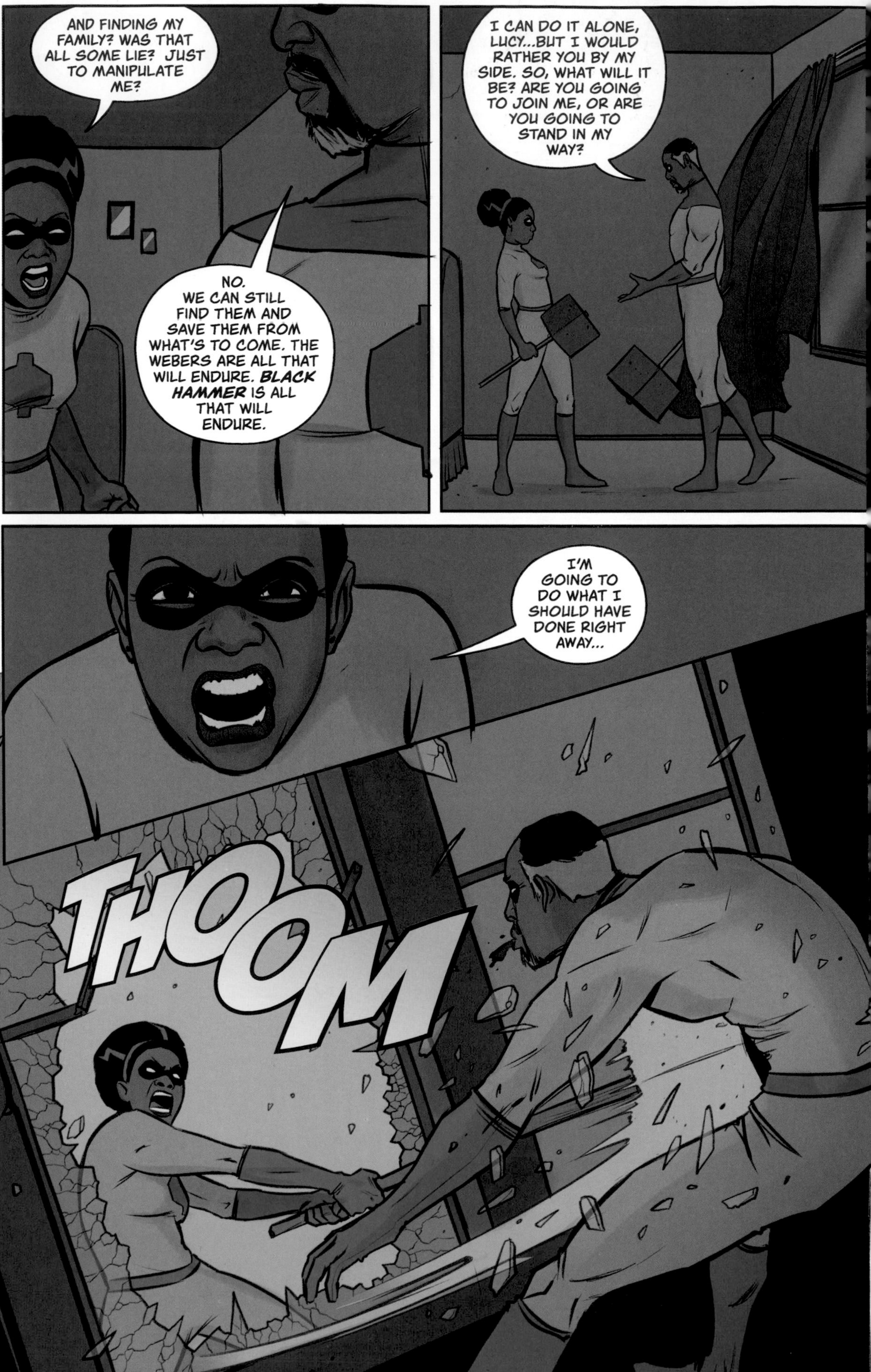

AND FINDING MY FAMILY? WAS THAT ALL SOME LIE? JUST TO MANIPULATE ME?
NO. WE CAN STILL FIND THEM AND SAVE THEM FROM WHAT'S TO COME. THE WEBERS ARE ALL THAT WILL ENDURE. *BLACK HAMMER* IS ALL THAT WILL ENDURE.
I CAN DO IT ALONE, LUCY...BUT I WOULD RATHER YOU BY MY SIDE. SO, WHAT WILL IT BE? ARE YOU GOING TO JOIN ME, OR ARE YOU GOING TO STAND IN MY WAY?
I'M GOING TO DO WHAT I SHOULD HAVE DONE RIGHT AWAY...
THOOM

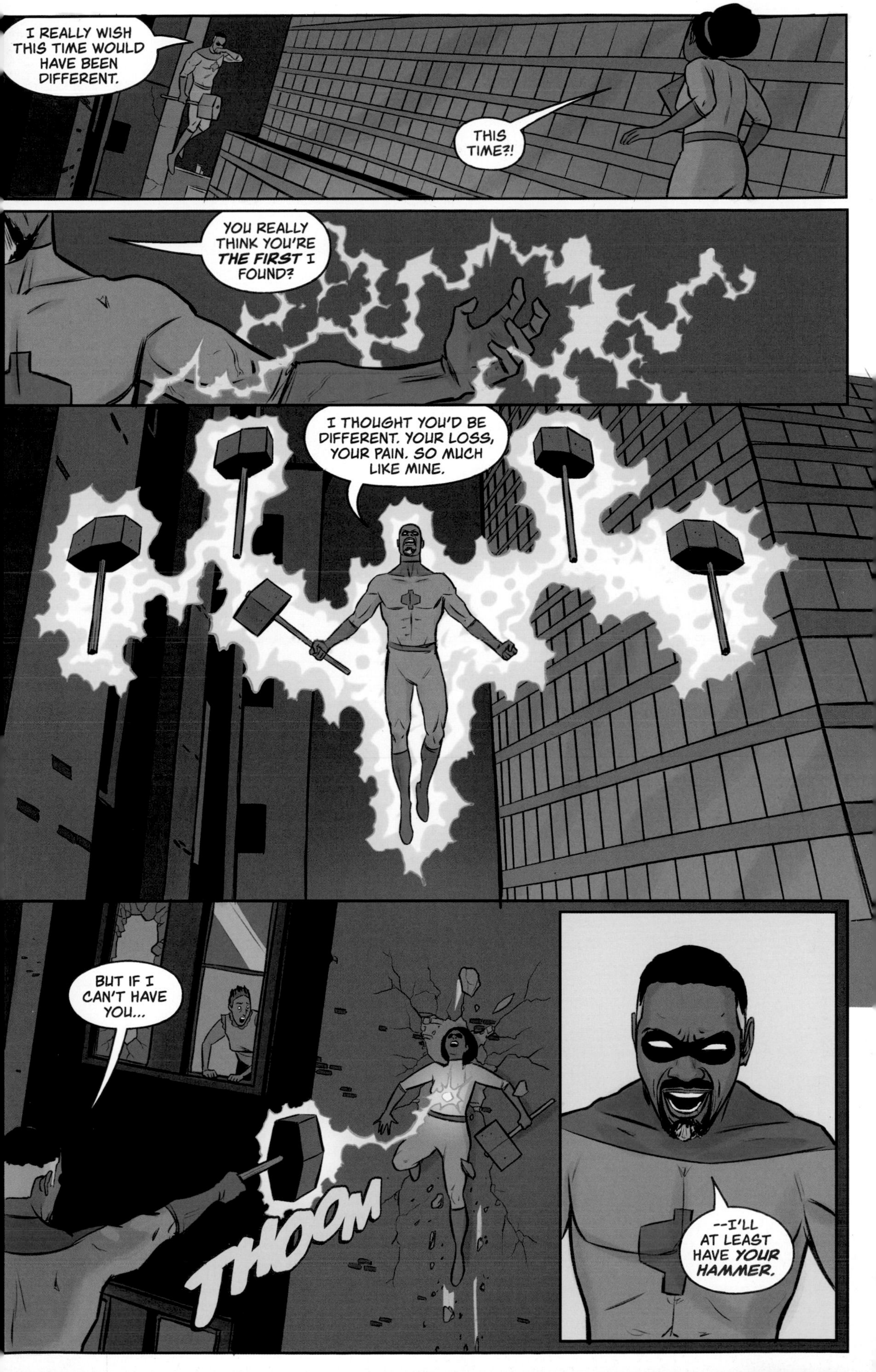

I REALLY WISH THIS TIME WOULD HAVE BEEN DIFFERENT.
THIS TIME?!
YOU REALLY THINK YOU'RE THE FIRST I FOUND?
I THOUGHT YOU'D BE DIFFERENT. YOUR LOSS, YOUR PAIN. SO MUCH LIKE MINE.
BUT IF I CAN'T HAVE YOU...
THOOM
--I'LL AT LEAST HAVE YOUR HAMMER.

ELSEWHERE.

KZZZZZACKT

UNGH!

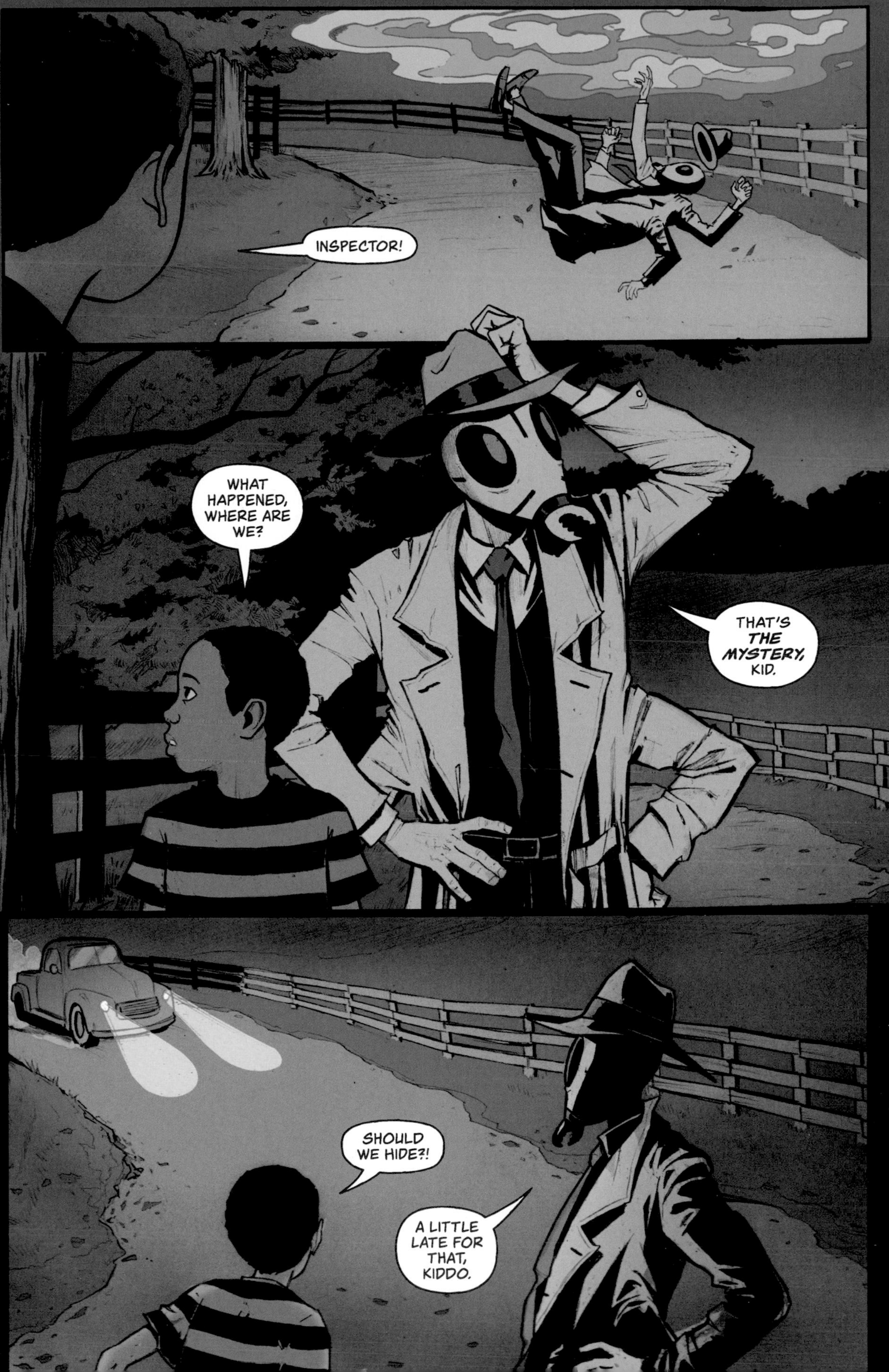
INSPECTOR!
WHAT HAPPENED, WHERE ARE WE?
THAT'S *THE MYSTERY,* KID.
SHOULD WE HIDE?!
A LITTLE LATE FOR THAT, KIDDO.

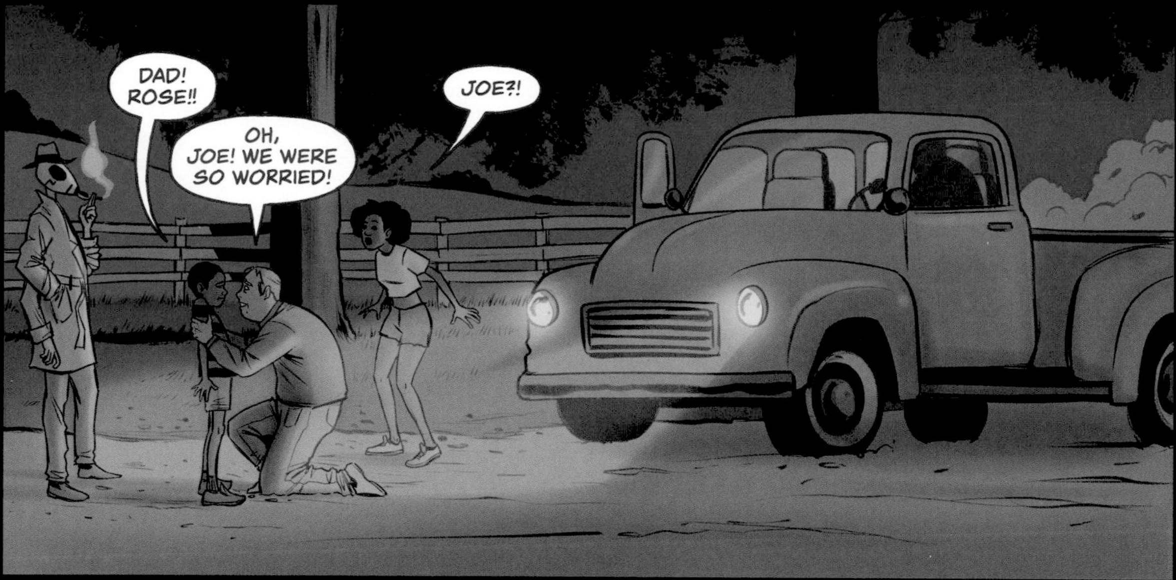
DAD! ROSE!!
OH, JOE! WE WERE SO WORRIED!
JOE?!

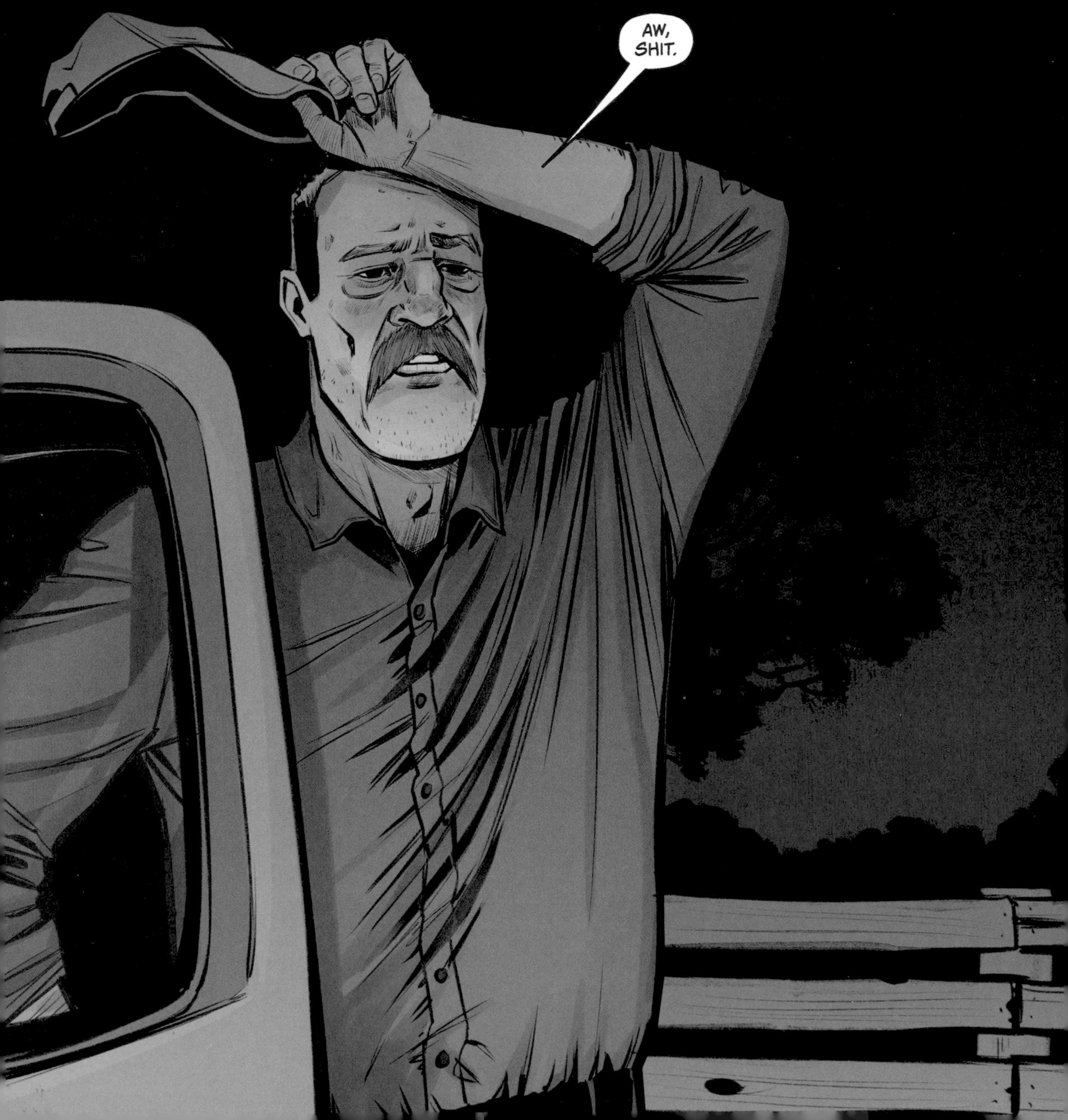
AW, SHIT.

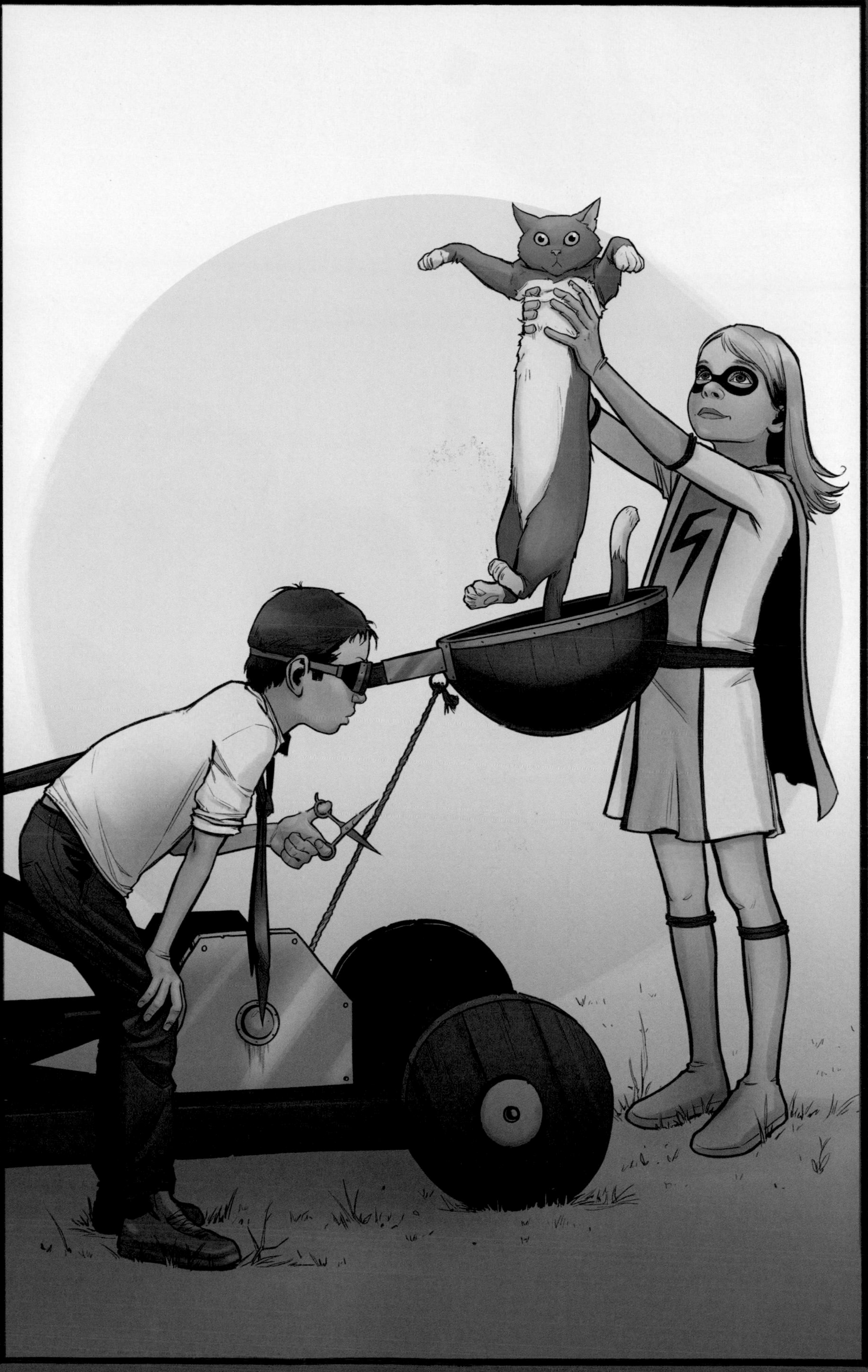

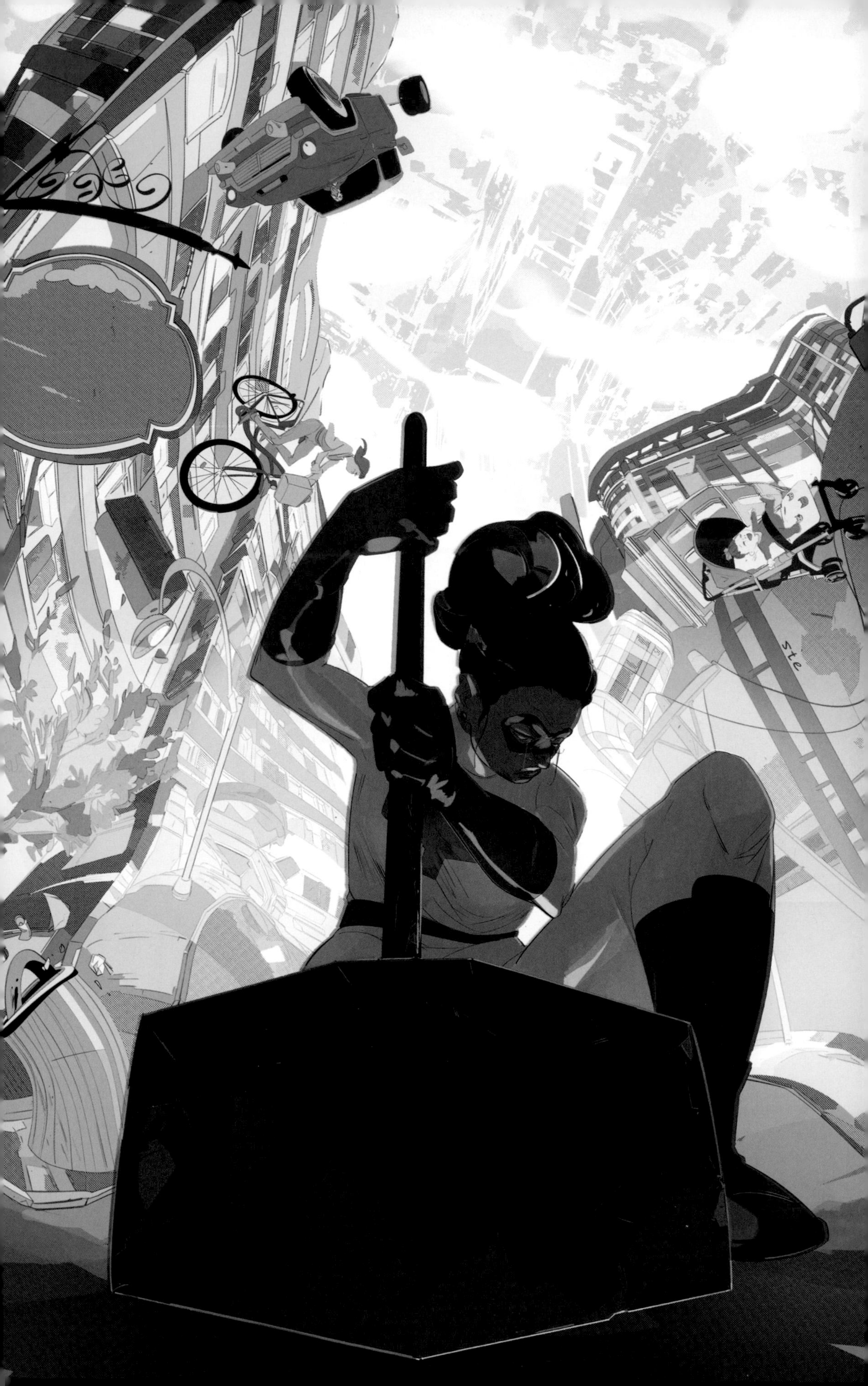

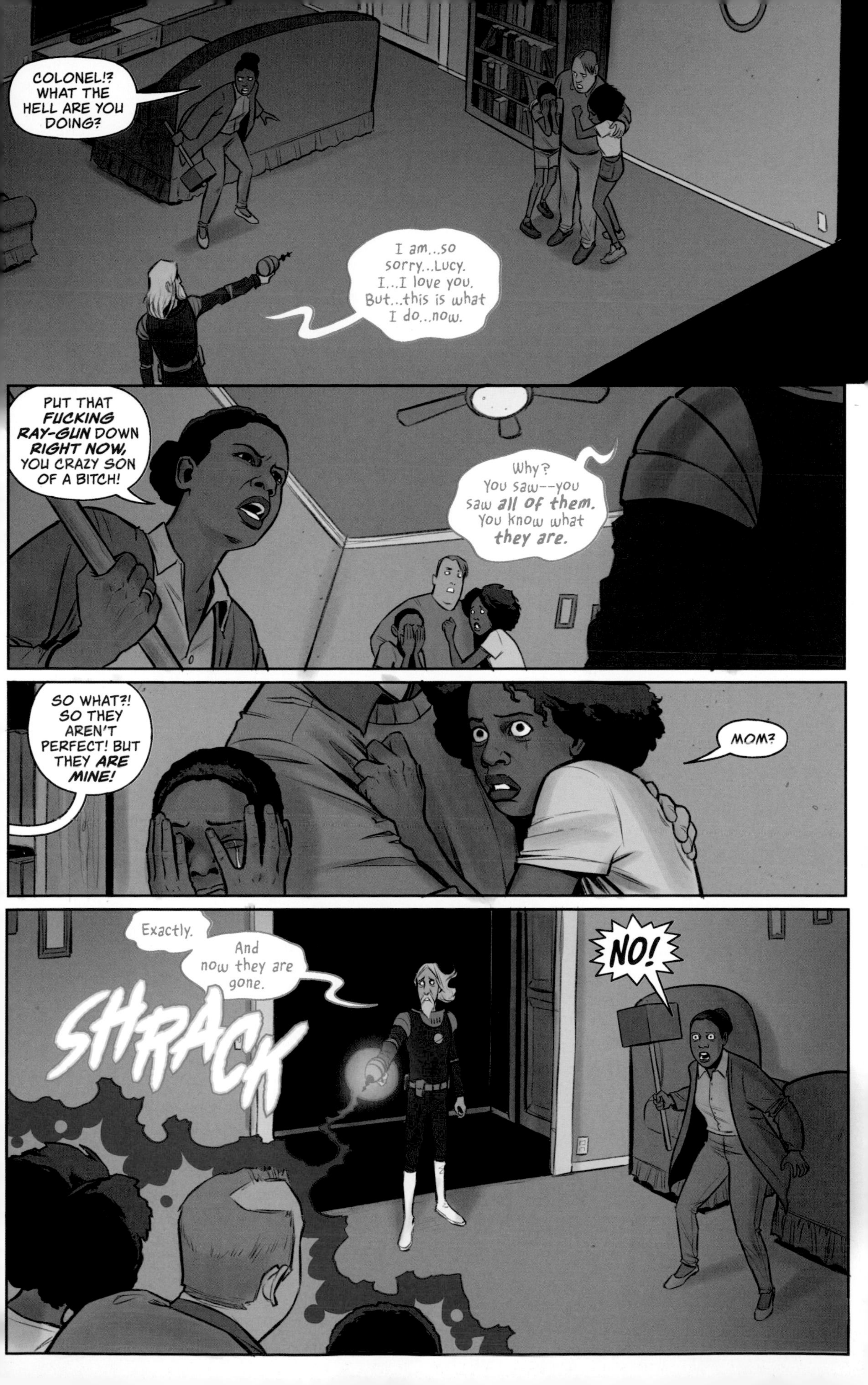
COLONEL!? WHAT THE HELL ARE YOU DOING?
I am...so sorry...Lucy. I...I love you. But...this is what I do...now.
PUT THAT **FUCKING RAY-GUN** DOWN **RIGHT NOW,** YOU CRAZY SON OF A BITCH!
Why? You saw--you saw **all of them.** You know what **they are.**
SO WHAT?! SO THEY AREN'T PERFECT! BUT THEY **ARE MINE!**
MOM?
Exactly.
And now they are gone.
SHRACK
NO!

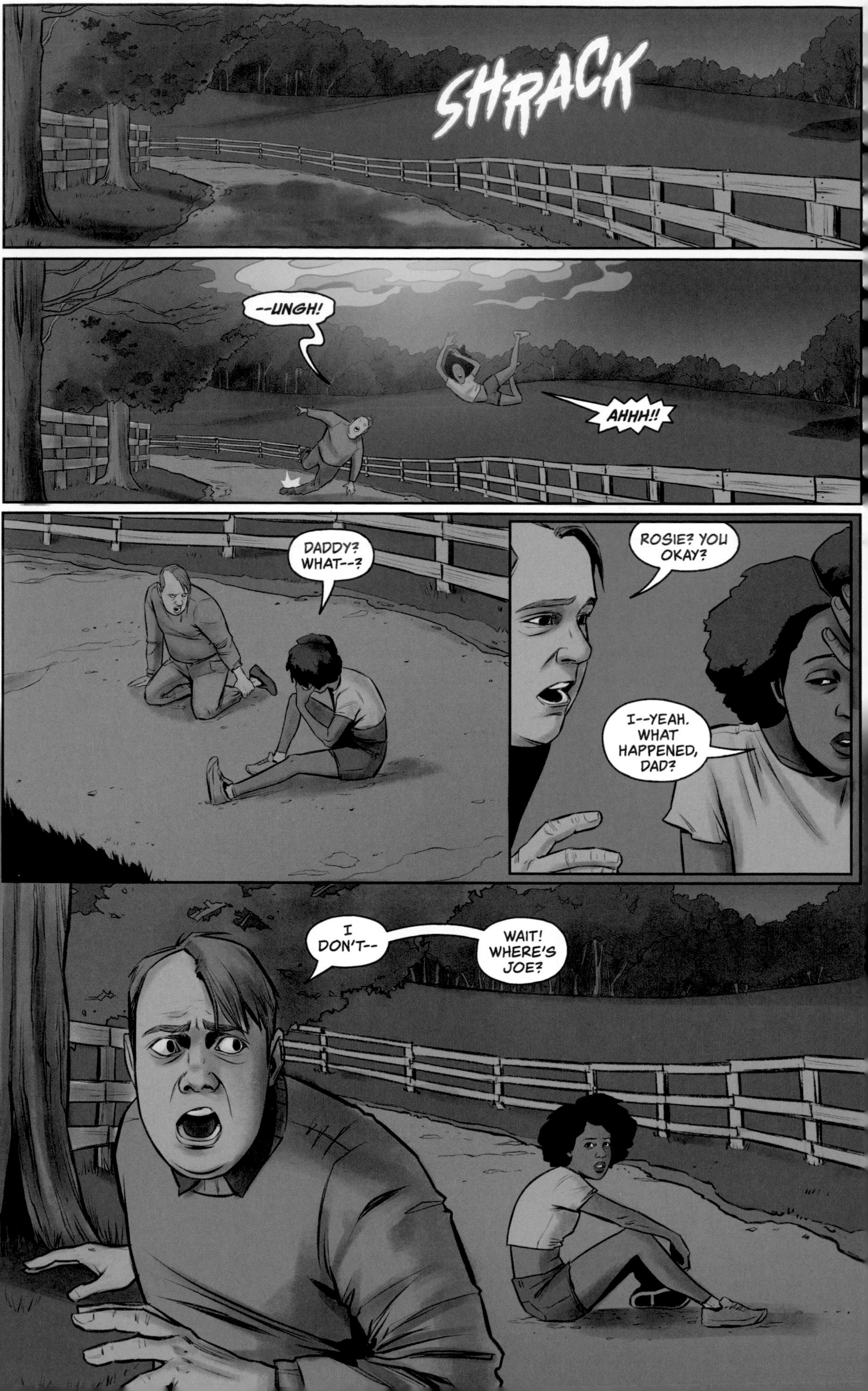
SHRACK
--UNGH!
AHHH!!
DADDY? WHAT--?
ROSIE? YOU OKAY?
I--YEAH. WHAT HAPPENED, DAD?
I DON'T--
WAIT! WHERE'S JOE?

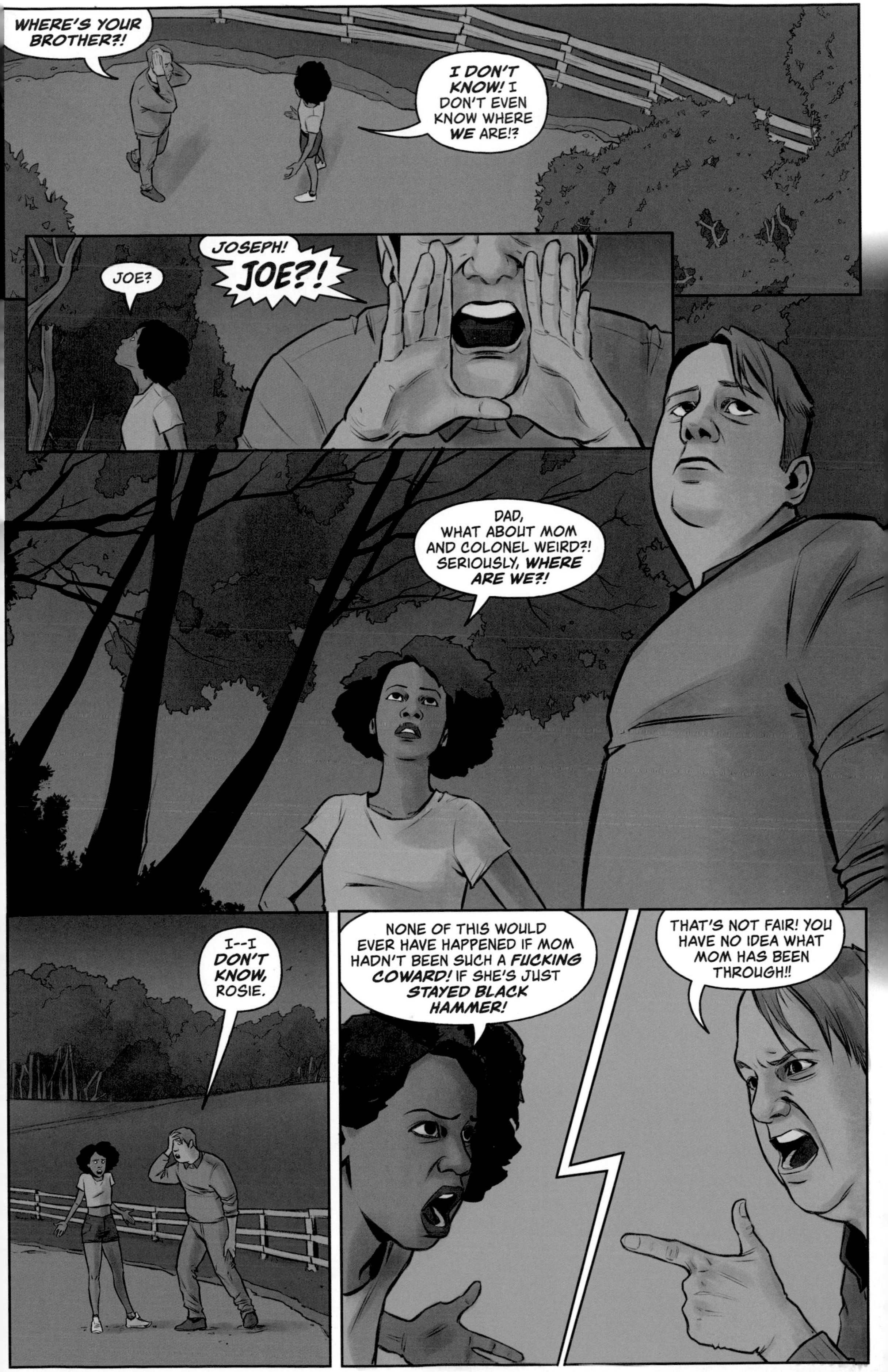
WHERE'S YOUR BROTHER?!
I DON'T KNOW! I DON'T EVEN KNOW WHERE WE ARE!?
JOE?
JOSEPH!
JOE?!
DAD, WHAT ABOUT MOM AND COLONEL WEIRD?! SERIOUSLY, WHERE ARE WE?!
I--I DON'T KNOW, ROSIE.
NONE OF THIS WOULD EVER HAVE HAPPENED IF MOM HADN'T BEEN SUCH A FUCKING COWARD! IF SHE'S JUST STAYED BLACK HAMMER!
THAT'S NOT FAIR! YOU HAVE NO IDEA WHAT MOM HAS BEEN THROUGH!!

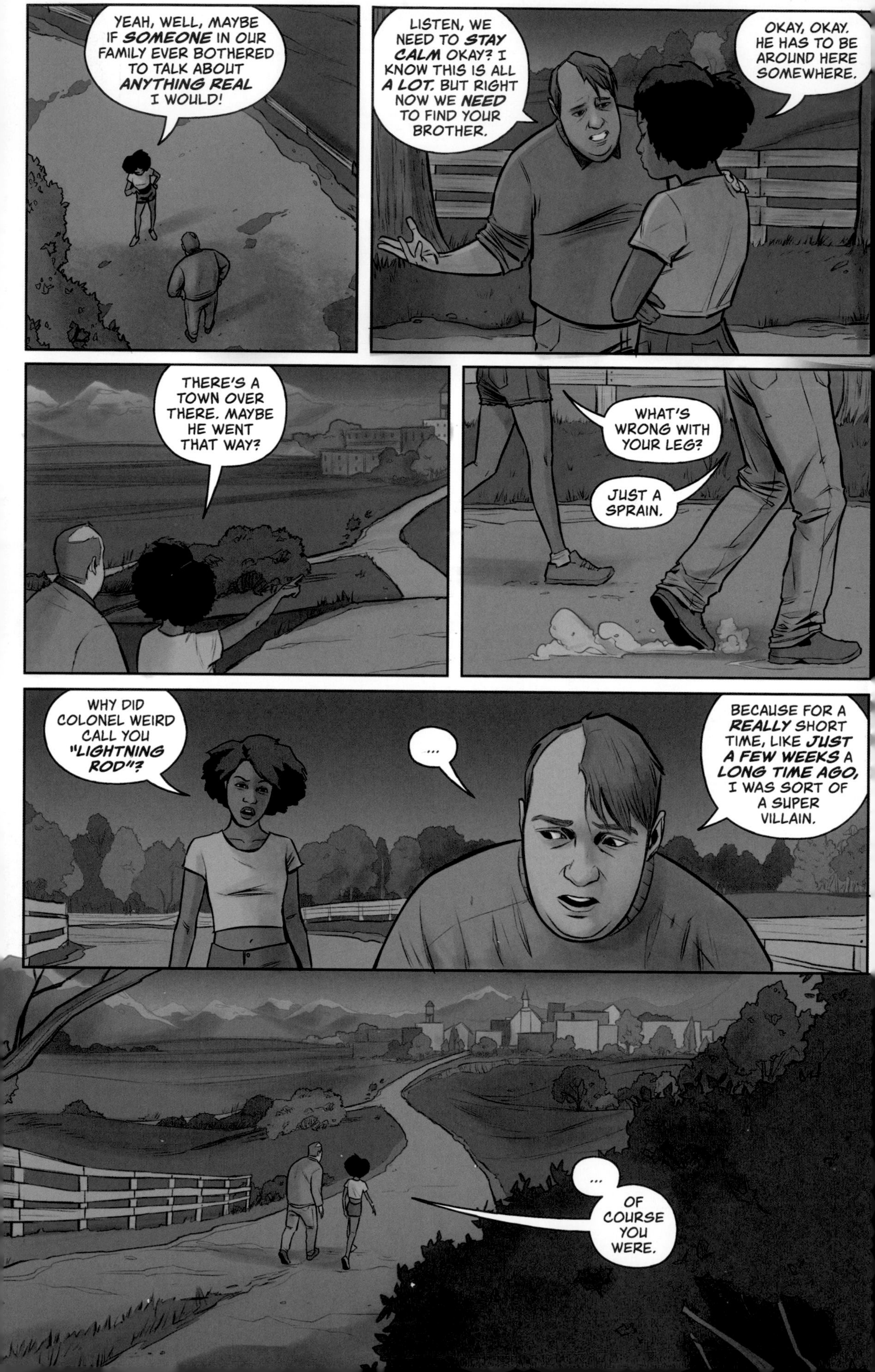
YEAH, WELL, MAYBE IF SOMEONE IN OUR FAMILY EVER BOTHERED TO TALK ABOUT ANYTHING REAL I WOULD!
LISTEN, WE NEED TO STAY CALM OKAY? I KNOW THIS IS ALL A LOT. BUT RIGHT NOW WE NEED TO FIND YOUR BROTHER.
OKAY, OKAY. HE HAS TO BE AROUND HERE SOMEWHERE.
THERE'S A TOWN OVER THERE. MAYBE HE WENT THAT WAY?
WHAT'S WRONG WITH YOUR LEG?
JUST A SPRAIN.
WHY DID COLONEL WEIRD CALL YOU "LIGHTNING ROD"?
...
BECAUSE FOR A REALLY SHORT TIME, LIKE JUST A FEW WEEKS A LONG TIME AGO, I WAS SORT OF A SUPER VILLAIN.
...
OF COURSE YOU WERE.

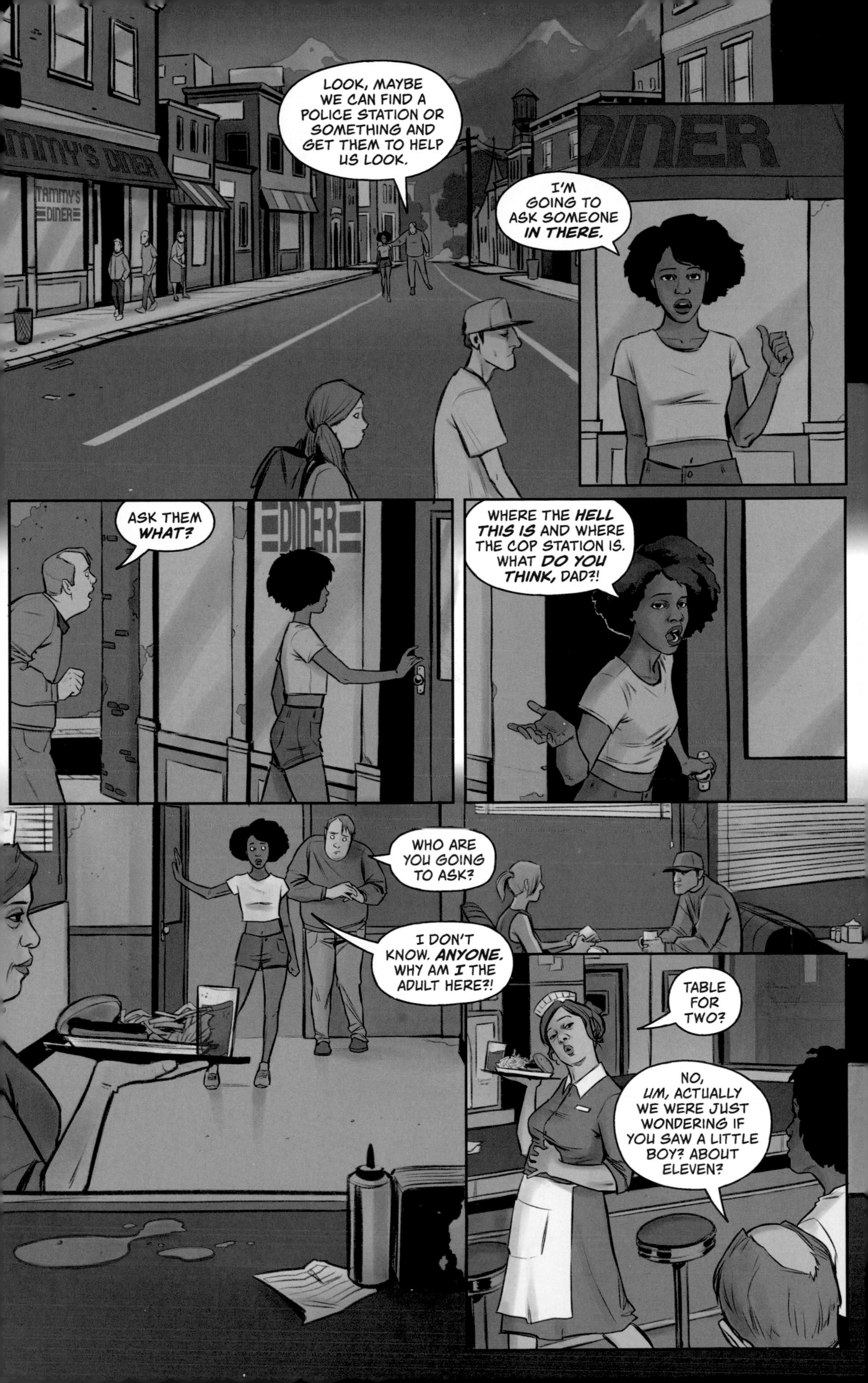
TAMMY'S DINER
LOOK, MAYBE WE CAN FIND A POLICE STATION OR SOMETHING AND GET THEM TO HELP US LOOK.
DINER
I'M GOING TO ASK SOMEONE *IN THERE.*
ASK THEM *WHAT?*
DINER
WHERE THE *HELL THIS IS* AND WHERE THE COP STATION IS. WHAT *DO YOU THINK,* DAD?!
WHO ARE YOU GOING TO ASK?
I DON'T KNOW. *ANYONE.* WHY AM *I* THE ADULT HERE?!
TABLE FOR TWO?
NO, *UM,* ACTUALLY WE WERE JUST WONDERING IF YOU SAW A LITTLE BOY? ABOUT ELEVEN?

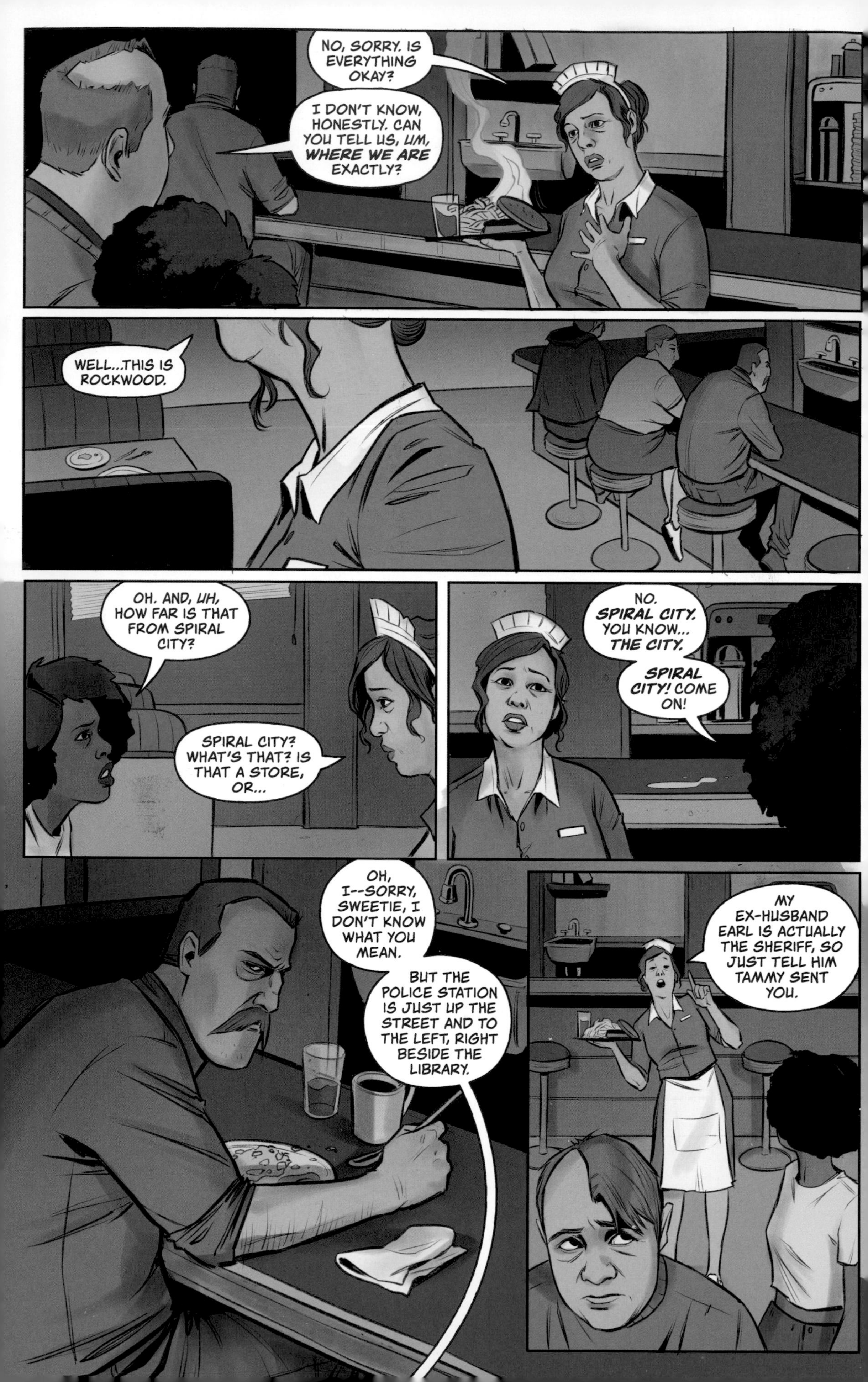
NO, SORRY. IS EVERYTHING OKAY?
I DON'T KNOW, HONESTLY. CAN YOU TELL US, *UM*, ***WHERE WE ARE*** EXACTLY?
WELL...THIS IS ROCKWOOD.
OH. AND, *UH*, HOW FAR IS THAT FROM SPIRAL CITY?
SPIRAL CITY? WHAT'S THAT? IS THAT A STORE, OR...
NO. ***SPIRAL CITY.*** YOU KNOW... ***THE CITY.***
SPIRAL CITY! COME ON!
OH, I--SORRY, SWEETIE, I DON'T KNOW WHAT YOU MEAN.
BUT THE POLICE STATION IS JUST UP THE STREET AND TO THE LEFT, RIGHT BESIDE THE LIBRARY.
MY EX-HUSBAND EARL IS ACTUALLY THE SHERIFF, SO JUST TELL HIM TAMMY SENT YOU.

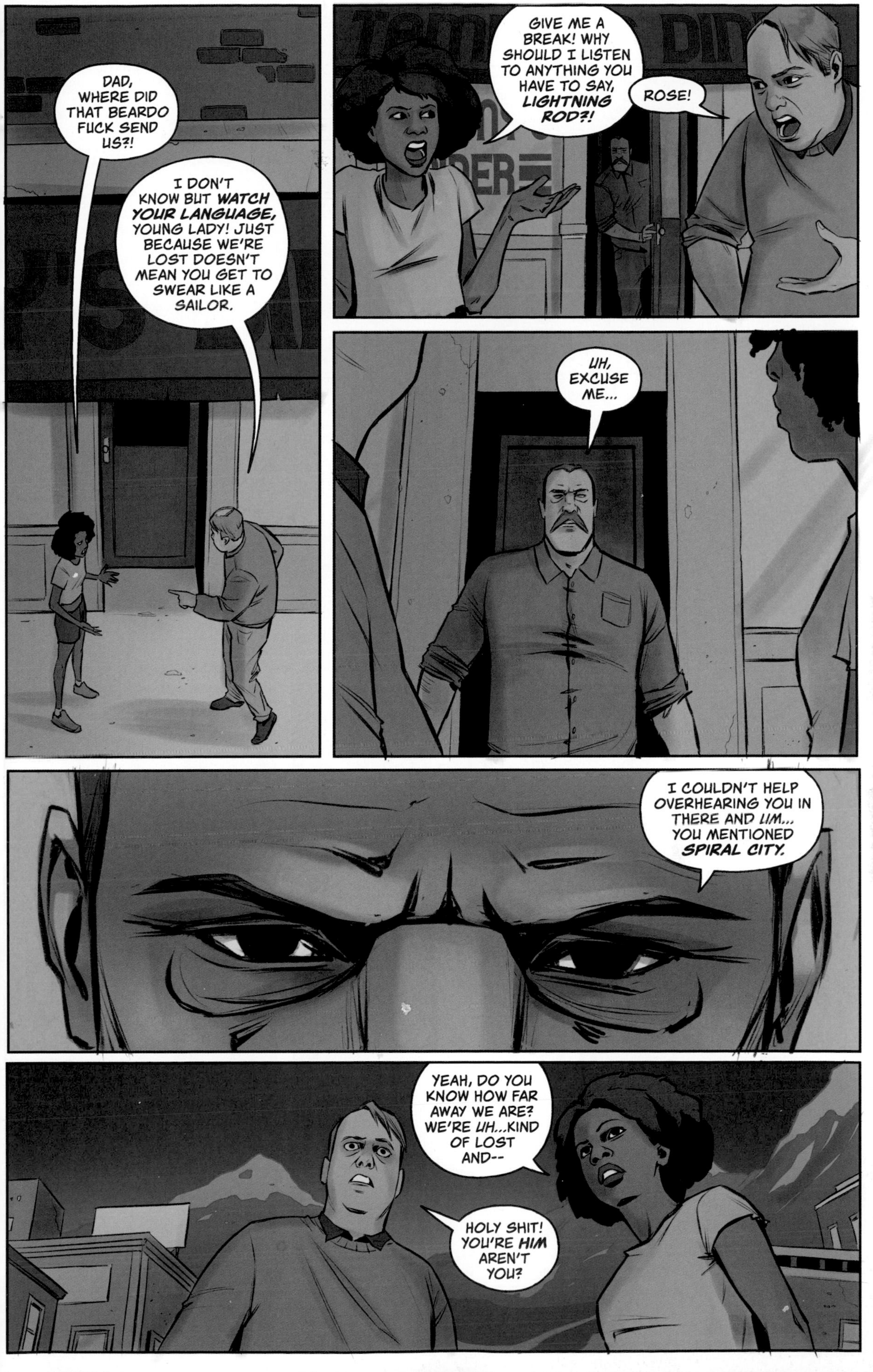
DAD, WHERE DID THAT BEARDO FUCK SEND US?!
I DON'T KNOW BUT WATCH YOUR LANGUAGE, YOUNG LADY! JUST BECAUSE WE'RE LOST DOESN'T MEAN YOU GET TO SWEAR LIKE A SAILOR.
GIVE ME A BREAK! WHY SHOULD I LISTEN TO ANYTHING YOU HAVE TO SAY, LIGHTNING ROD?!
ROSE!
UH, EXCUSE ME...
I COULDN'T HELP OVERHEARING YOU IN THERE AND UM... YOU MENTIONED SPIRAL CITY.
YEAH, DO YOU KNOW HOW FAR AWAY WE ARE? WE'RE UH...KIND OF LOST AND--
HOLY SHIT! YOU'RE HIM AREN'T YOU?

SORRY, I DON'T KNOW WHAT YOU MEAN THERE, BUDDY, BUT--

ABRAHAM SLAM. *YOU'RE ABRAHAM SLAM!*

KEEP YOUR *GODDAMN VOICE DOWN!*

HEY!

I DON'T KNOW WHO YOU TWO ARE, BUT WE DO NOT SAY THAT NAME AROUND HERE, UNDERSTAND?!

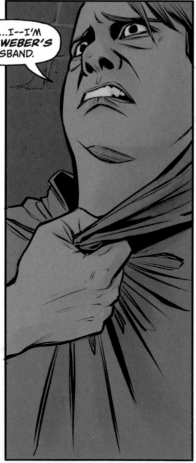

ABE...I--I'M *LUCY WEBER'S* HUSBAND.

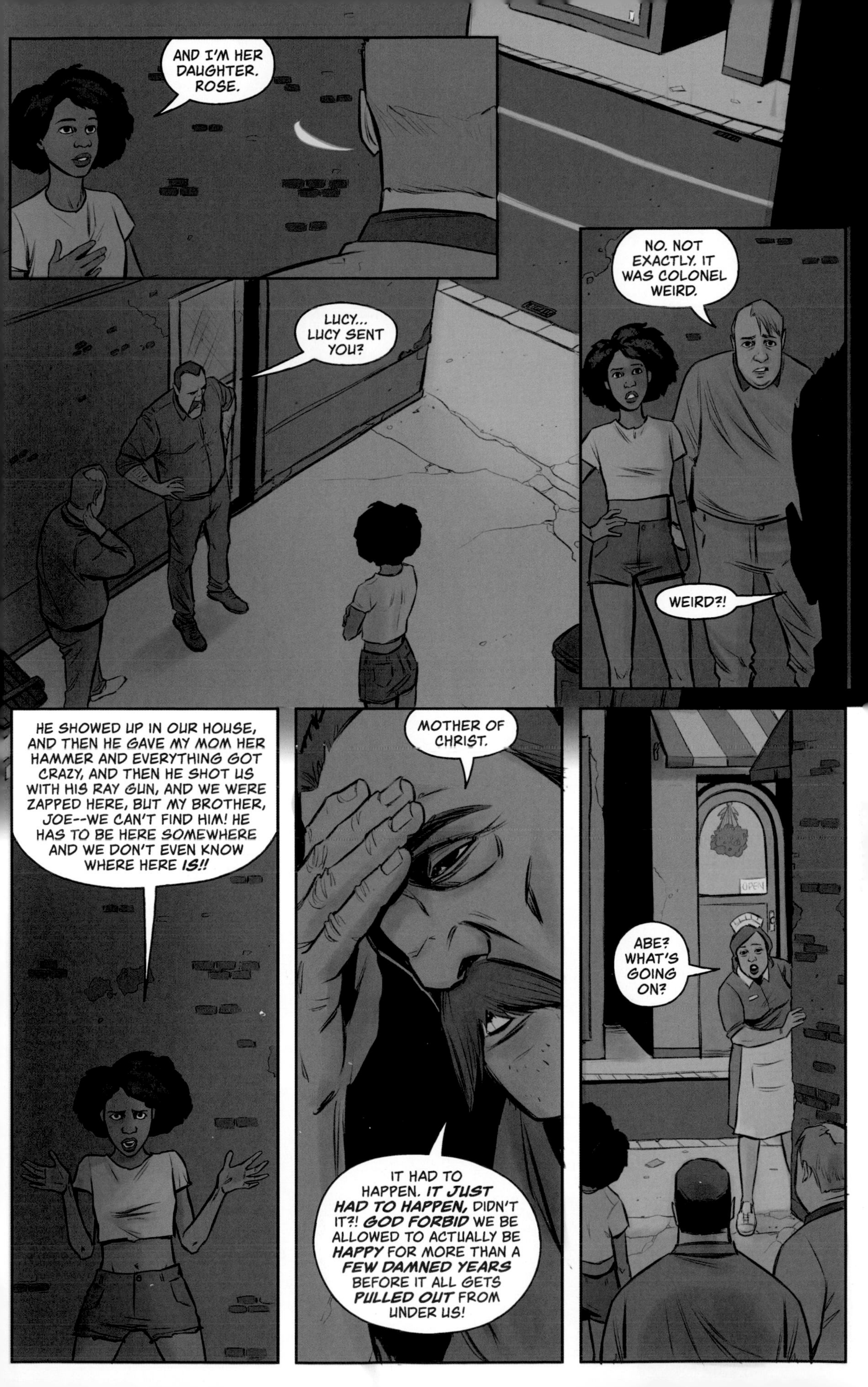
AND I'M HER DAUGHTER. ROSE.
LUCY... LUCY SENT YOU?
NO. NOT EXACTLY. IT WAS COLONEL WEIRD.
WEIRD?!
HE SHOWED UP IN OUR HOUSE, AND THEN HE GAVE MY MOM HER HAMMER AND EVERYTHING GOT CRAZY, AND THEN HE SHOT US WITH HIS RAY GUN, AND WE WERE ZAPPED HERE, BUT MY BROTHER, JOE--WE CAN'T FIND HIM! HE HAS TO BE HERE SOMEWHERE AND WE DON'T EVEN KNOW WHERE HERE IS!!
MOTHER OF CHRIST.
IT HAD TO HAPPEN. IT JUST HAD TO HAPPEN, DIDN'T IT?! GOD FORBID WE BE ALLOWED TO ACTUALLY BE HAPPY FOR MORE THAN A FEW DAMNED YEARS BEFORE IT ALL GETS PULLED OUT FROM UNDER US!
OPEN
ABE? WHAT'S GOING ON?

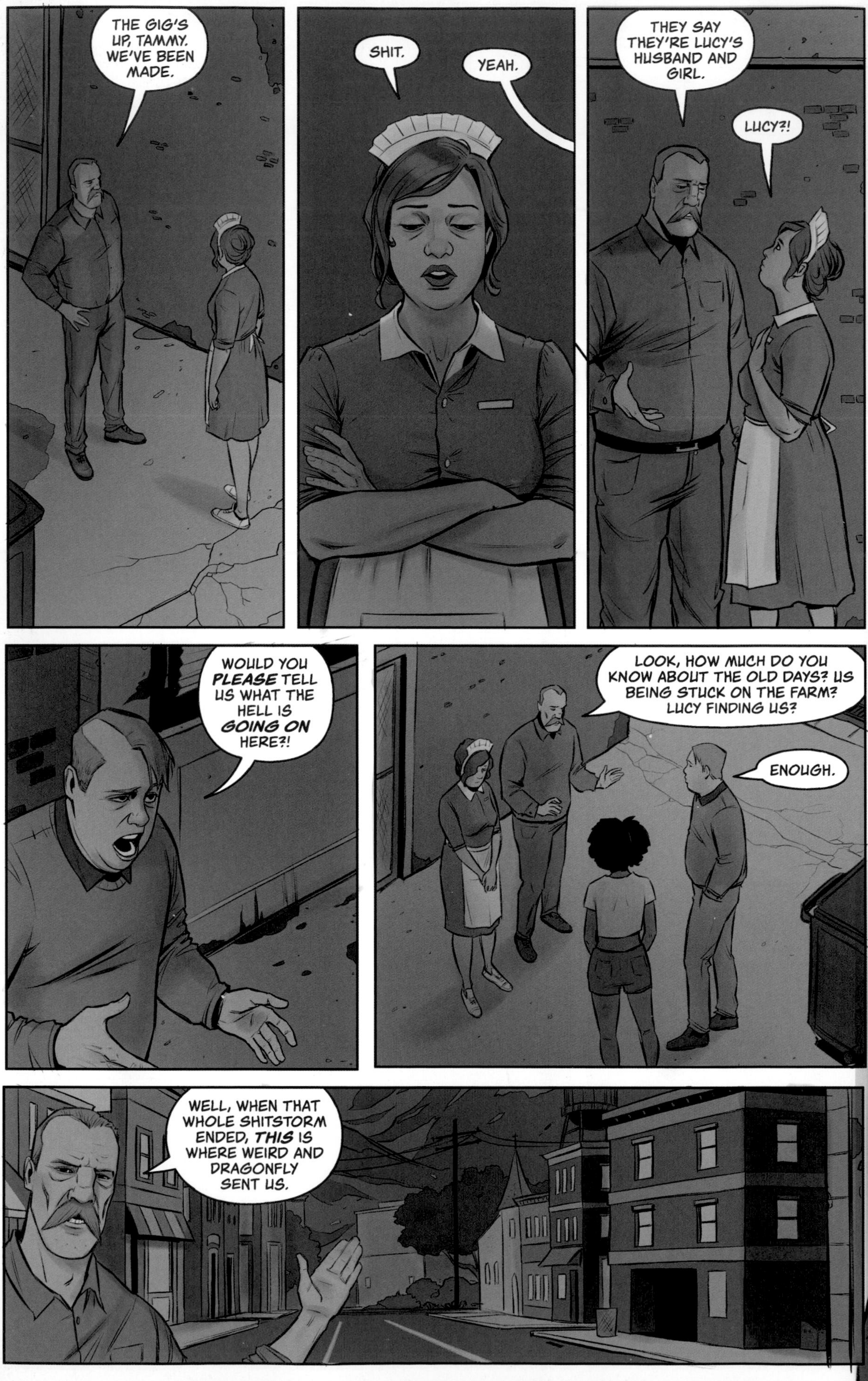
THE GIG'S UP, TAMMY. WE'VE BEEN MADE.
SHIT.
YEAH.
THEY SAY THEY'RE LUCY'S HUSBAND AND GIRL.
LUCY?!
WOULD YOU *PLEASE* TELL US WHAT THE HELL IS *GOING ON* HERE?!
LOOK, HOW MUCH DO YOU KNOW ABOUT THE OLD DAYS? US BEING STUCK ON THE FARM? LUCY FINDING US?
ENOUGH.
WELL, WHEN THAT WHOLE SHITSTORM ENDED, *THIS* IS WHERE WEIRD AND DRAGONFLY SENT US.

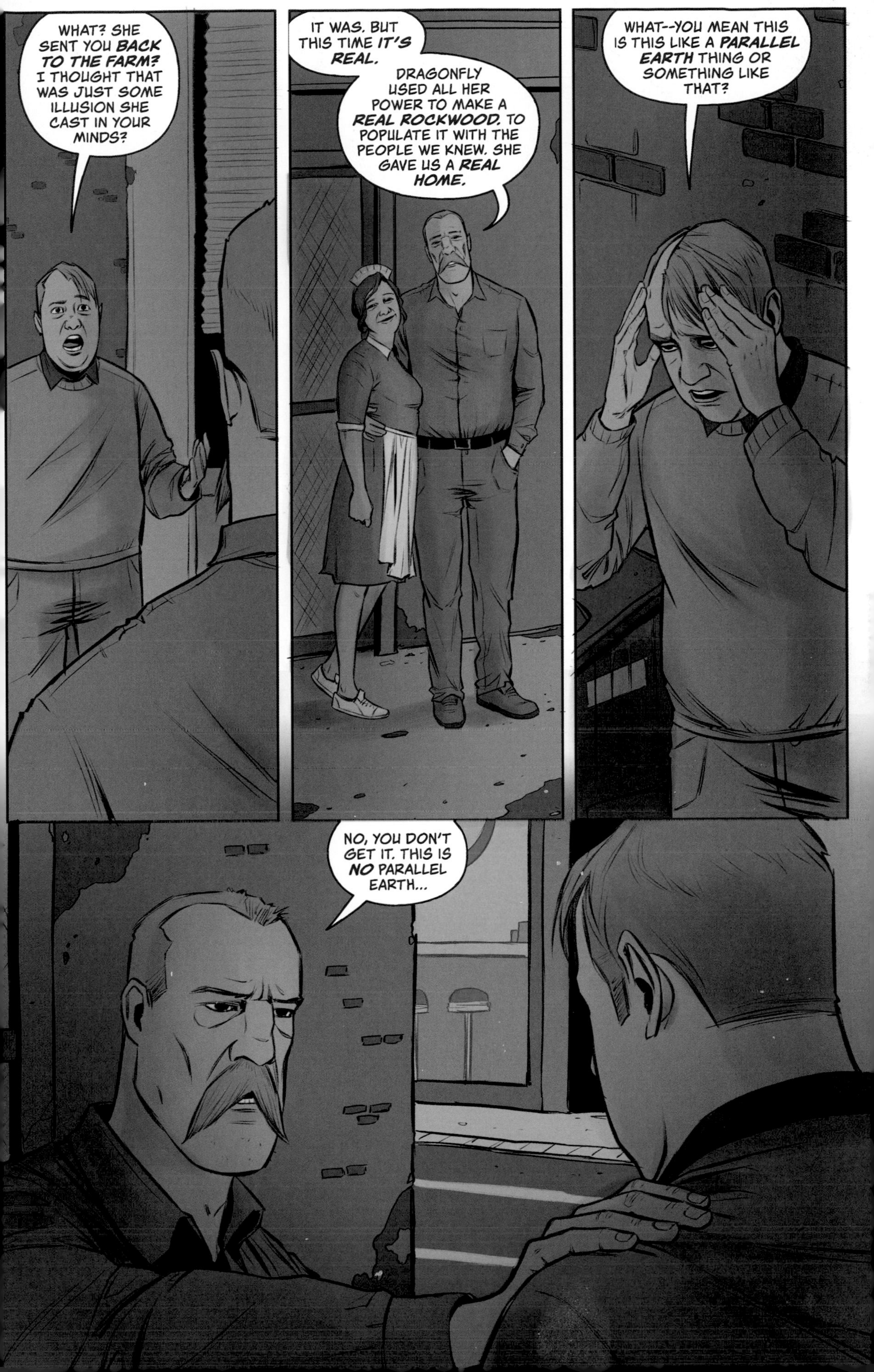

WHAT? SHE SENT YOU BACK TO THE FARM? I THOUGHT THAT WAS JUST SOME ILLUSION SHE CAST IN YOUR MINDS?
IT WAS. BUT THIS TIME IT'S REAL.
DRAGONFLY USED ALL HER POWER TO MAKE A REAL ROCKWOOD. TO POPULATE IT WITH THE PEOPLE WE KNEW. SHE GAVE US A REAL HOME.
WHAT--YOU MEAN THIS IS THIS LIKE A PARALLEL EARTH THING OR SOMETHING LIKE THAT?
NO, YOU DON'T GET IT. THIS IS NO PARALLEL EARTH...

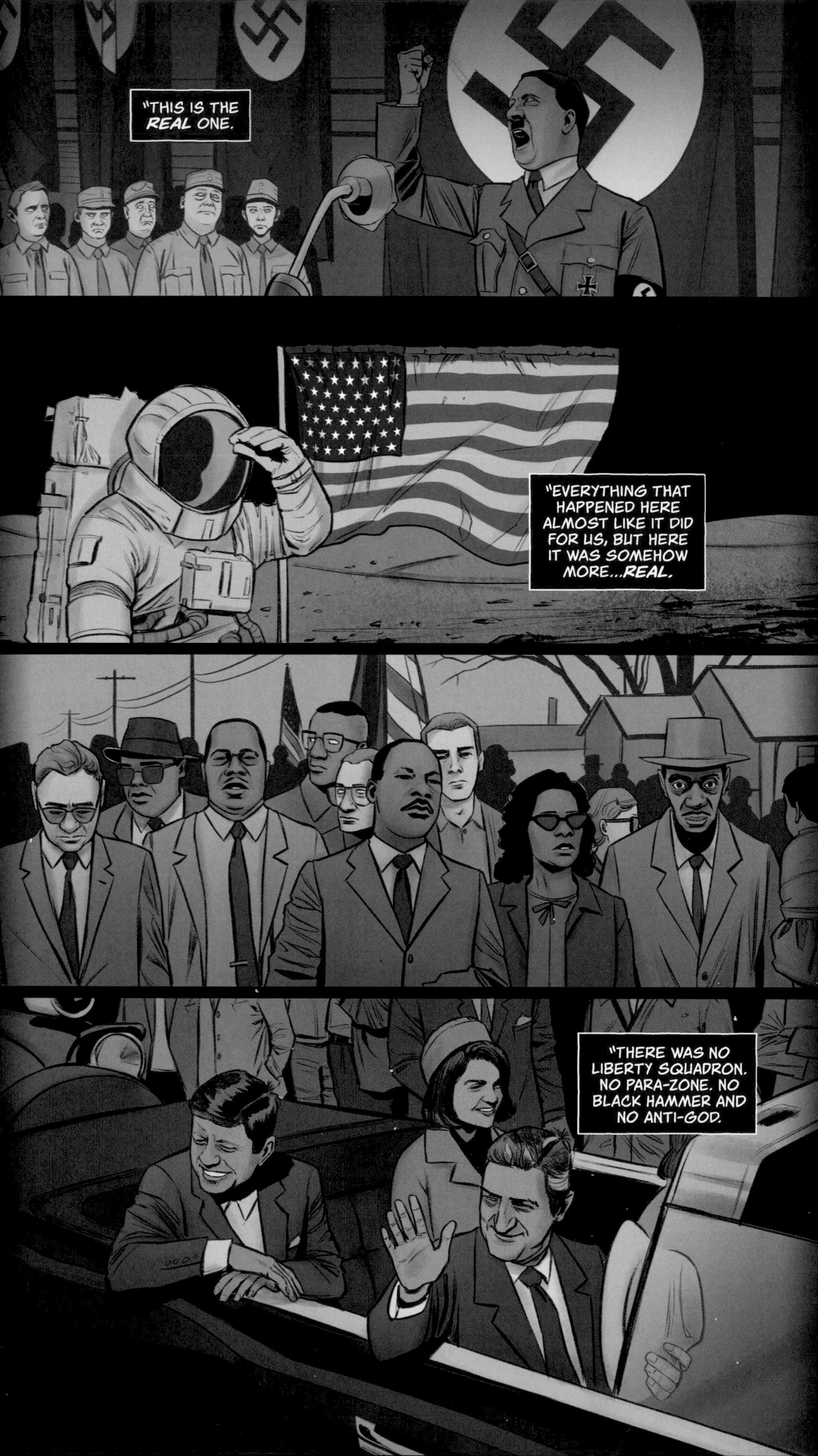

"THIS IS THE *REAL* ONE.
"EVERYTHING THAT HAPPENED HERE ALMOST LIKE IT DID FOR US, BUT HERE IT WAS SOMEHOW MORE...*REAL*.
"THERE WAS NO LIBERTY SQUADRON. NO PARA-ZONE. NO BLACK HAMMER AND NO ANTI-GOD.

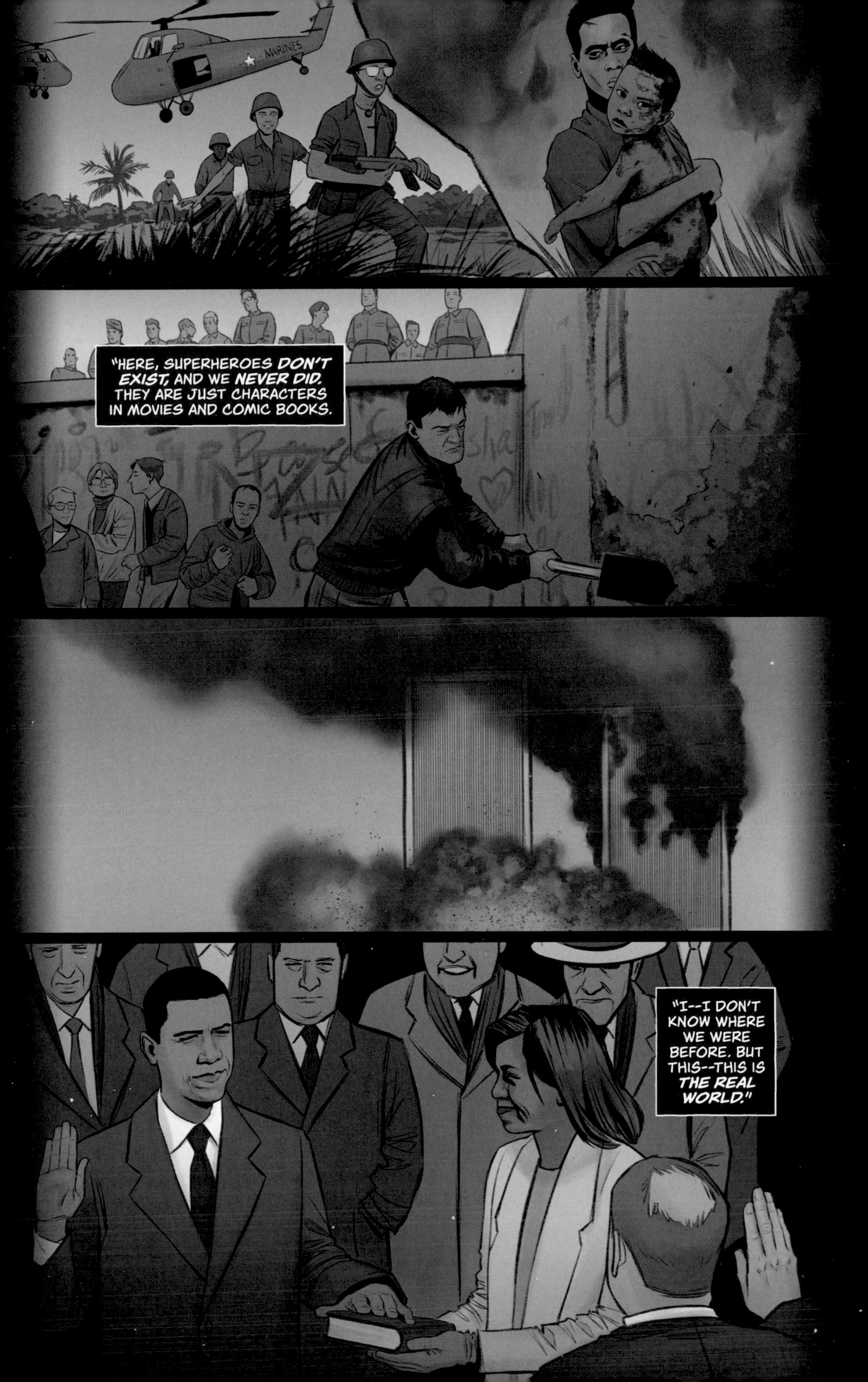

MARINES
"HERE, SUPERHEROES DON'T EXIST, AND WE NEVER DID. THEY ARE JUST CHARACTERS IN MOVIES AND COMIC BOOKS.
"I--I DON'T KNOW WHERE WE WERE BEFORE. BUT THIS--THIS IS THE REAL WORLD."

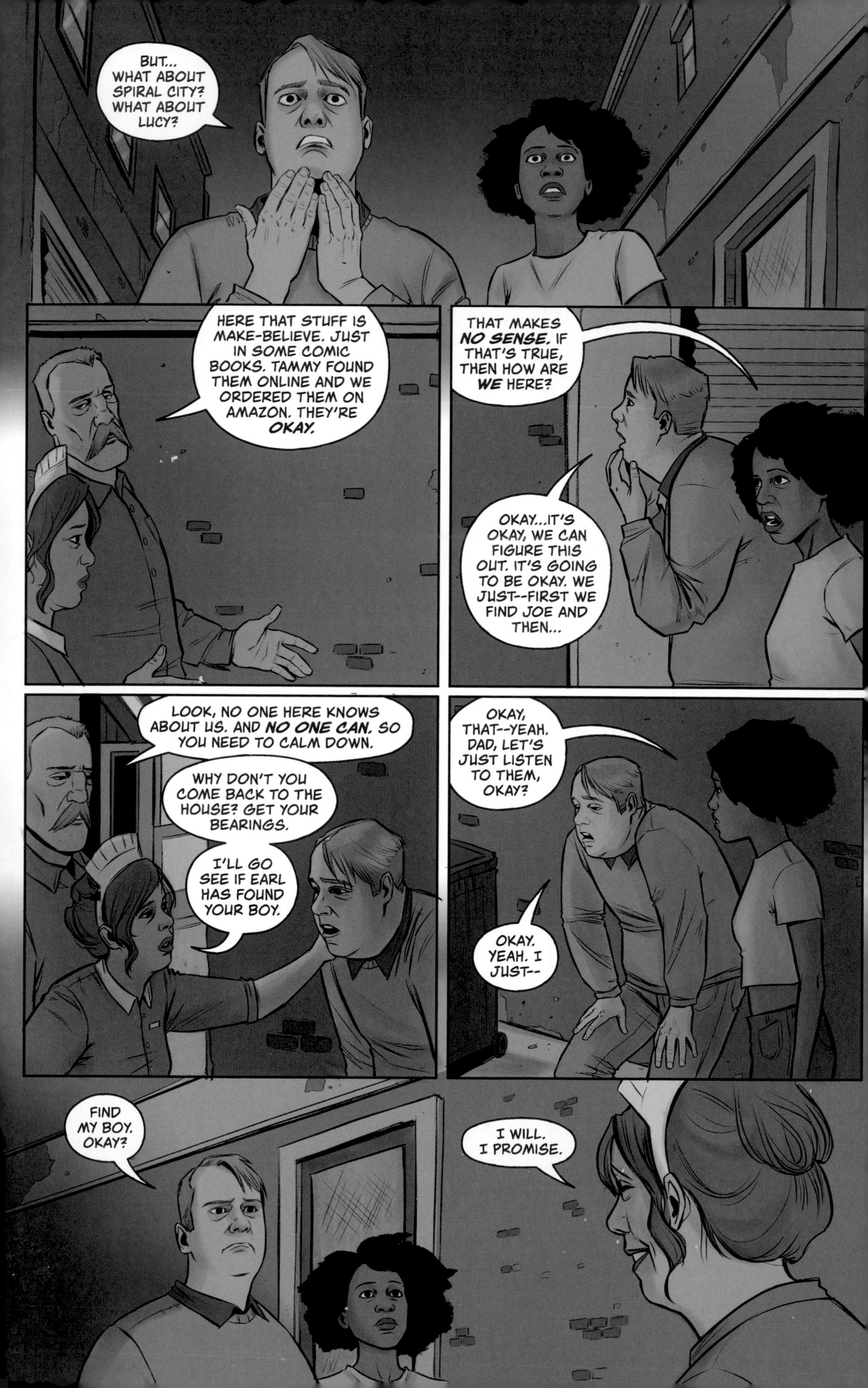
BUT... WHAT ABOUT SPIRAL CITY? WHAT ABOUT LUCY?
HERE THAT STUFF IS MAKE-BELIEVE. JUST IN SOME COMIC BOOKS. TAMMY FOUND THEM ONLINE AND WE ORDERED THEM ON AMAZON. THEY'RE OKAY.
THAT MAKES NO SENSE. IF THAT'S TRUE, THEN HOW ARE WE HERE?
OKAY...IT'S OKAY, WE CAN FIGURE THIS OUT. IT'S GOING TO BE OKAY. WE JUST--FIRST WE FIND JOE AND THEN...
LOOK, NO ONE HERE KNOWS ABOUT US. AND NO ONE CAN. SO YOU NEED TO CALM DOWN.
WHY DON'T YOU COME BACK TO THE HOUSE? GET YOUR BEARINGS.
I'LL GO SEE IF EARL HAS FOUND YOUR BOY.
OKAY, THAT--YEAH. DAD, LET'S JUST LISTEN TO THEM, OKAY?
OKAY. YEAH. I JUST--
FIND MY BOY. OKAY?
I WILL. I PROMISE.

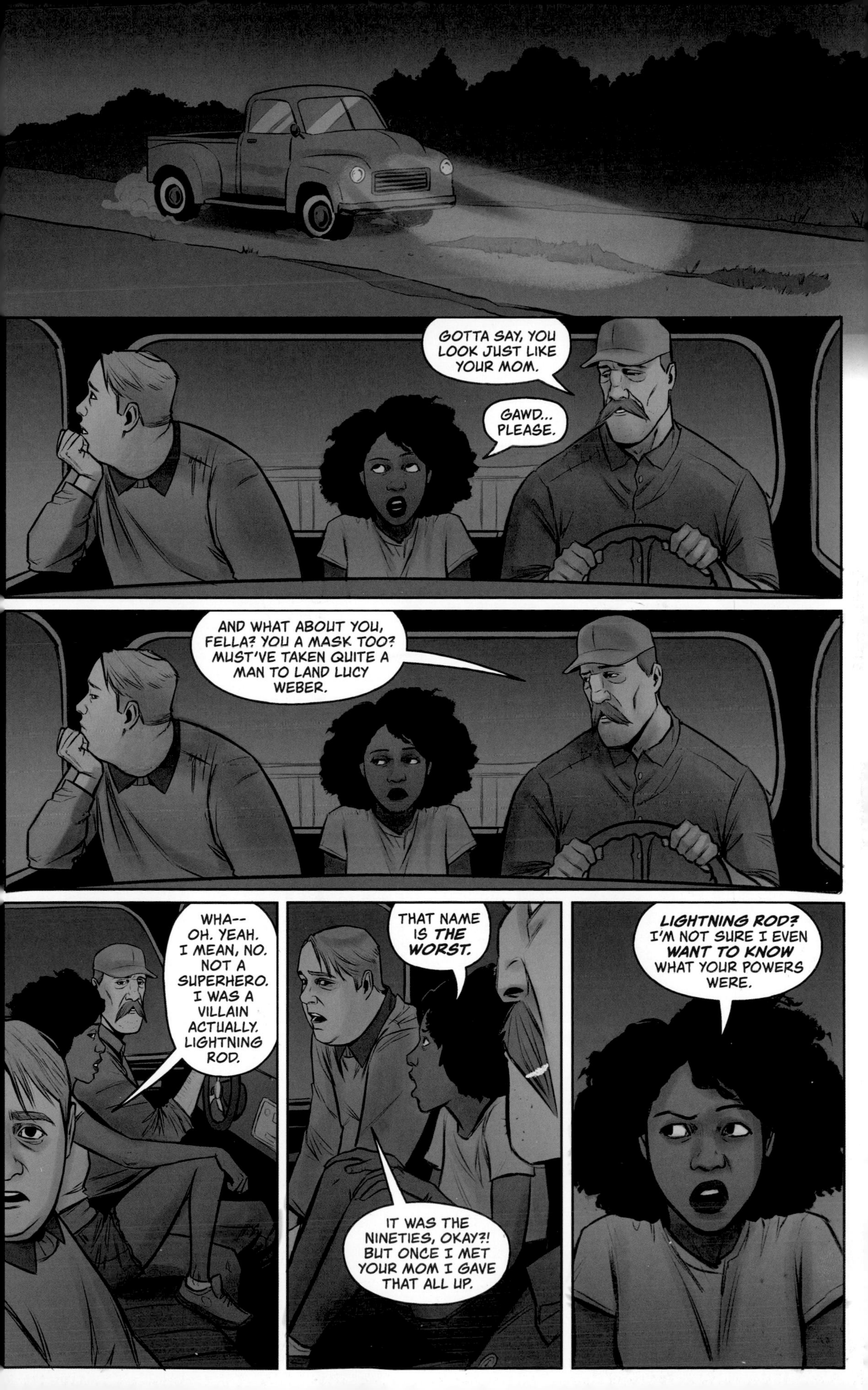
GOTTA SAY, YOU LOOK JUST LIKE YOUR MOM.
GAWD... PLEASE.
AND WHAT ABOUT YOU, FELLA? YOU A MASK TOO? MUST'VE TAKEN QUITE A MAN TO LAND LUCY WEBER.
WHA-- OH. YEAH. I MEAN, NO. NOT A SUPERHERO. I WAS A VILLAIN ACTUALLY. LIGHTNING ROD.
THAT NAME IS THE WORST.
IT WAS THE NINETIES, OKAY?! BUT ONCE I MET YOUR MOM I GAVE THAT ALL UP.
LIGHTNING ROD? I'M NOT SURE I EVEN WANT TO KNOW WHAT YOUR POWERS WERE.

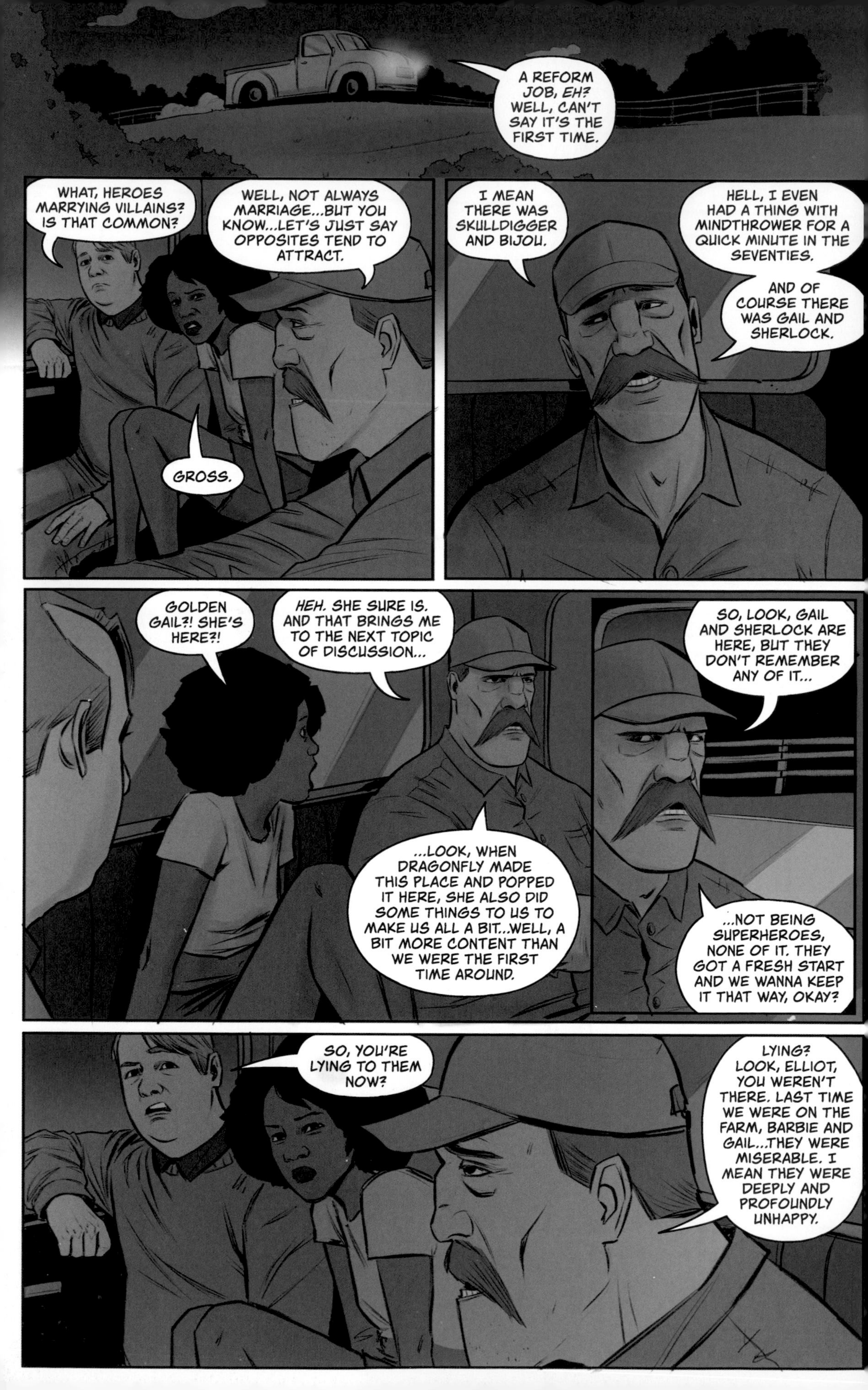
A REFORM JOB, EH? WELL, CAN'T SAY IT'S THE FIRST TIME.
WHAT, HEROES MARRYING VILLAINS? IS THAT COMMON?
WELL, NOT ALWAYS MARRIAGE...BUT YOU KNOW...LET'S JUST SAY OPPOSITES TEND TO ATTRACT.
GROSS.
I MEAN THERE WAS SKULLDIGGER AND BIJOU.
HELL, I EVEN HAD A THING WITH MINDTHROWER FOR A QUICK MINUTE IN THE SEVENTIES.
AND OF COURSE THERE WAS GAIL AND SHERLOCK.
GOLDEN GAIL?! SHE'S HERE?!
HEH. SHE SURE IS. AND THAT BRINGS ME TO THE NEXT TOPIC OF DISCUSSION...
...LOOK, WHEN DRAGONFLY MADE THIS PLACE AND POPPED IT HERE, SHE ALSO DID SOME THINGS TO US TO MAKE US ALL A BIT...WELL, A BIT MORE CONTENT THAN WE WERE THE FIRST TIME AROUND.
SO, LOOK, GAIL AND SHERLOCK ARE HERE, BUT THEY DON'T REMEMBER ANY OF IT...
...NOT BEING SUPERHEROES, NONE OF IT. THEY GOT A FRESH START AND WE WANNA KEEP IT THAT WAY, OKAY?
SO, YOU'RE LYING TO THEM NOW?
LYING? LOOK, ELLIOT, YOU WEREN'T THERE. LAST TIME WE WERE ON THE FARM, BARBIE AND GAIL...THEY WERE MISERABLE. I MEAN THEY WERE DEEPLY AND PROFOUNDLY UNHAPPY.

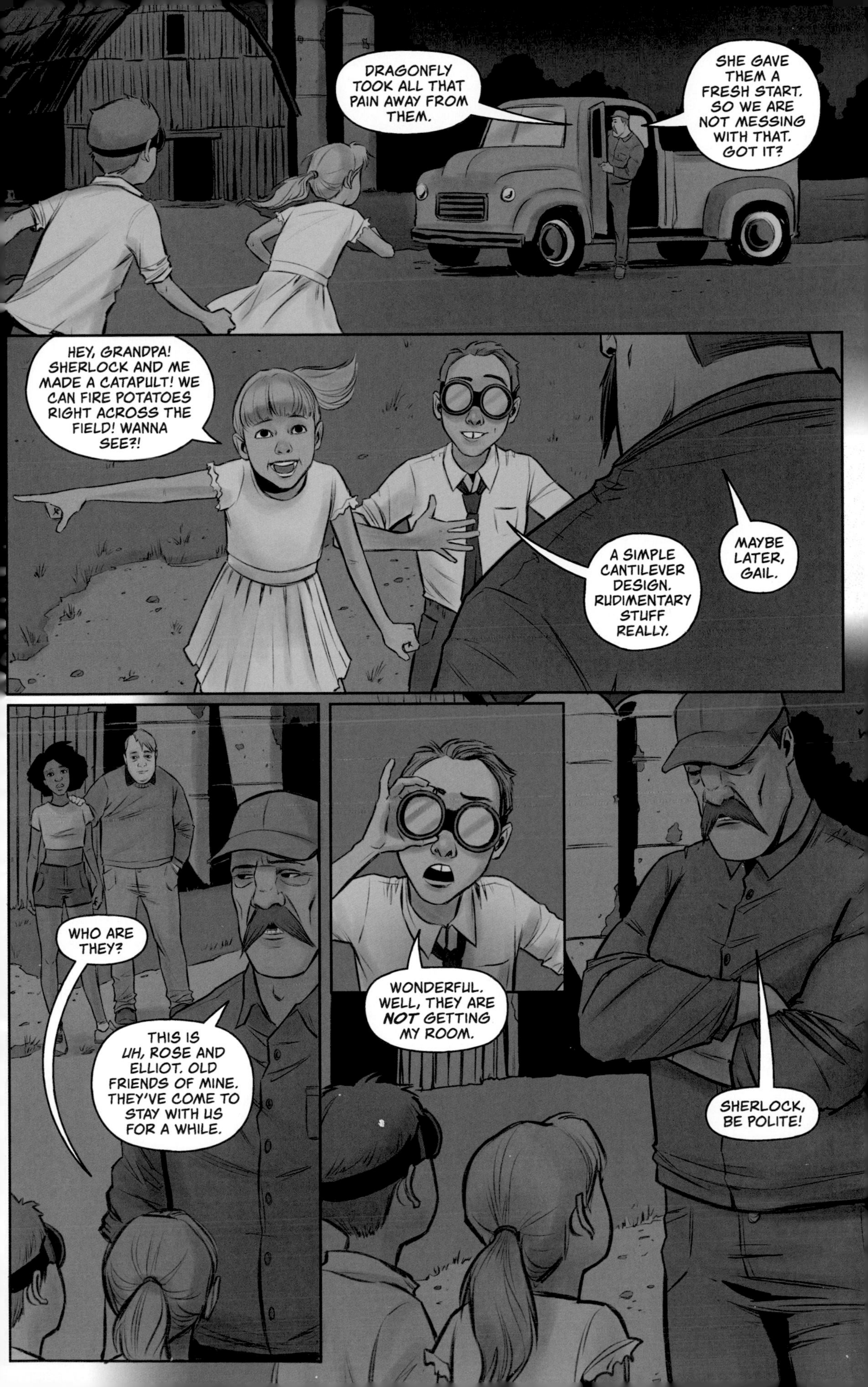
DRAGONFLY TOOK ALL THAT PAIN AWAY FROM THEM.
SHE GAVE THEM A FRESH START. SO WE ARE NOT MESSING WITH THAT. GOT IT?
HEY, GRANDPA! SHERLOCK AND ME MADE A CATAPULT! WE CAN FIRE POTATOES RIGHT ACROSS THE FIELD! WANNA SEE?!
A SIMPLE CANTILEVER DESIGN. RUDIMENTARY STUFF REALLY.
MAYBE LATER, GAIL.
WHO ARE THEY?
THIS IS UH, ROSE AND ELLIOT. OLD FRIENDS OF MINE. THEY'VE COME TO STAY WITH US FOR A WHILE.
WONDERFUL. WELL, THEY ARE *NOT* GETTING MY ROOM.
SHERLOCK, BE POLITE!

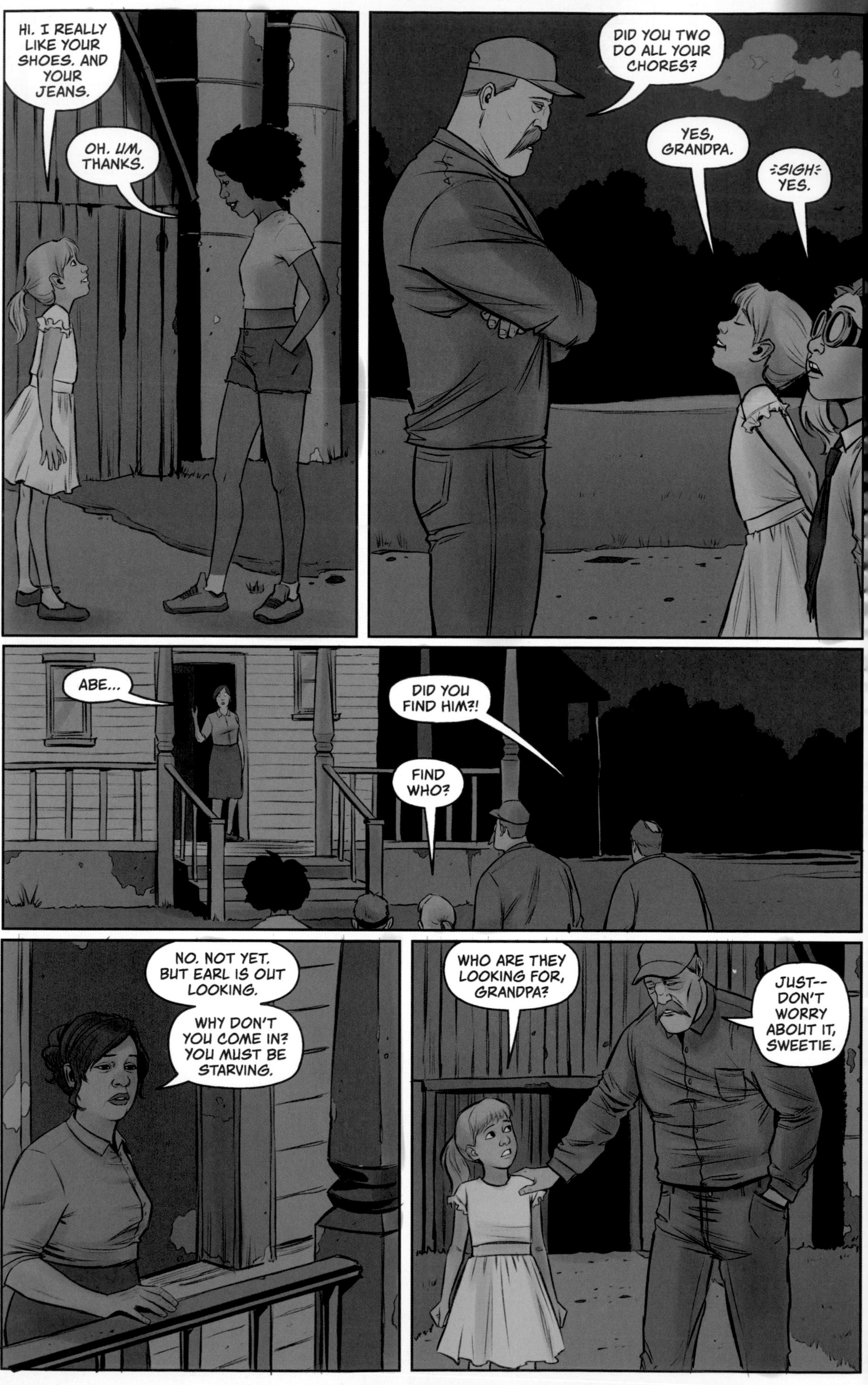
HI. I REALLY LIKE YOUR SHOES. AND YOUR JEANS.
OH. UM, THANKS.
DID YOU TWO DO ALL YOUR CHORES?
YES, GRANDPA.
SIGH YES.
ABE...
DID YOU FIND HIM?!
FIND WHO?
NO. NOT YET. BUT EARL IS OUT LOOKING.
WHY DON'T YOU COME IN? YOU MUST BE STARVING.
WHO ARE THEY LOOKING FOR, GRANDPA?
JUST-- DON'T WORRY ABOUT IT, SWEETIE.

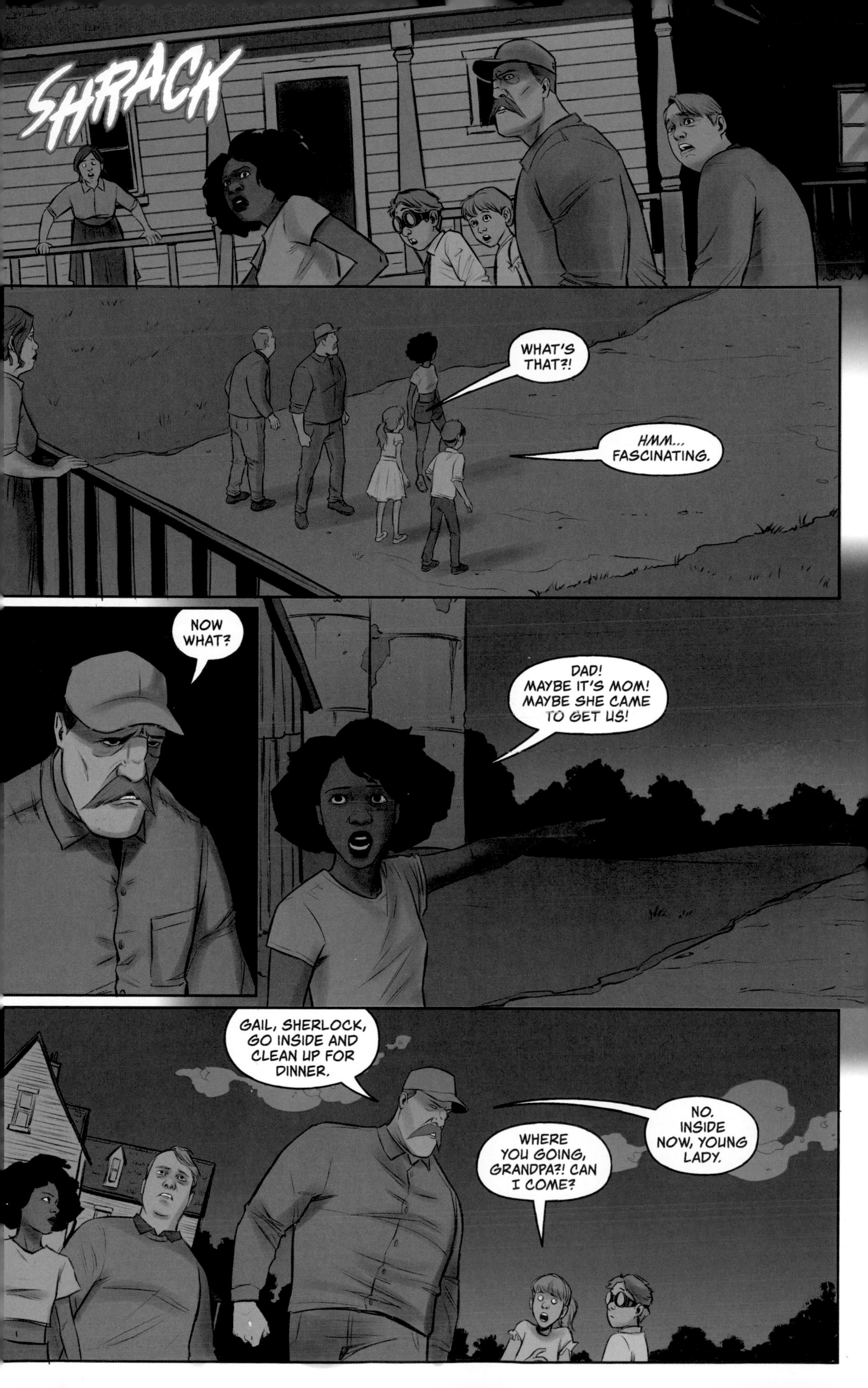
SHRACK
WHAT'S THAT?!
HMM... FASCINATING.
NOW WHAT?
DAD! MAYBE IT'S MOM! MAYBE SHE CAME TO GET US!
GAIL, SHERLOCK, GO INSIDE AND CLEAN UP FOR DINNER.
WHERE YOU GOING, GRANDPA?! CAN I COME?
NO. INSIDE NOW, YOUNG LADY.

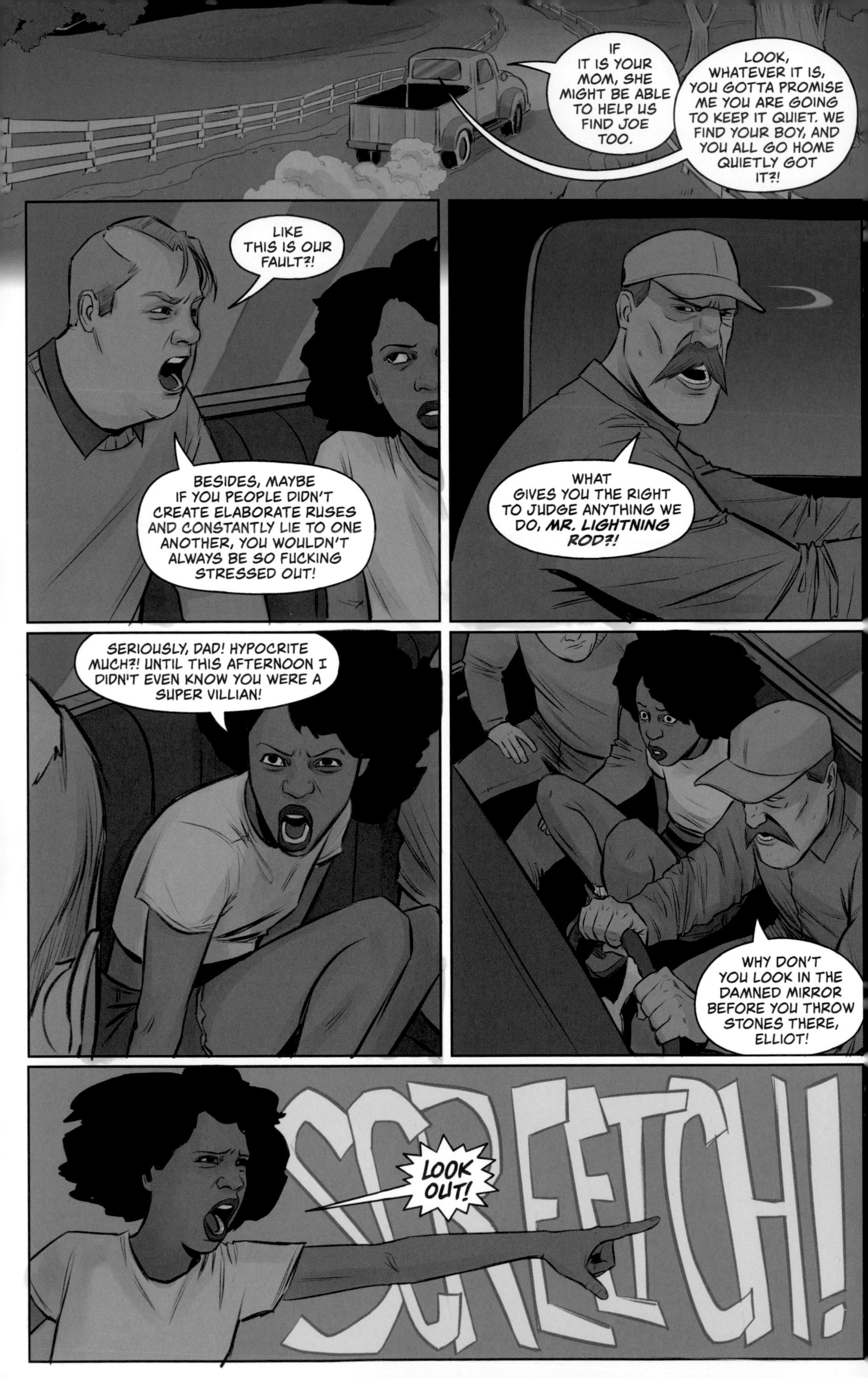
IF IT IS YOUR MOM, SHE MIGHT BE ABLE TO HELP US FIND JOE TOO.
LOOK, WHATEVER IT IS, YOU GOTTA PROMISE ME YOU ARE GOING TO KEEP IT QUIET. WE FIND YOUR BOY, AND YOU ALL GO HOME QUIETLY GOT IT?!
LIKE THIS IS OUR FAULT?!
BESIDES, MAYBE IF YOU PEOPLE DIDN'T CREATE ELABORATE RUSES AND CONSTANTLY LIE TO ONE ANOTHER, YOU WOULDN'T ALWAYS BE SO FUCKING STRESSED OUT!
WHAT GIVES YOU THE RIGHT TO JUDGE ANYTHING WE DO, MR. LIGHTNING ROD?!
SERIOUSLY, DAD! HYPOCRITE MUCH?! UNTIL THIS AFTERNOON I DIDN'T EVEN KNOW YOU WERE A SUPER VILLIAN!
WHY DON'T YOU LOOK IN THE DAMNED MIRROR BEFORE YOU THROW STONES THERE, ELLIOT!
SCREETCH!
LOOK OUT!

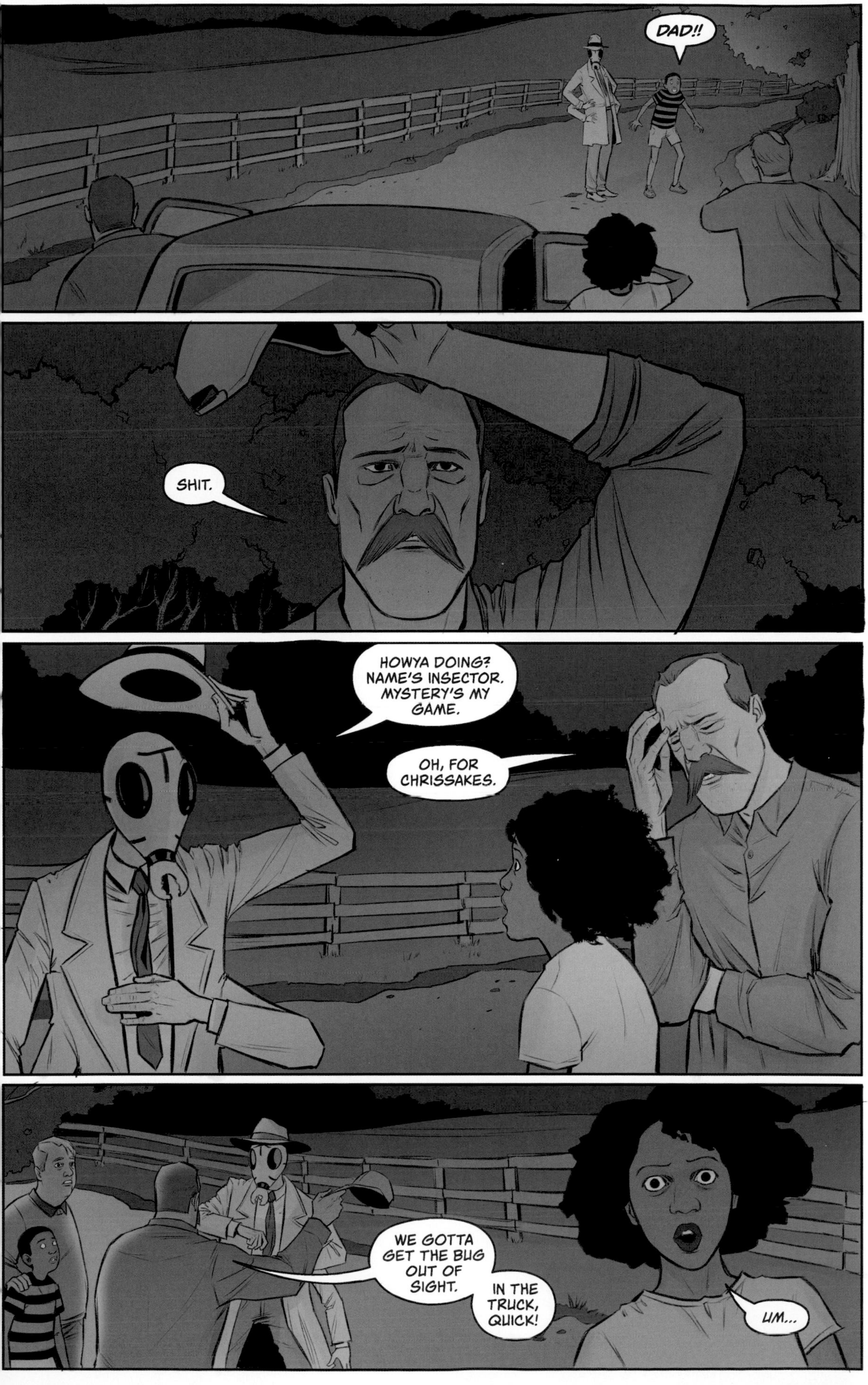
DAD!!
SHIT.
HOWYA DOING? NAME'S INSECTOR. MYSTERY'S MY GAME.
OH, FOR CHRISSAKES.
WE GOTTA GET THE BUG OUT OF SIGHT.
IN THE TRUCK, QUICK!
UM...

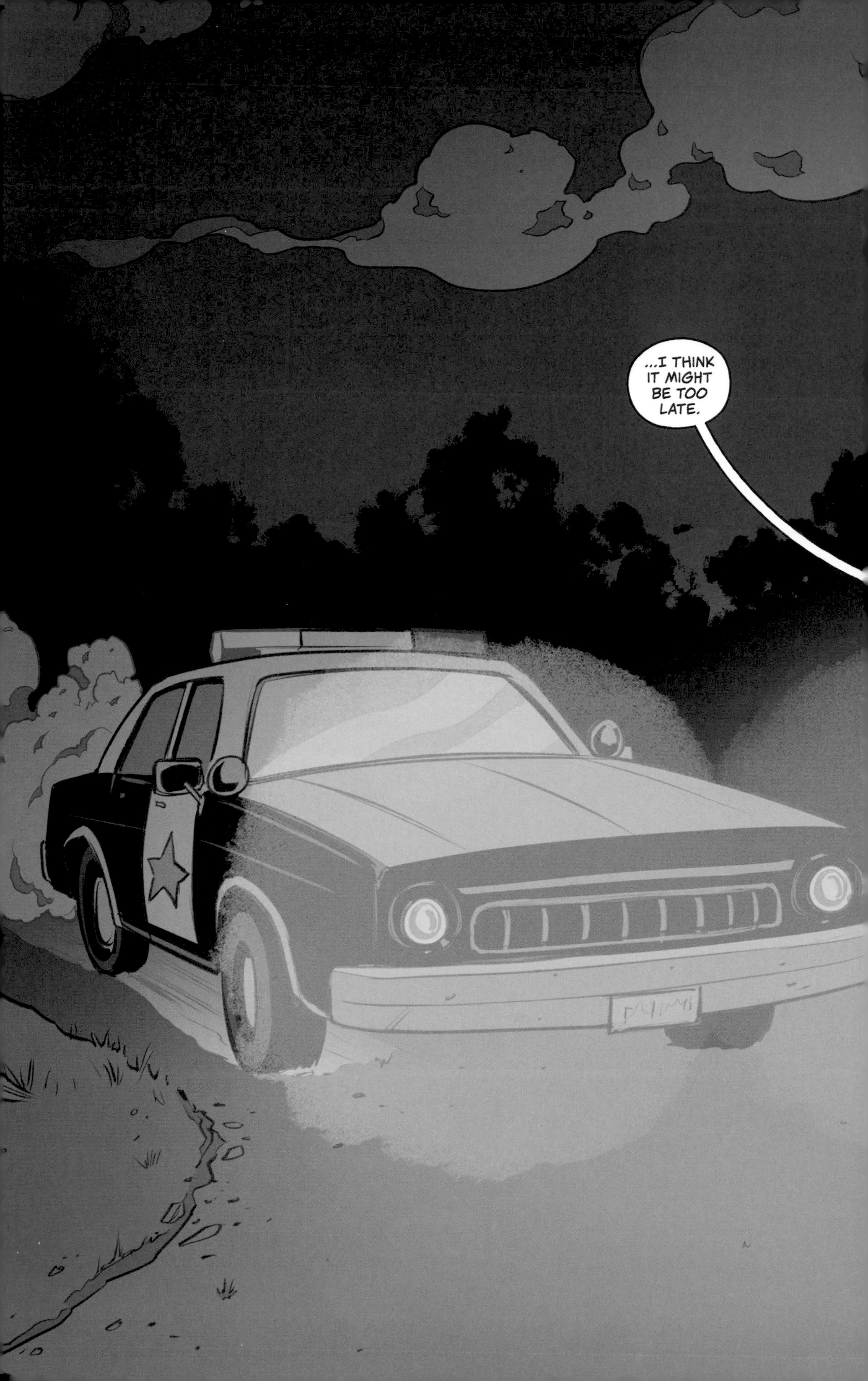
...I THINK IT MIGHT BE TOO LATE.

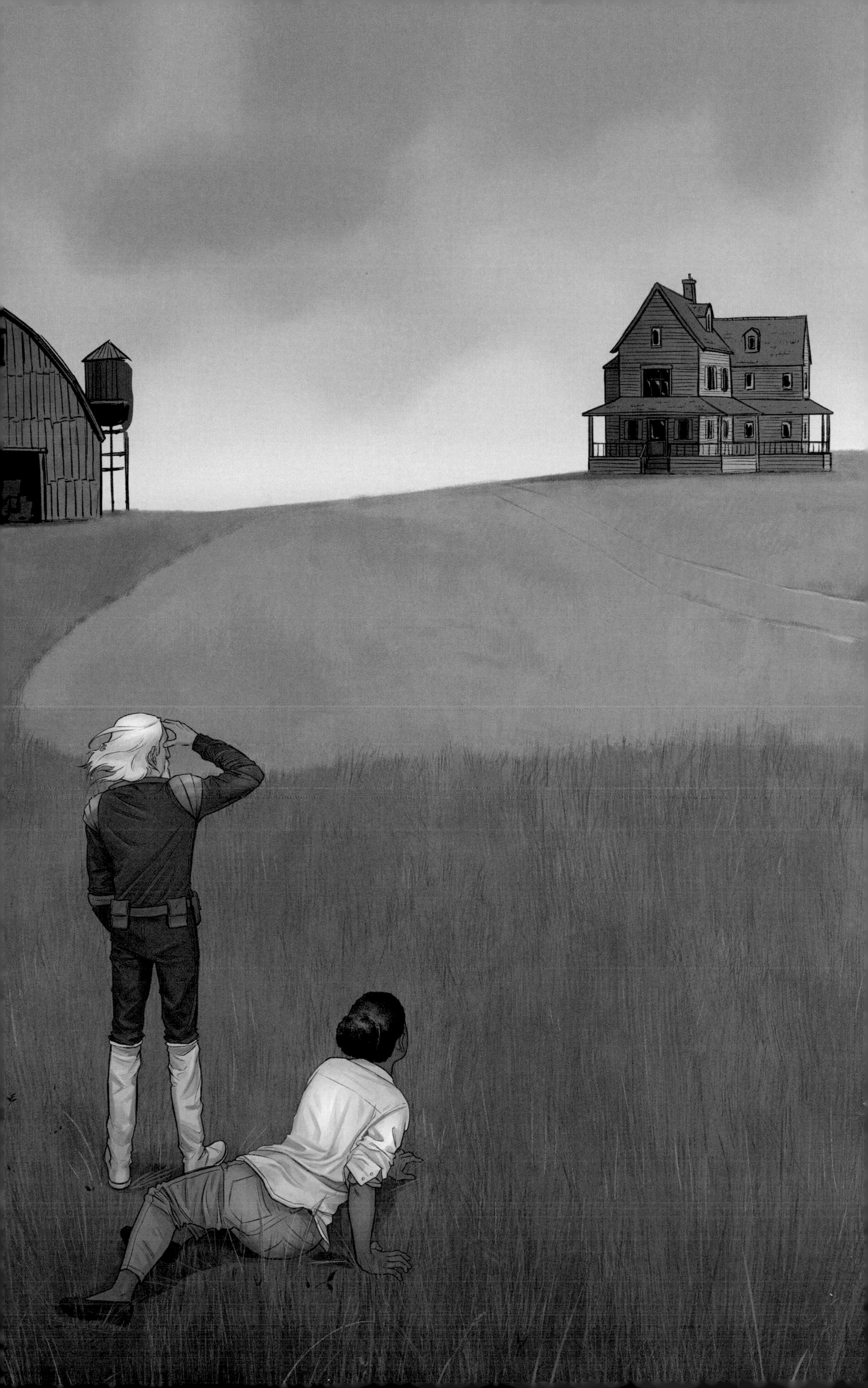

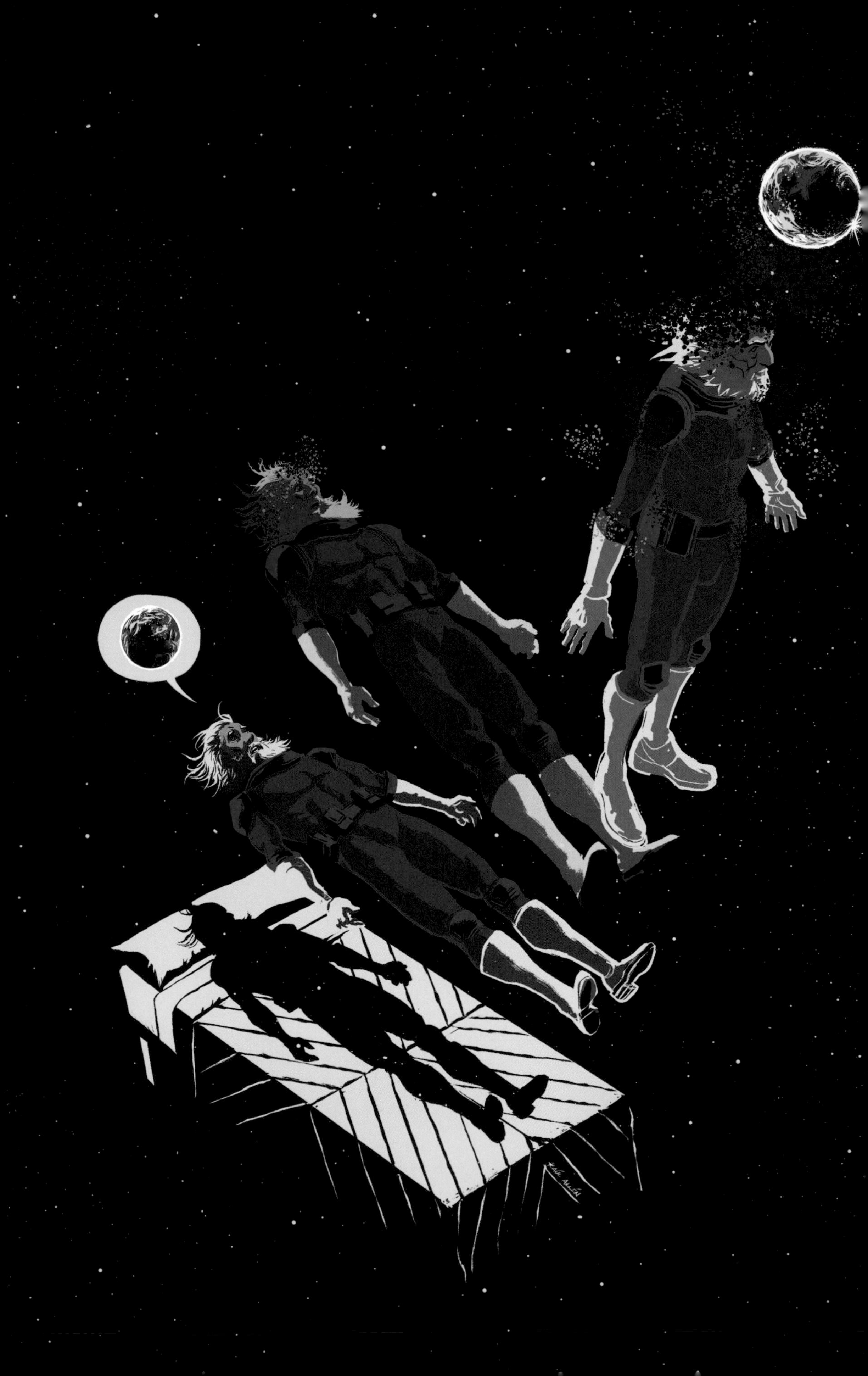

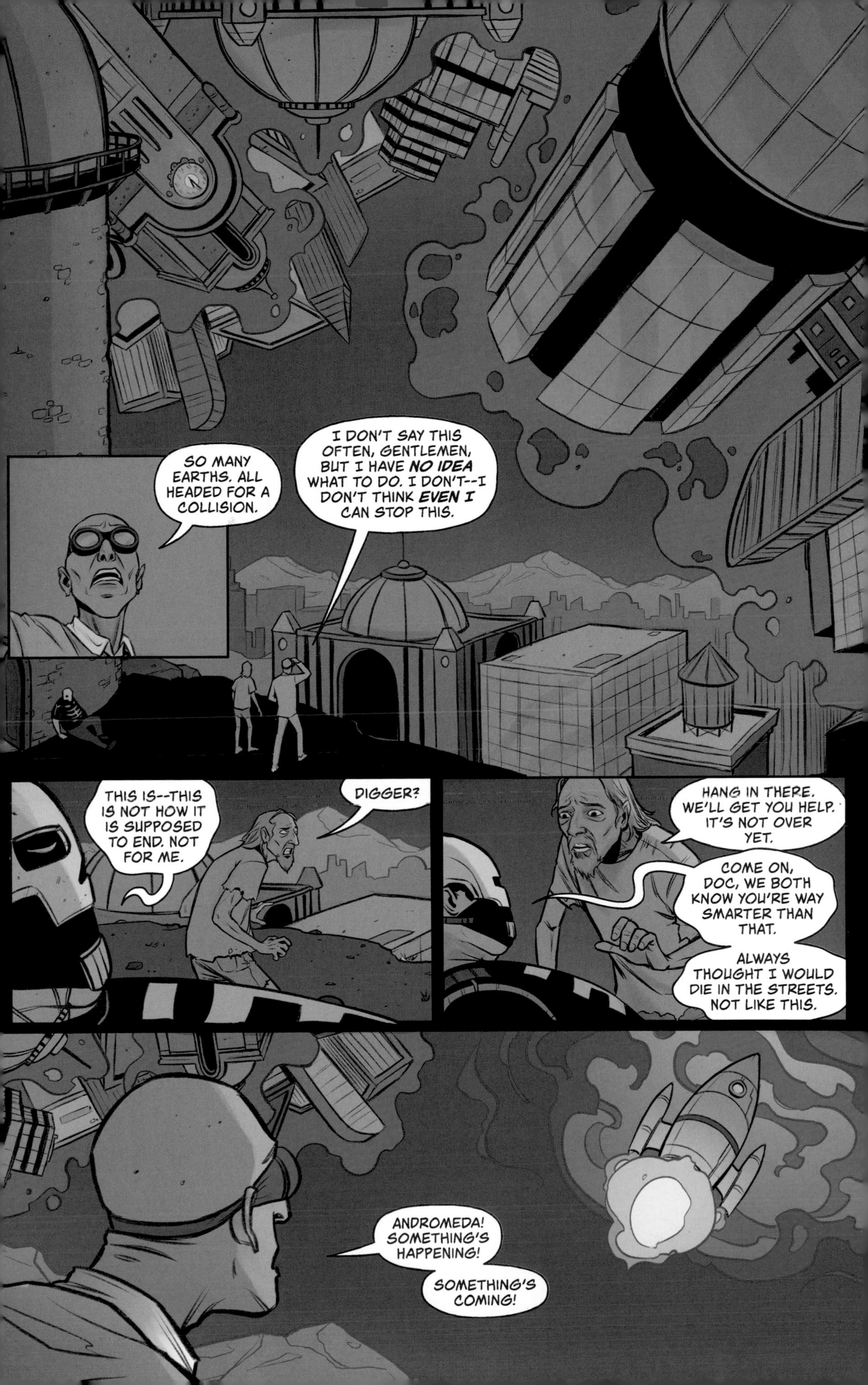
SO MANY EARTHS. ALL HEADED FOR A COLLISION.
I DON'T SAY THIS OFTEN, GENTLEMEN, BUT I HAVE NO IDEA WHAT TO DO. I DON'T--I DON'T THINK EVEN I CAN STOP THIS.
THIS IS--THIS IS NOT HOW IT IS SUPPOSED TO END. NOT FOR ME.
DIGGER?
HANG IN THERE. WE'LL GET YOU HELP. IT'S NOT OVER YET.
COME ON, DOC, WE BOTH KNOW YOU'RE WAY SMARTER THAN THAT.
ALWAYS THOUGHT I WOULD DIE IN THE STREETS. NOT LIKE THIS.
ANDROMEDA! SOMETHING'S HAPPENING!
SOMETHING'S COMING!

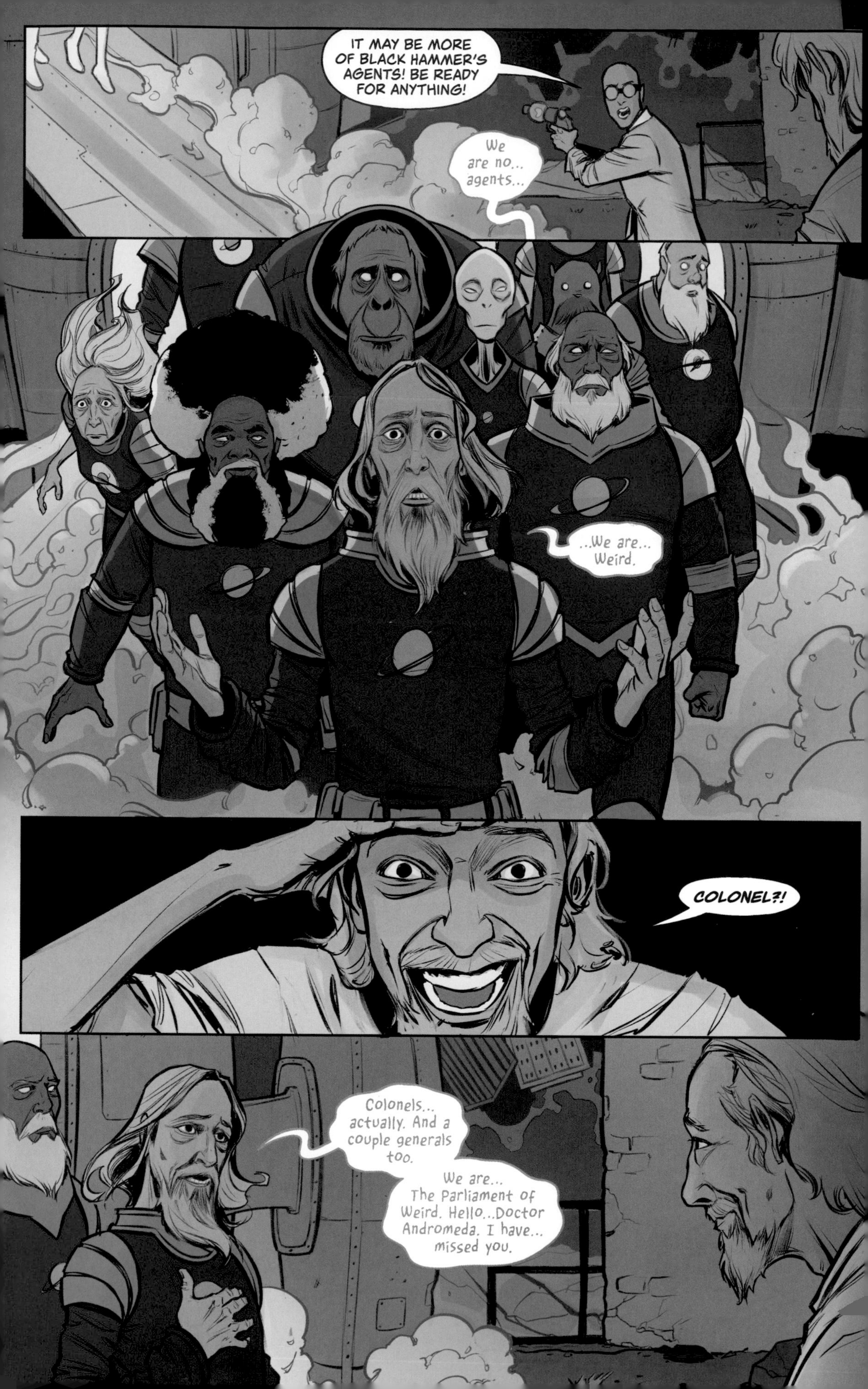
IT MAY BE MORE OF BLACK HAMMER'S AGENTS! BE READY FOR ANYTHING!
We are no... agents...
...We are... Weird.
COLONEL?!
Colonels... actually. And a couple generals too.
We are... The Parliament of Weird. Hello...Doctor Andromeda. I have... missed you.

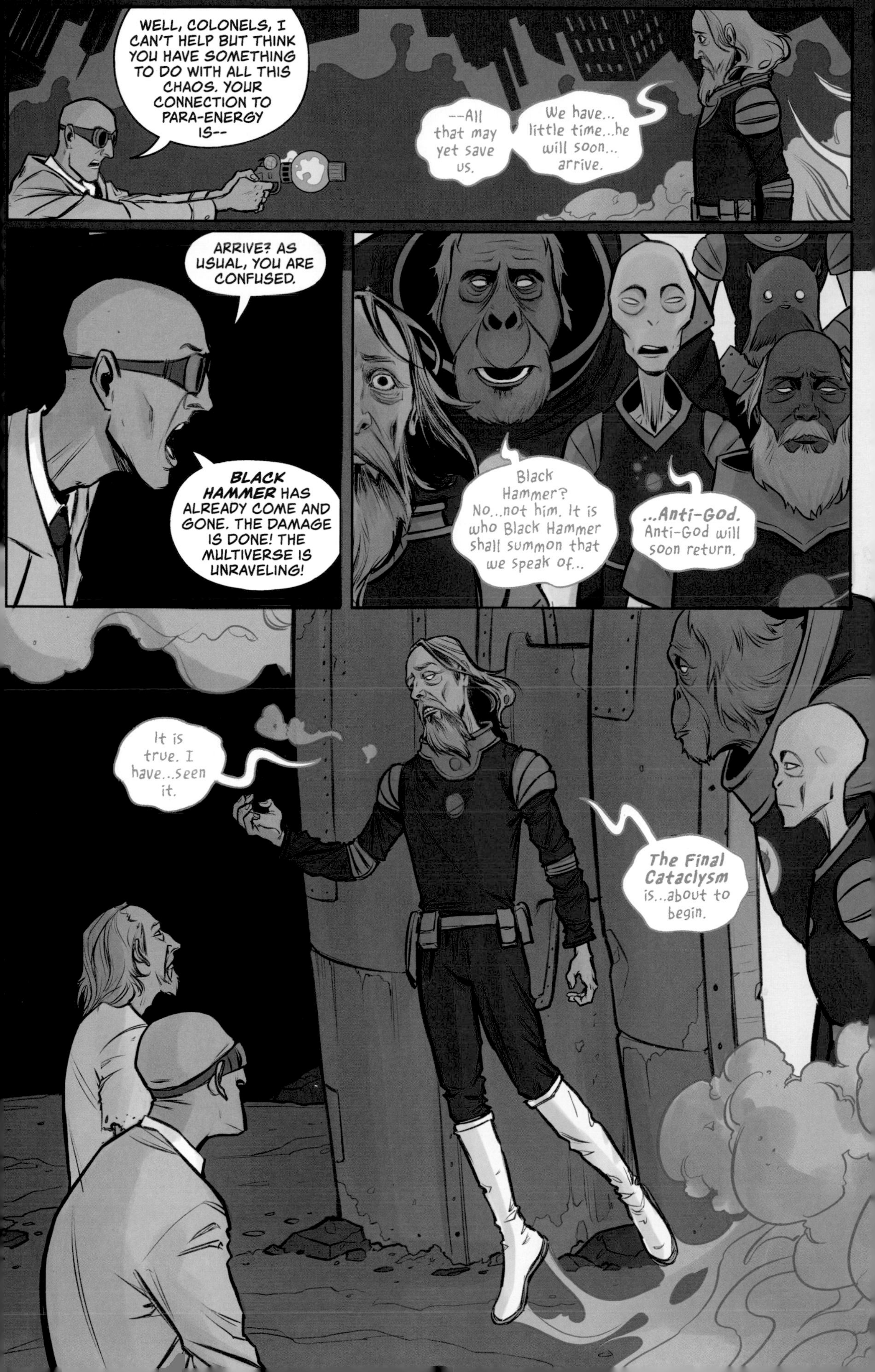
WELL, COLONELS, I CAN'T HELP BUT THINK YOU HAVE SOMETHING TO DO WITH ALL THIS CHAOS. YOUR CONNECTION TO PARA-ENERGY IS--
We have... little time...he will soon... arrive.
--All that may yet save us.
ARRIVE? AS USUAL, YOU ARE CONFUSED.
BLACK HAMMER HAS ALREADY COME AND GONE. THE DAMAGE IS DONE! THE MULTIVERSE IS UNRAVELING!
Black Hammer? No...not him. It is who Black Hammer shall summon that we speak of...
...Anti-God. Anti-God will soon return.
It is true. I have...seen it.
The Final Cataclysm is...about to begin.

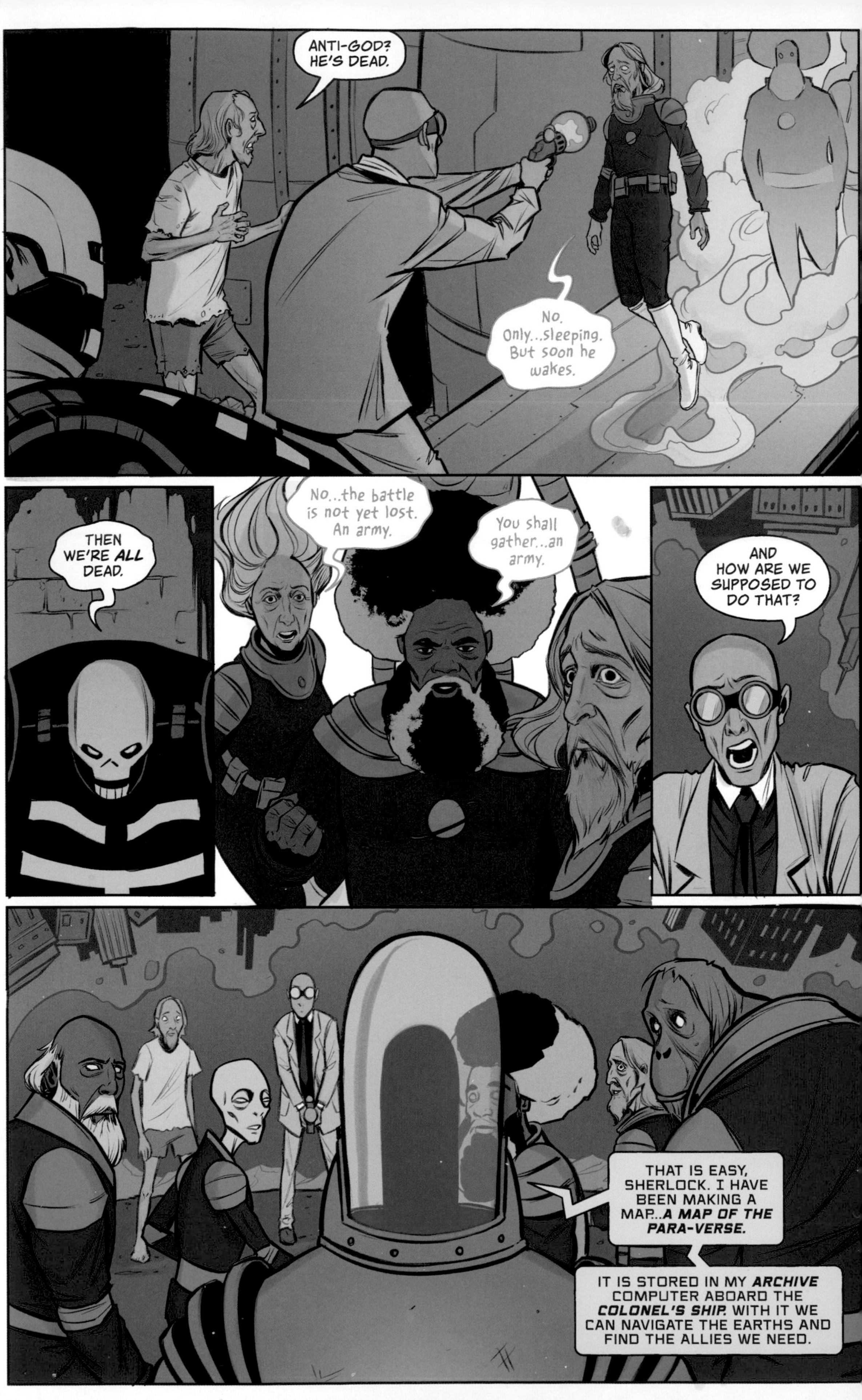
ANTI-GOD? HE'S DEAD.
No. Only...sleeping. But soon he wakes.
THEN WE'RE ALL DEAD.
No...the battle is not yet lost. An army.
You shall gather...an army.
AND HOW ARE WE SUPPOSED TO DO THAT?
THAT IS EASY, SHERLOCK. I HAVE BEEN MAKING A MAP...A MAP OF THE PARA-VERSE.
IT IS STORED IN MY ARCHIVE COMPUTER ABOARD THE COLONEL'S SHIP. WITH IT WE CAN NAVIGATE THE EARTHS AND FIND THE ALLIES WE NEED.

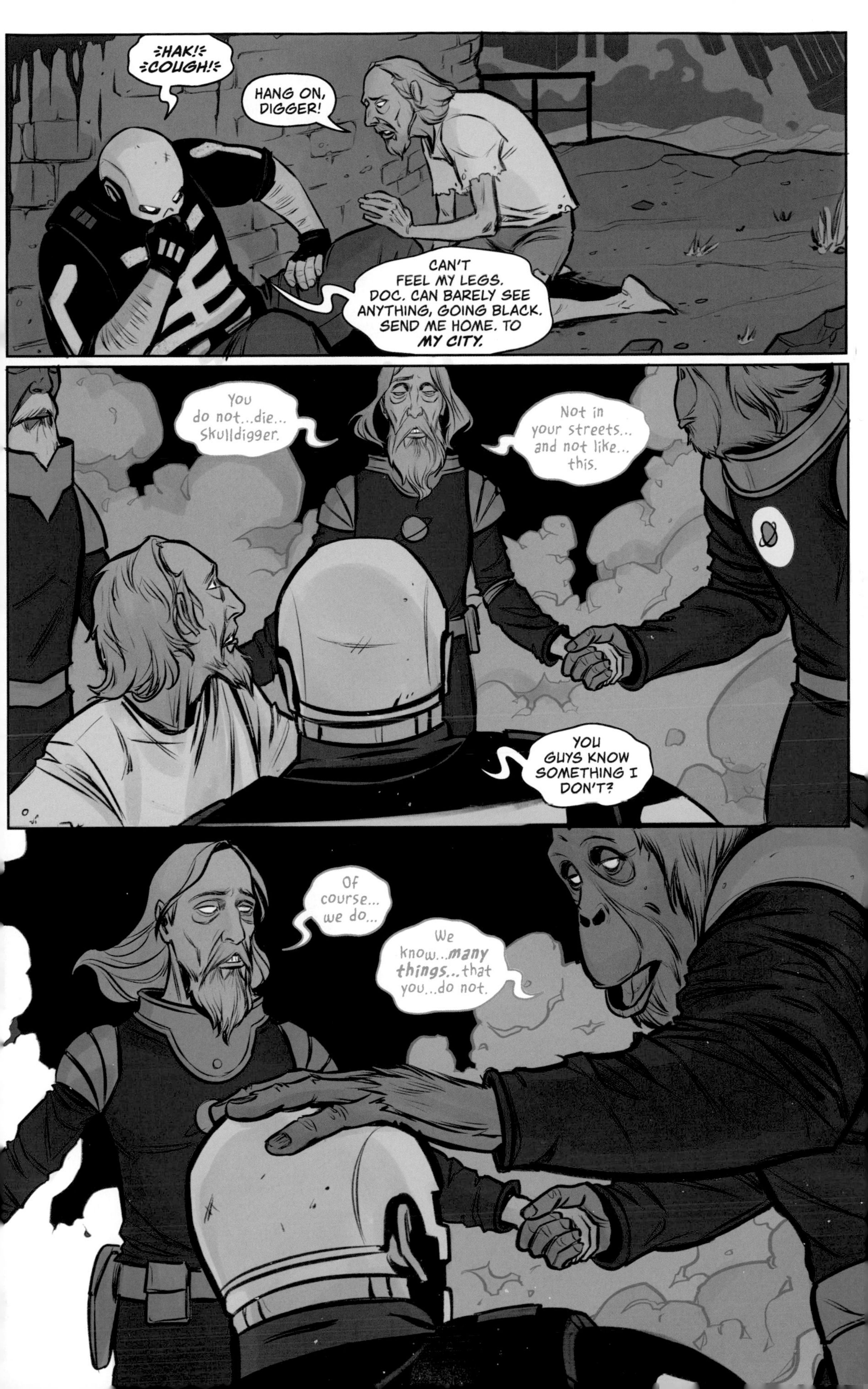

HAK! COUGH!
HANG ON, DIGGER!
CAN'T FEEL MY LEGS. DOC. CAN BARELY SEE ANYTHING, GOING BLACK. SEND ME HOME. TO *MY CITY.*
You do not...die... Skulldigger.
Not in your streets... and not like... this.
YOU GUYS KNOW SOMETHING I DON'T?
Of course... we do...
We know...*many things*...that you...do not.

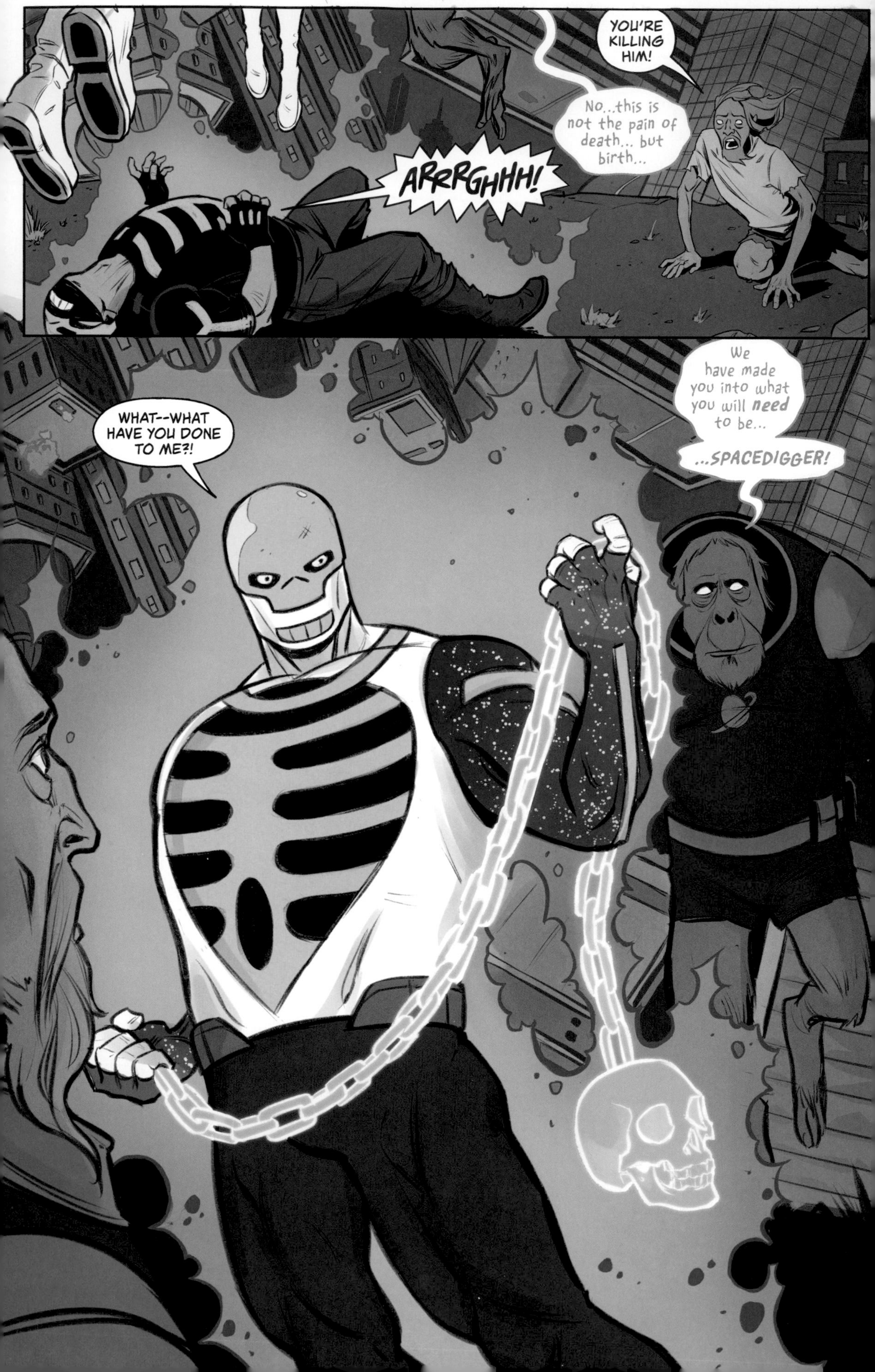
YOU'RE KILLING HIM!
No...this is not the pain of death... but birth...
ARRRGHHH!
WHAT--WHAT HAVE YOU DONE TO ME?!
We have made you into what you will need to be...
...SPACEDIGGER!

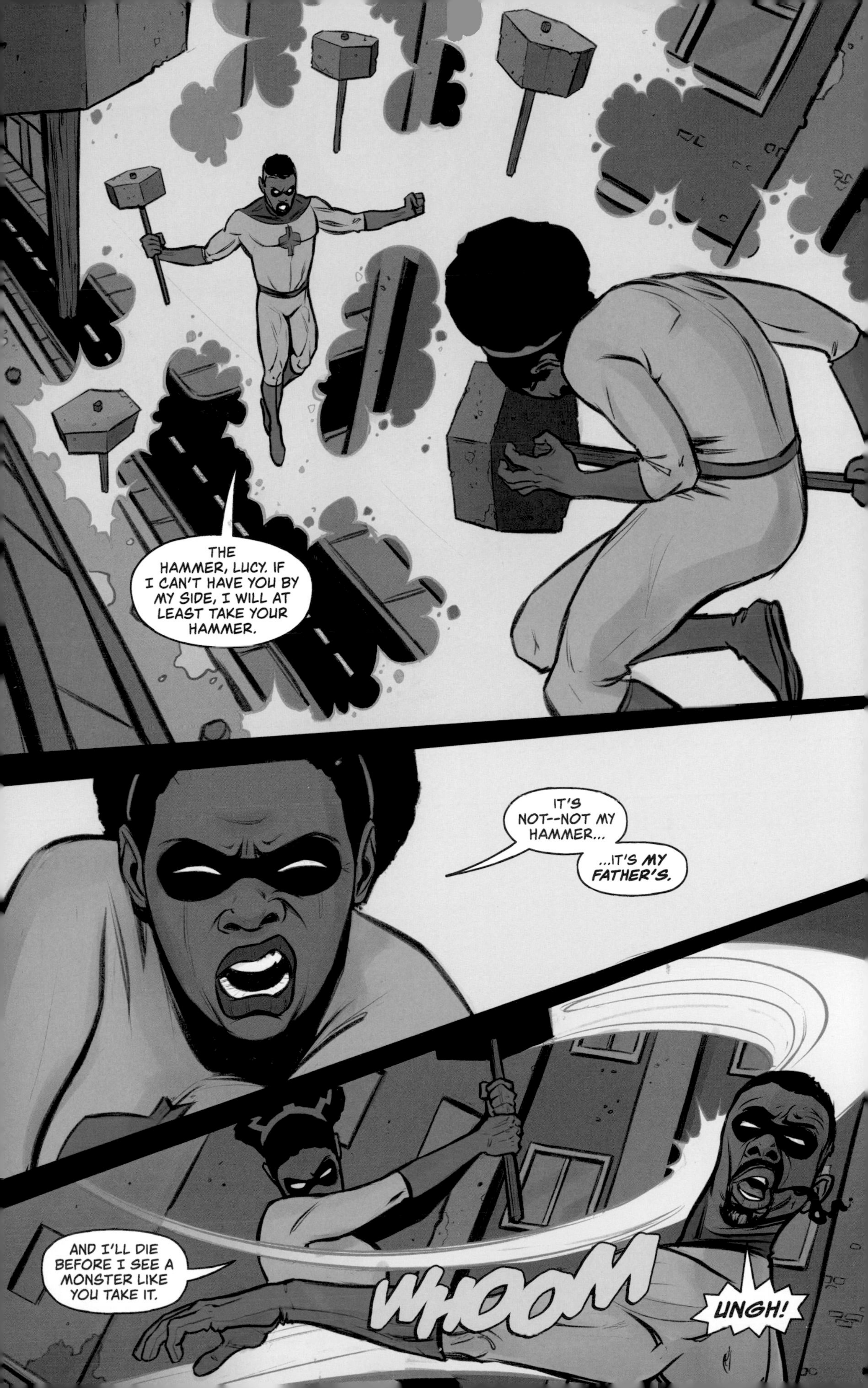
THE HAMMER, LUCY. IF I CAN'T HAVE YOU BY MY SIDE, I WILL AT LEAST TAKE YOUR HAMMER.
IT'S NOT--NOT MY HAMMER...
...IT'S MY FATHER'S.
AND I'LL DIE BEFORE I SEE A MONSTER LIKE YOU TAKE IT.
WHOOM
UNGH!

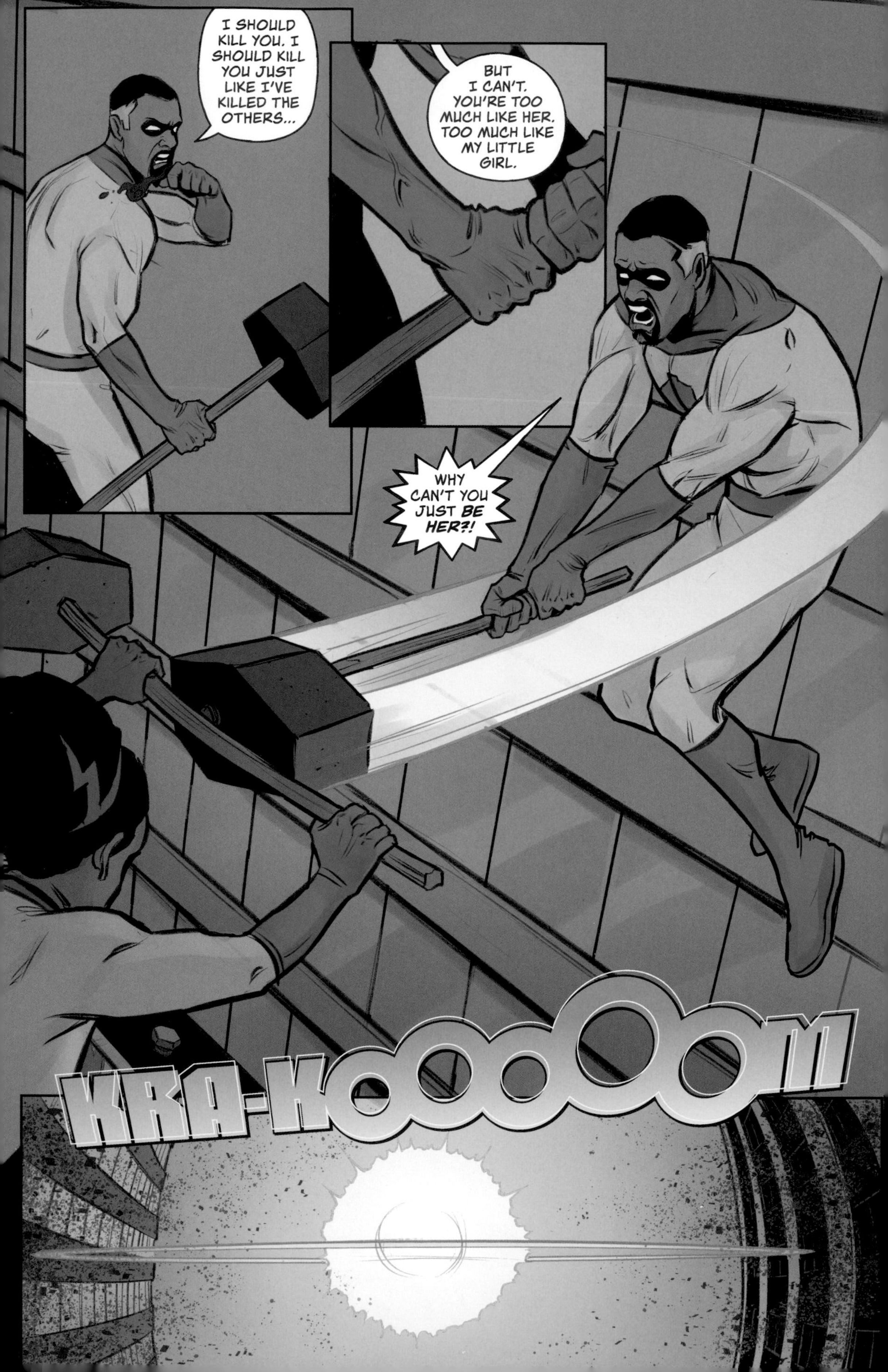
I SHOULD KILL YOU. I SHOULD KILL YOU JUST LIKE I'VE KILLED THE OTHERS...
BUT I CAN'T. YOU'RE TOO MUCH LIKE HER. TOO MUCH LIKE MY LITTLE GIRL.
WHY CAN'T YOU JUST *BE HER?!*
KRA-KOOOOOOM

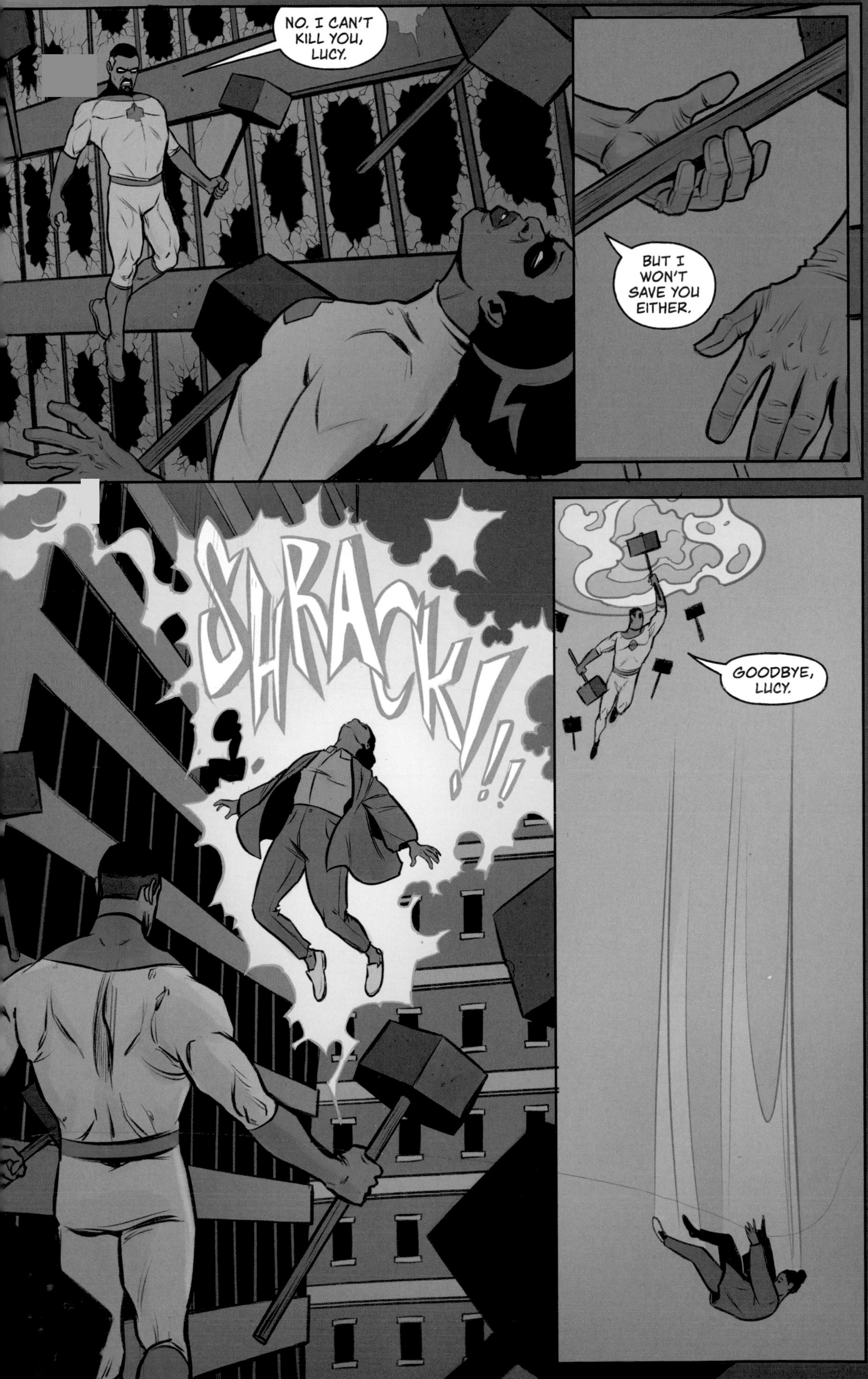
NO. I CAN'T KILL YOU, LUCY.
BUT I WON'T SAVE YOU EITHER.
SHRACK!!!
GOODBYE, LUCY.

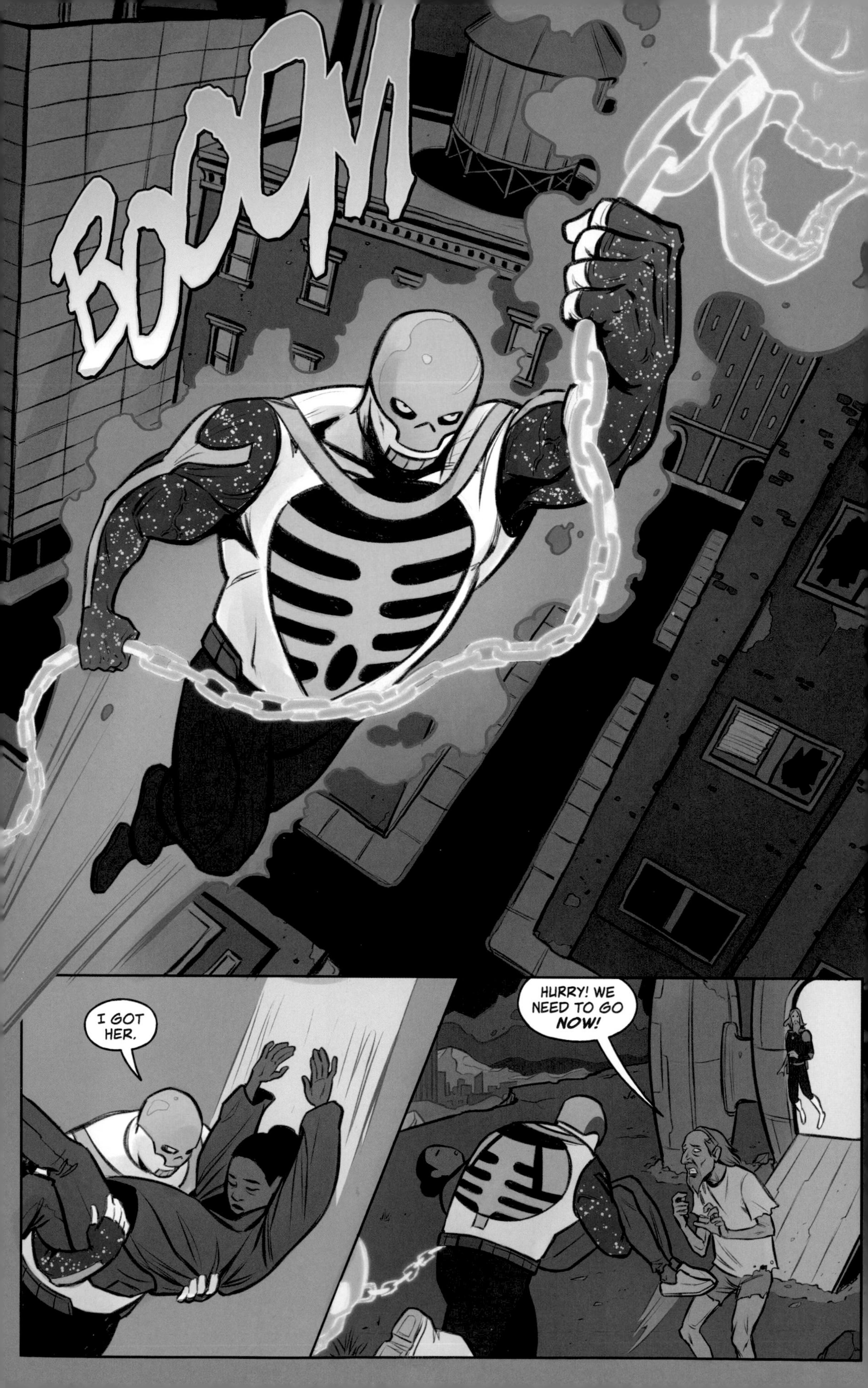
BOOM
I GOT HER.
HURRY! WE NEED TO GO NOW!

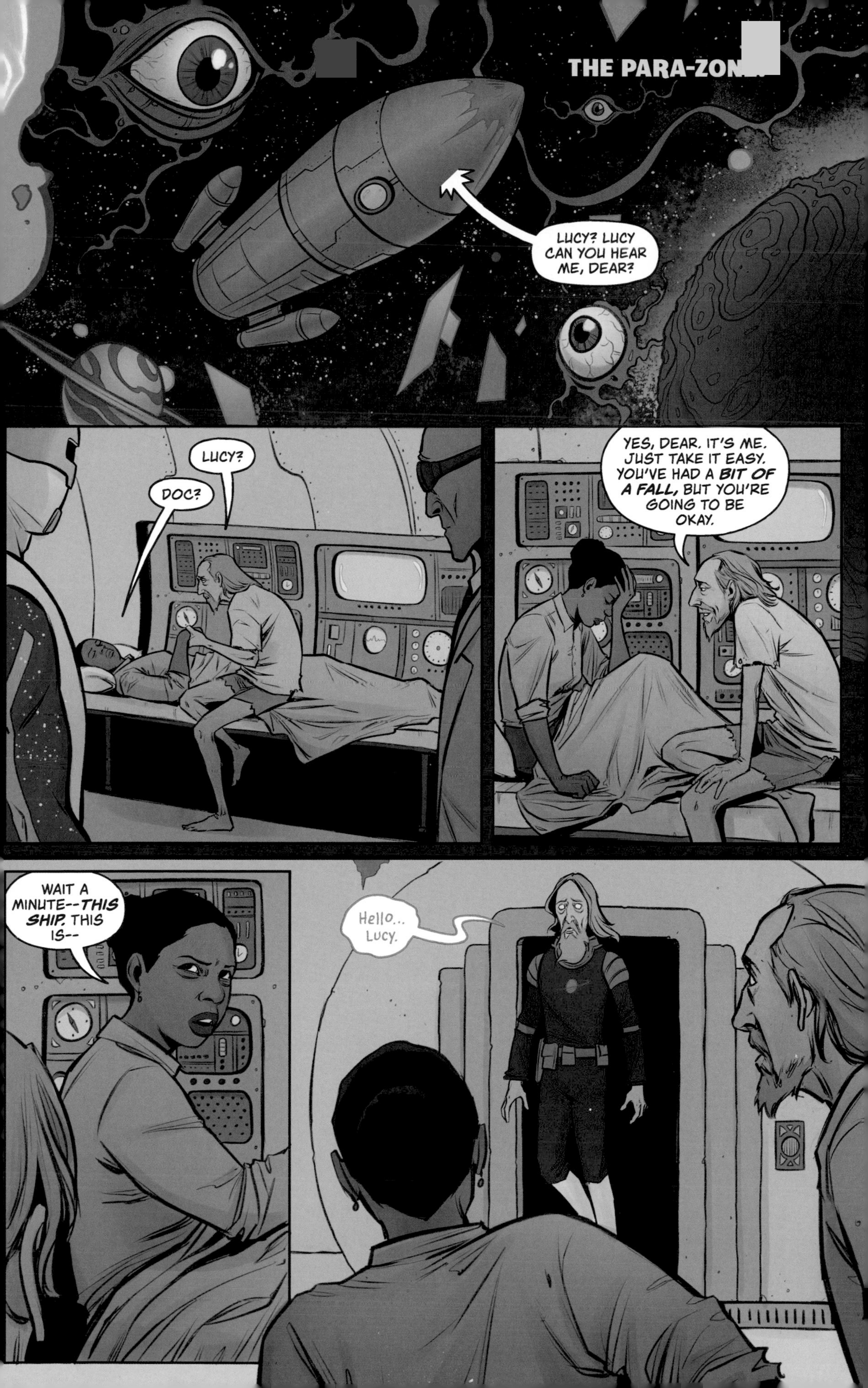
THE PARA-ZON
LUCY? LUCY CAN YOU HEAR ME, DEAR?
LUCY?
DOC?
YES, DEAR. IT'S ME. JUST TAKE IT EASY. YOU'VE HAD A ***BIT OF A FALL,*** BUT YOU'RE GOING TO BE OKAY.
WAIT A MINUTE--***THIS SHIP.*** THIS IS--
Hello... Lucy.

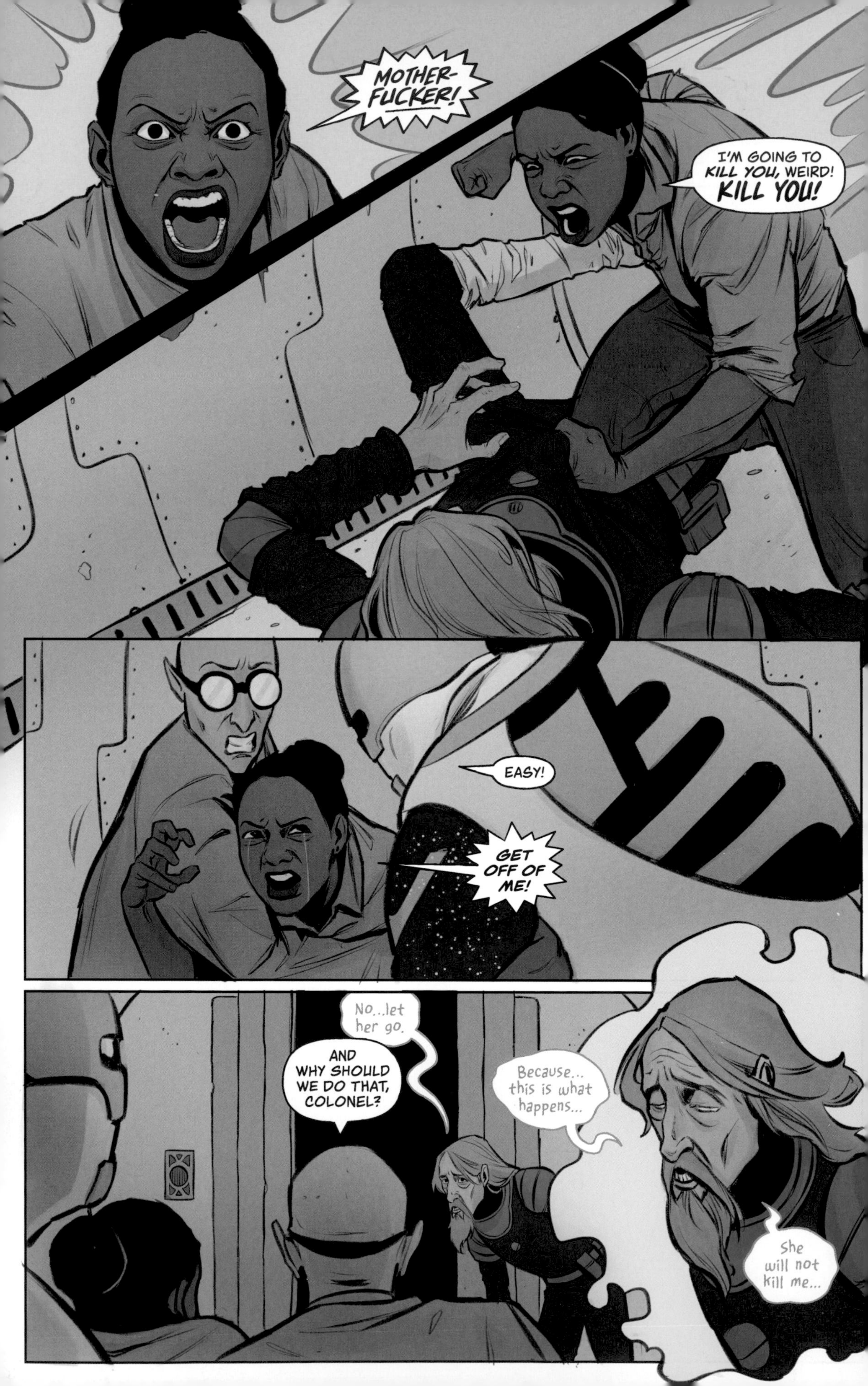
MOTHER-FUCKER!
I'M GOING TO KILL YOU, WEIRD! KILL YOU!
EASY!
GET OFF OF ME!
No...let her go.
AND WHY SHOULD WE DO THAT, COLONEL?
Because... this is what happens...
She will not kill me...

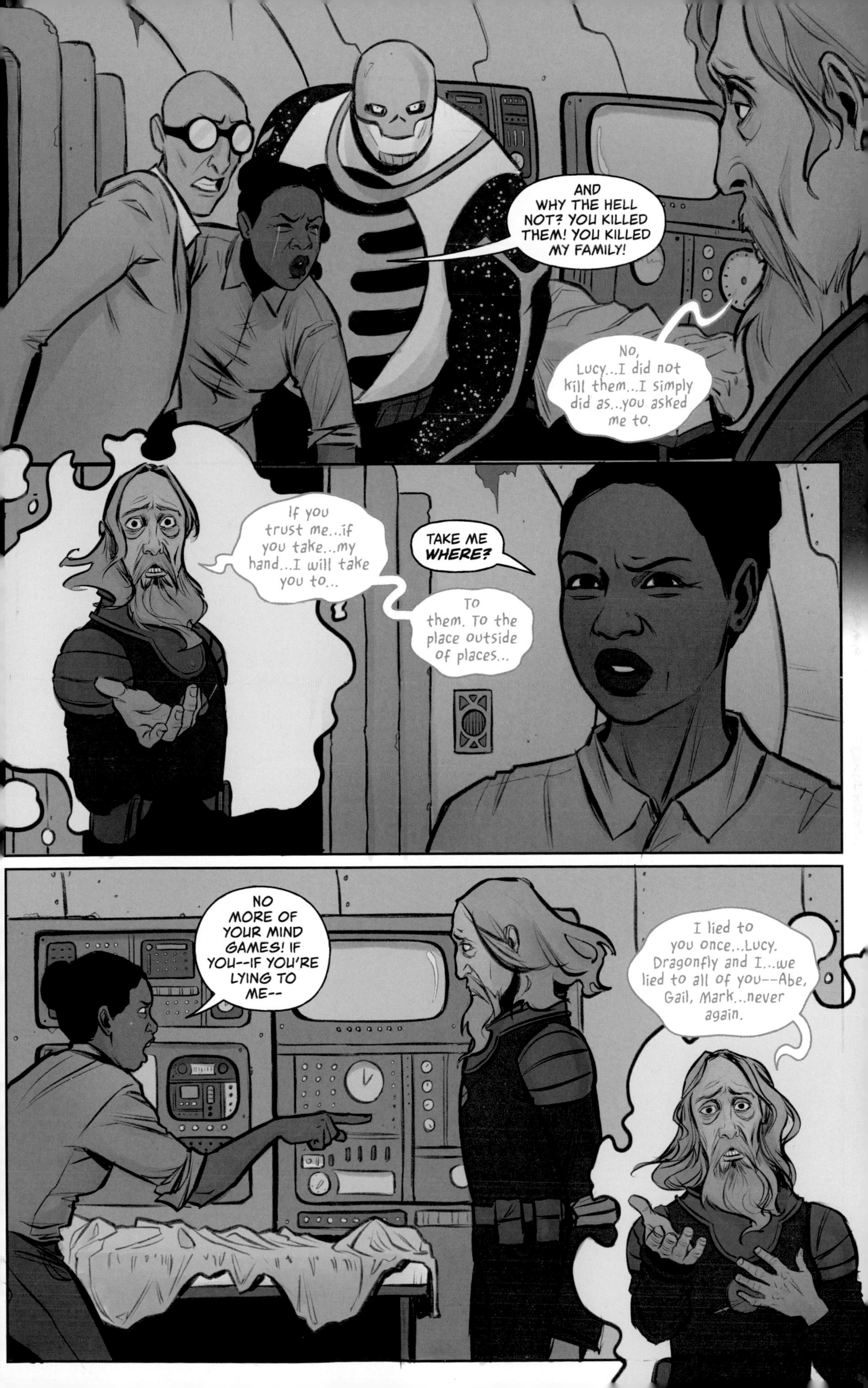
AND WHY THE HELL NOT? YOU KILLED THEM! YOU KILLED MY FAMILY!
No, Lucy...I did not kill them...I simply did as...you asked me to.
If you trust me...if you take...my hand...I will take you to...
TAKE ME WHERE?
To them. To the place outside of places...
NO MORE OF YOUR MIND GAMES! IF YOU--IF YOU'RE LYING TO ME--
I lied to you once...Lucy. Dragonfly and I...we lied to all of you--Abe, Gail, Mark...never again.

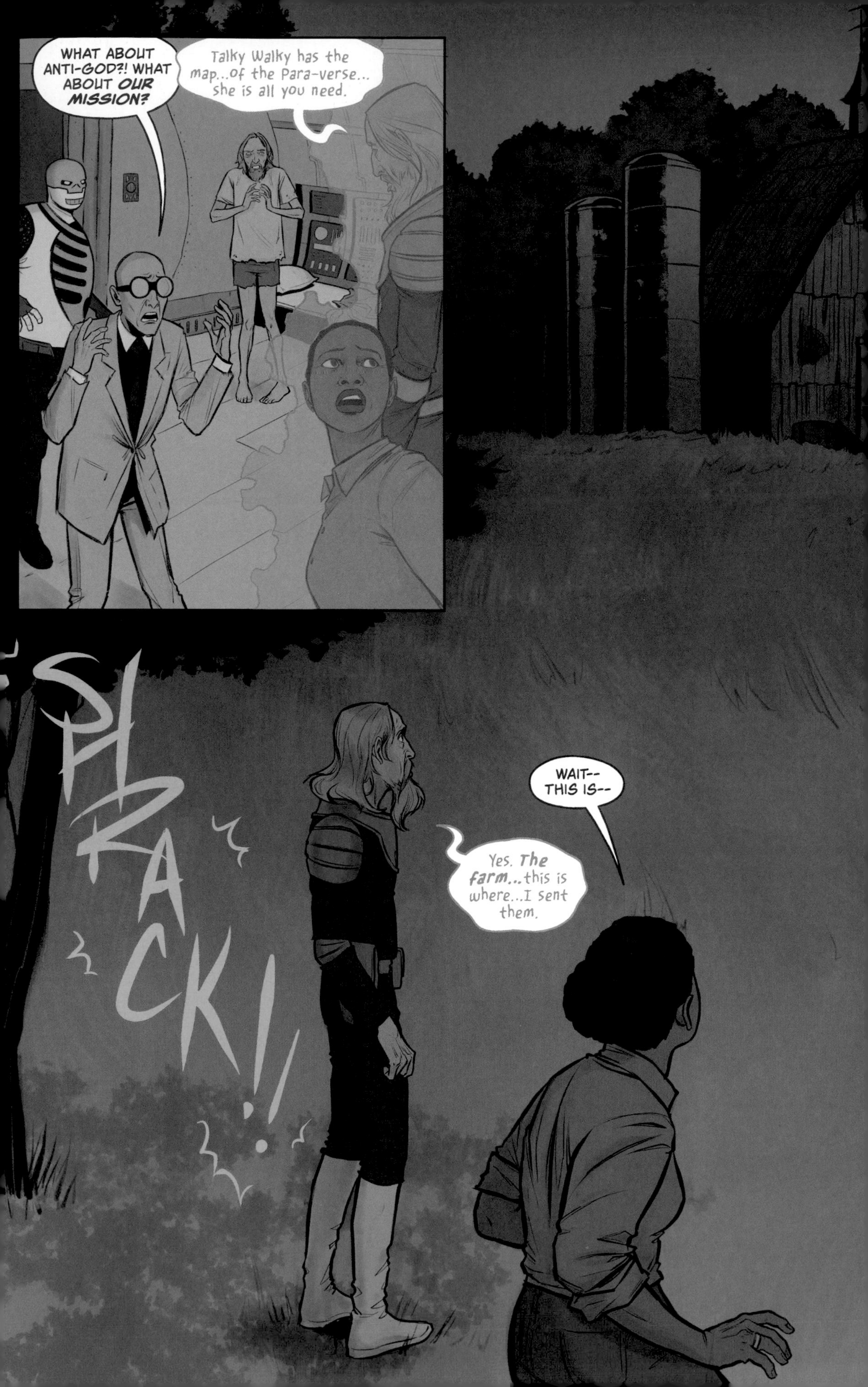
WHAT ABOUT ANTI-GOD?! WHAT ABOUT OUR MISSION?
Talky Walky has the map...of the Para-verse... she is all you need.
PHRACK!!
WAIT-- THIS IS--
Yes. The farm...this is where...I sent them.

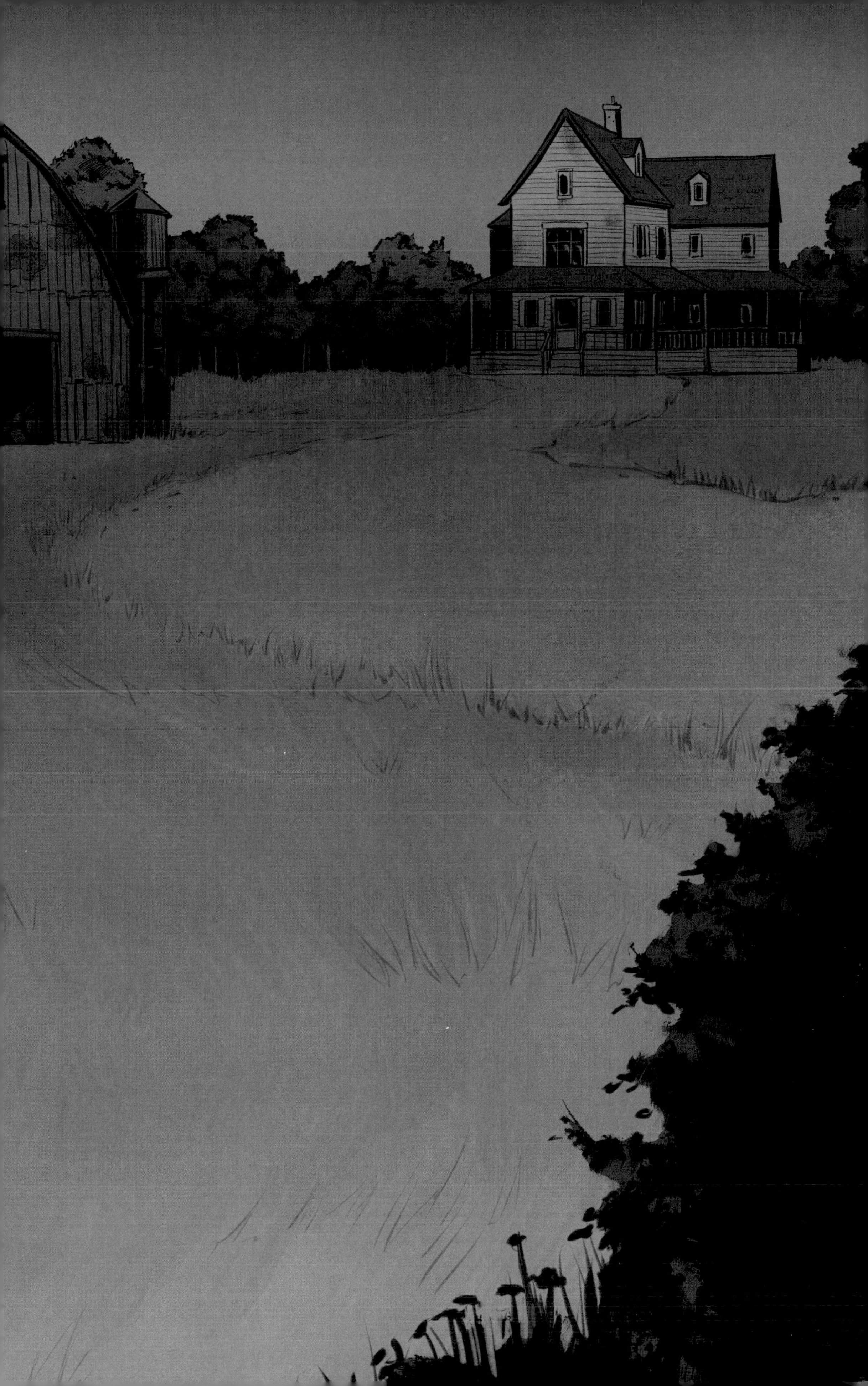

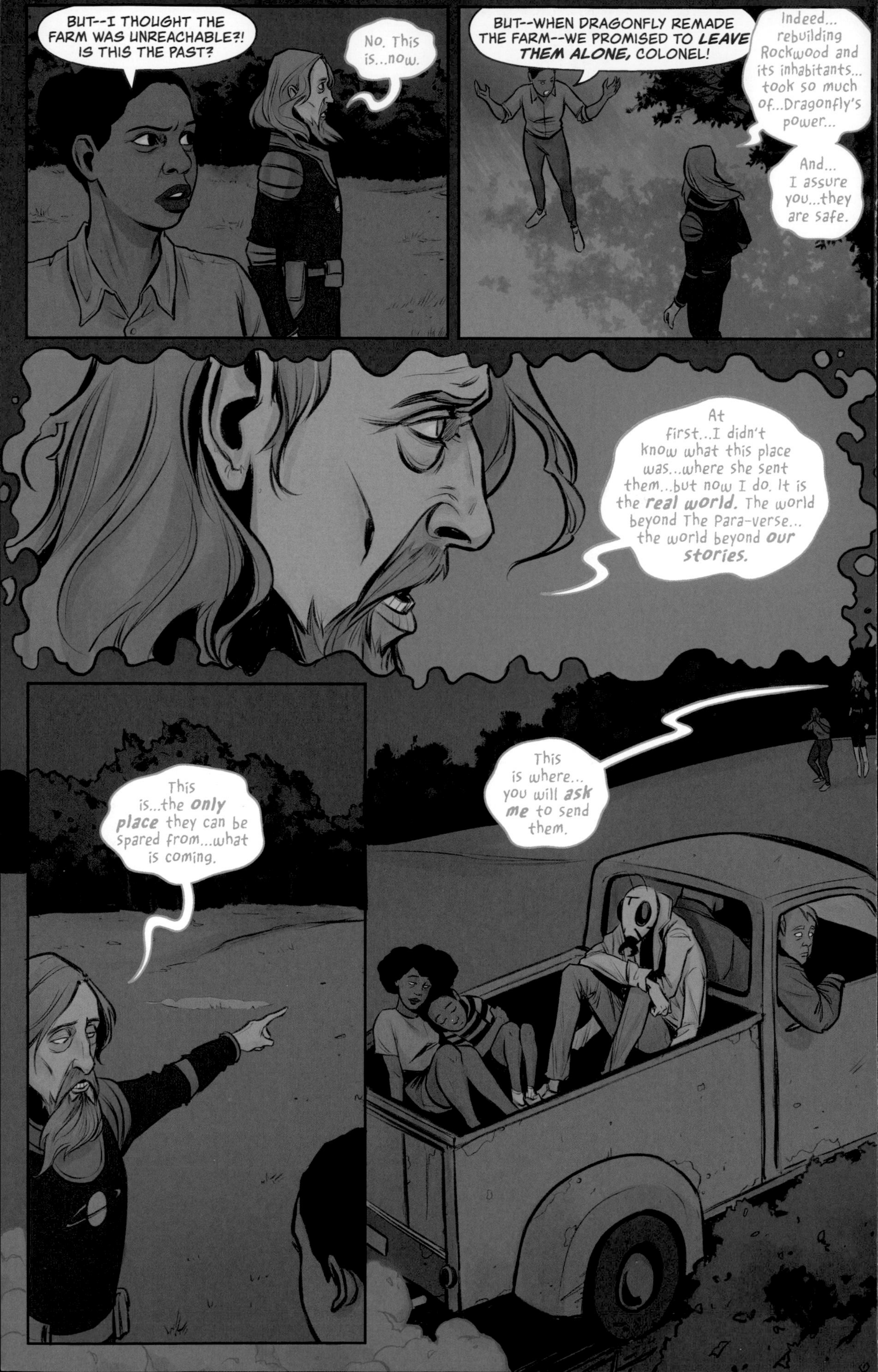
BUT--I THOUGHT THE FARM WAS UNREACHABLE?! IS THIS THE PAST?
No. This is...now.
BUT--WHEN DRAGONFLY REMADE THE FARM--WE PROMISED TO LEAVE THEM ALONE, COLONEL!
Indeed... rebuilding Rockwood and its inhabitants... took so much of...Dragonfly's power...
And... I assure you...they are safe.
At first...I didn't know what this place was...where she sent them...but now I do. It is the real world. The world beyond The Para-verse... the world beyond our stories.
This is...the only place they can be spared from...what is coming.
This is where... you will ask me to send them.

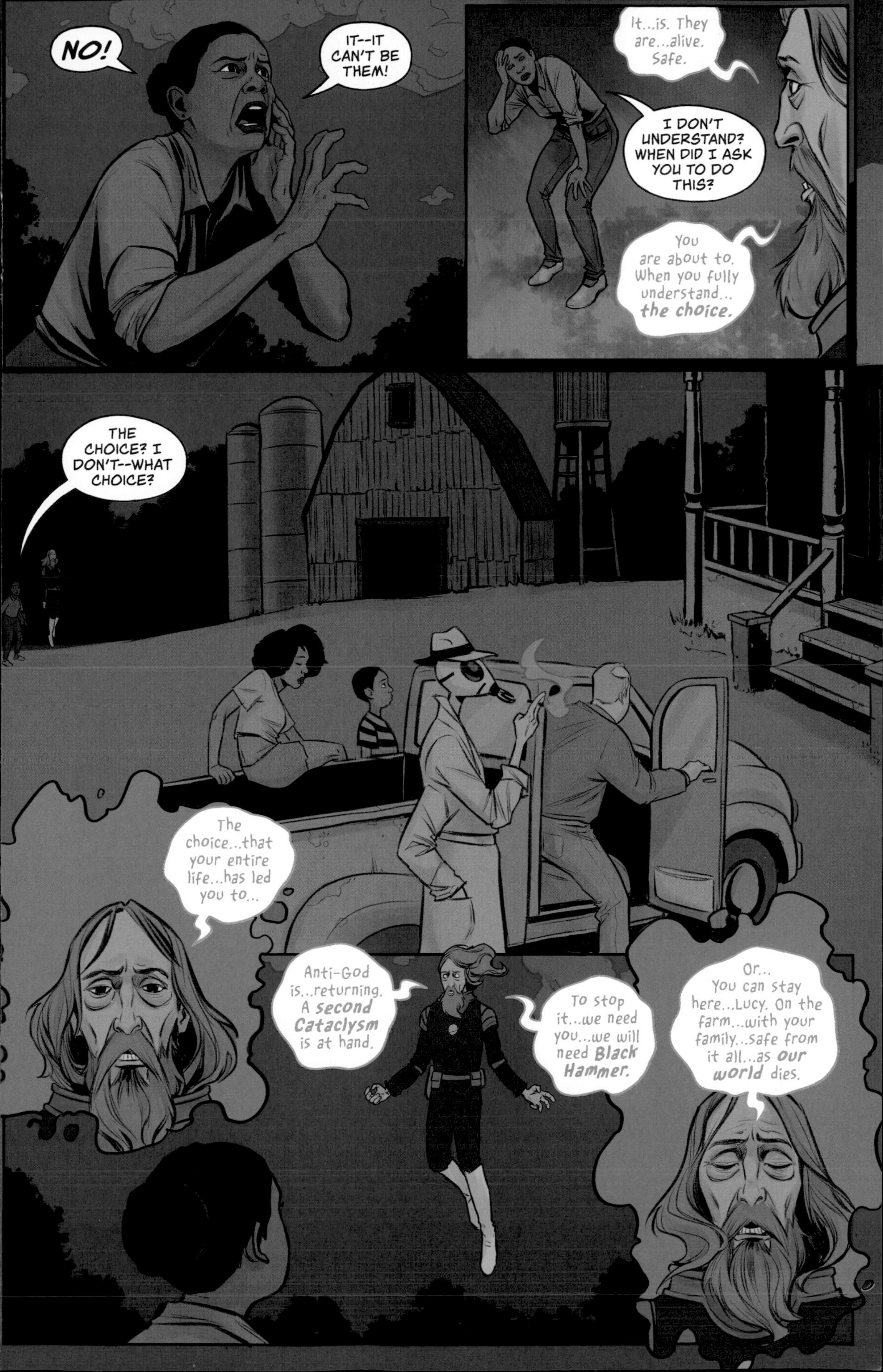
NO!
IT--IT CAN'T BE THEM!
It...is. They are...alive. Safe.
I DON'T UNDERSTAND? WHEN DID I ASK YOU TO DO THIS?
You are about to. When you fully understand... **the choice.**
THE CHOICE? I DON'T--WHAT CHOICE?
The choice...that your entire life...has led you to...
Anti-God is...returning. A **second Cataclysm** is at hand.
To stop it...we need you...we will need **Black Hammer.**
Or... You can stay here...Lucy. On the farm...with your family...safe from it all...as **our world** dies.

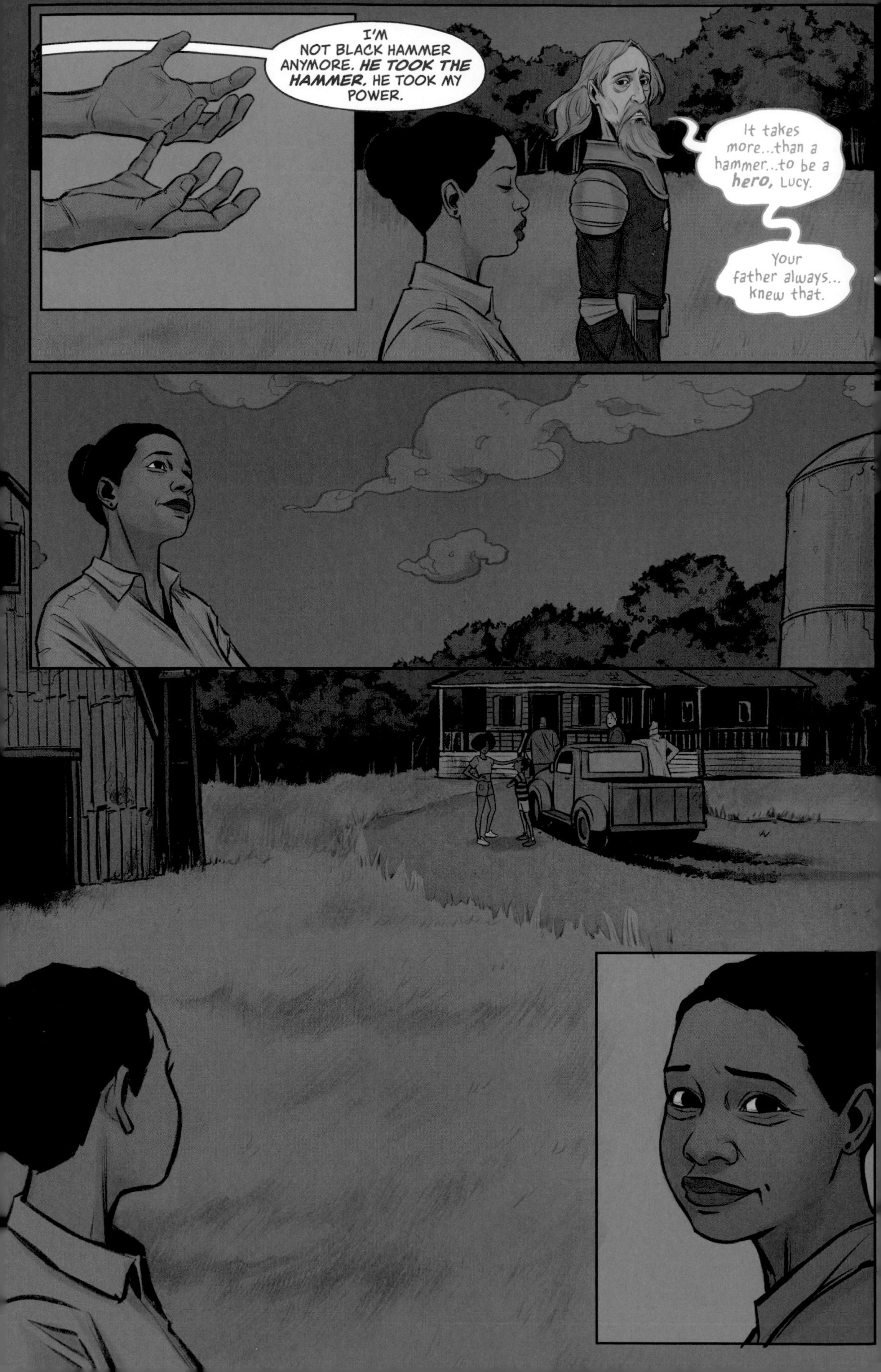
I'M NOT BLACK HAMMER ANYMORE. HE TOOK THE HAMMER. HE TOOK MY POWER.
It takes more...than a hammer...to be a hero, Lucy.
Your father always... knew that.

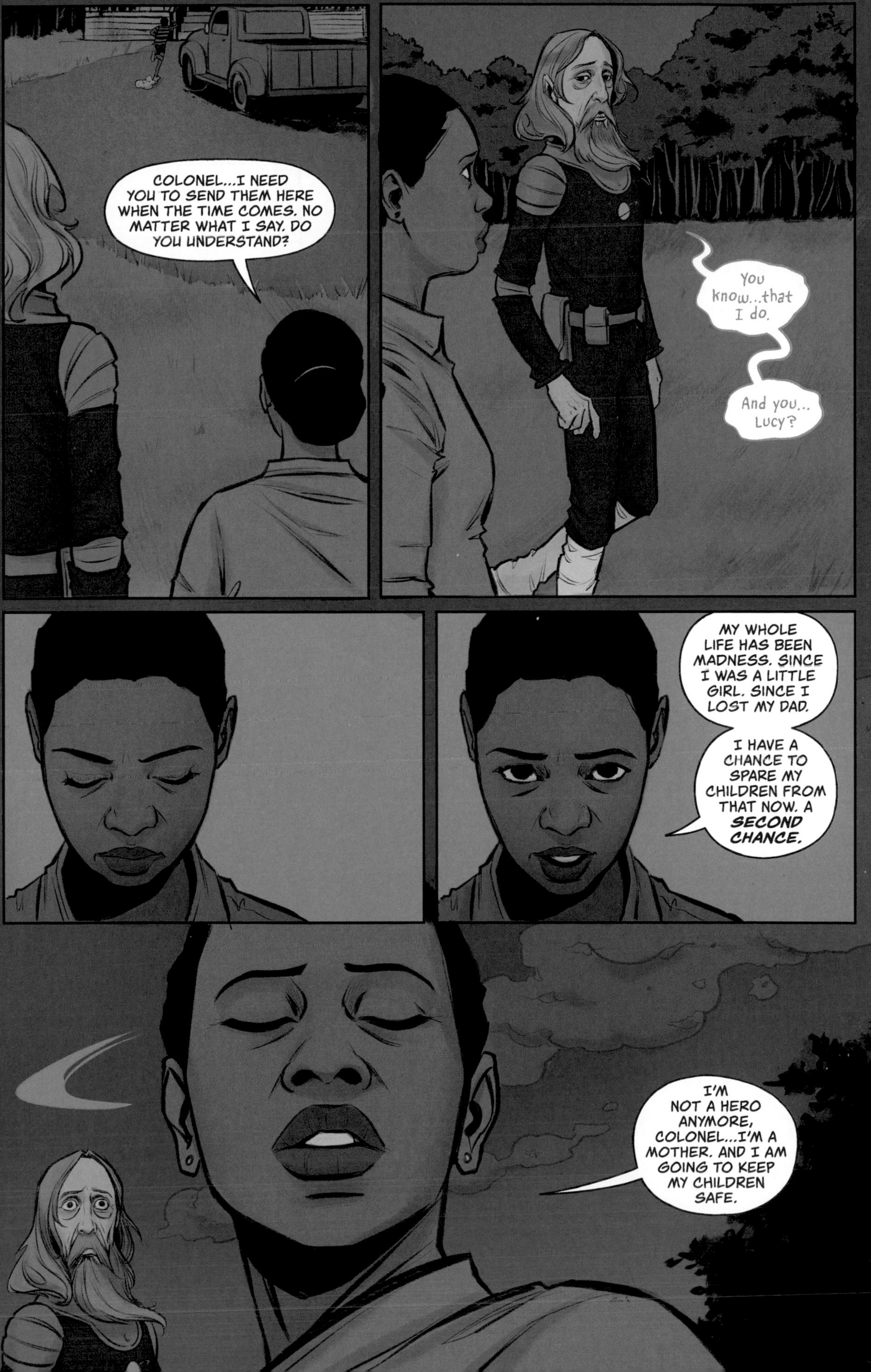
COLONEL...I NEED YOU TO SEND THEM HERE WHEN THE TIME COMES. NO MATTER WHAT I SAY. DO YOU UNDERSTAND?
You know...that I do.
And you... Lucy?
MY WHOLE LIFE HAS BEEN MADNESS. SINCE I WAS A LITTLE GIRL. SINCE I LOST MY DAD.
I HAVE A CHANCE TO SPARE MY CHILDREN FROM THAT NOW. A *SECOND CHANCE.*
I'M NOT A HERO ANYMORE, COLONEL...I'M A MOTHER. AND I AM GOING TO KEEP MY CHILDREN SAFE.

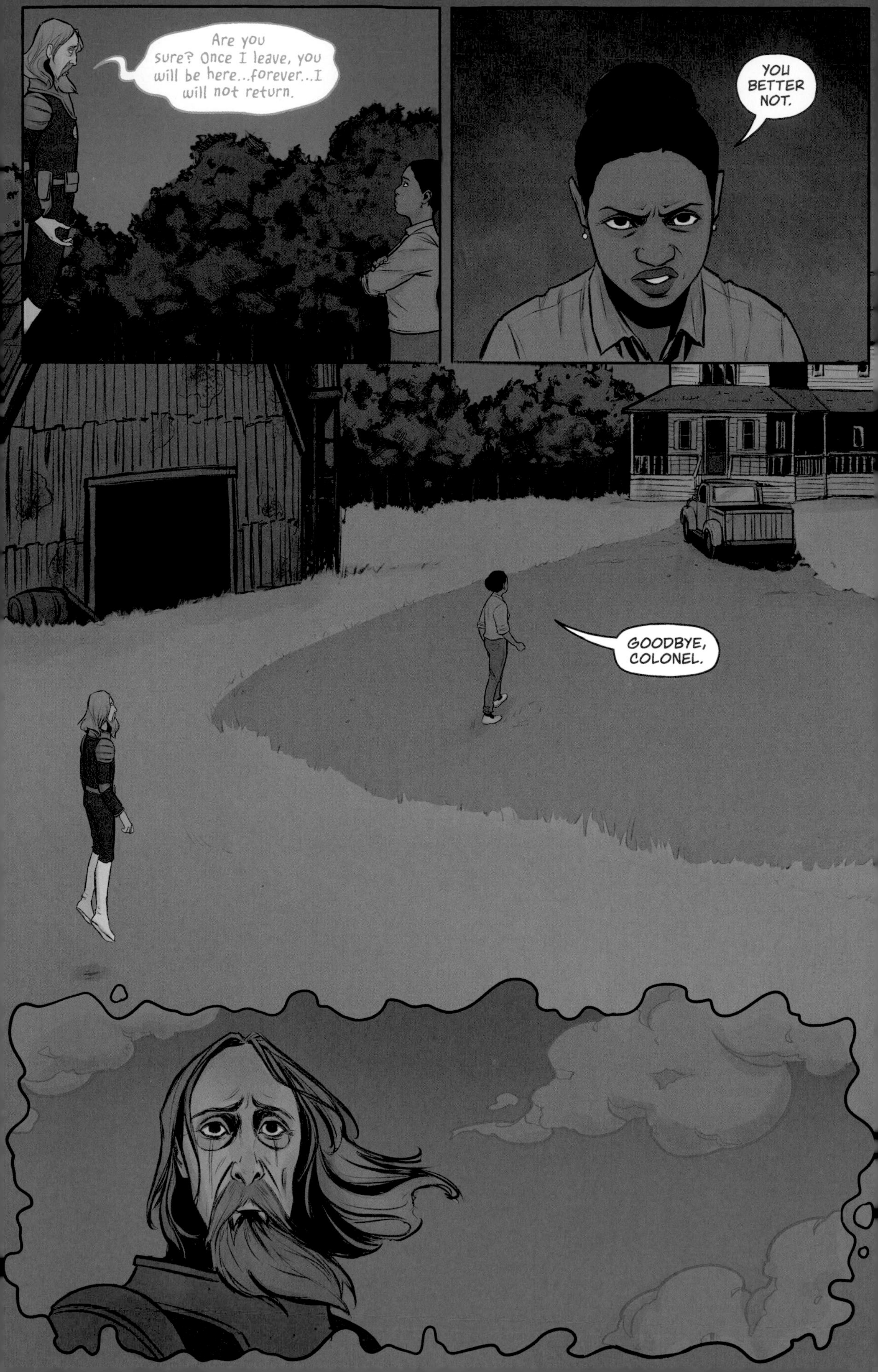
Are you sure? Once I leave, you will be here...forever...I will not return.
YOU BETTER NOT.
GOODBYE, COLONEL.

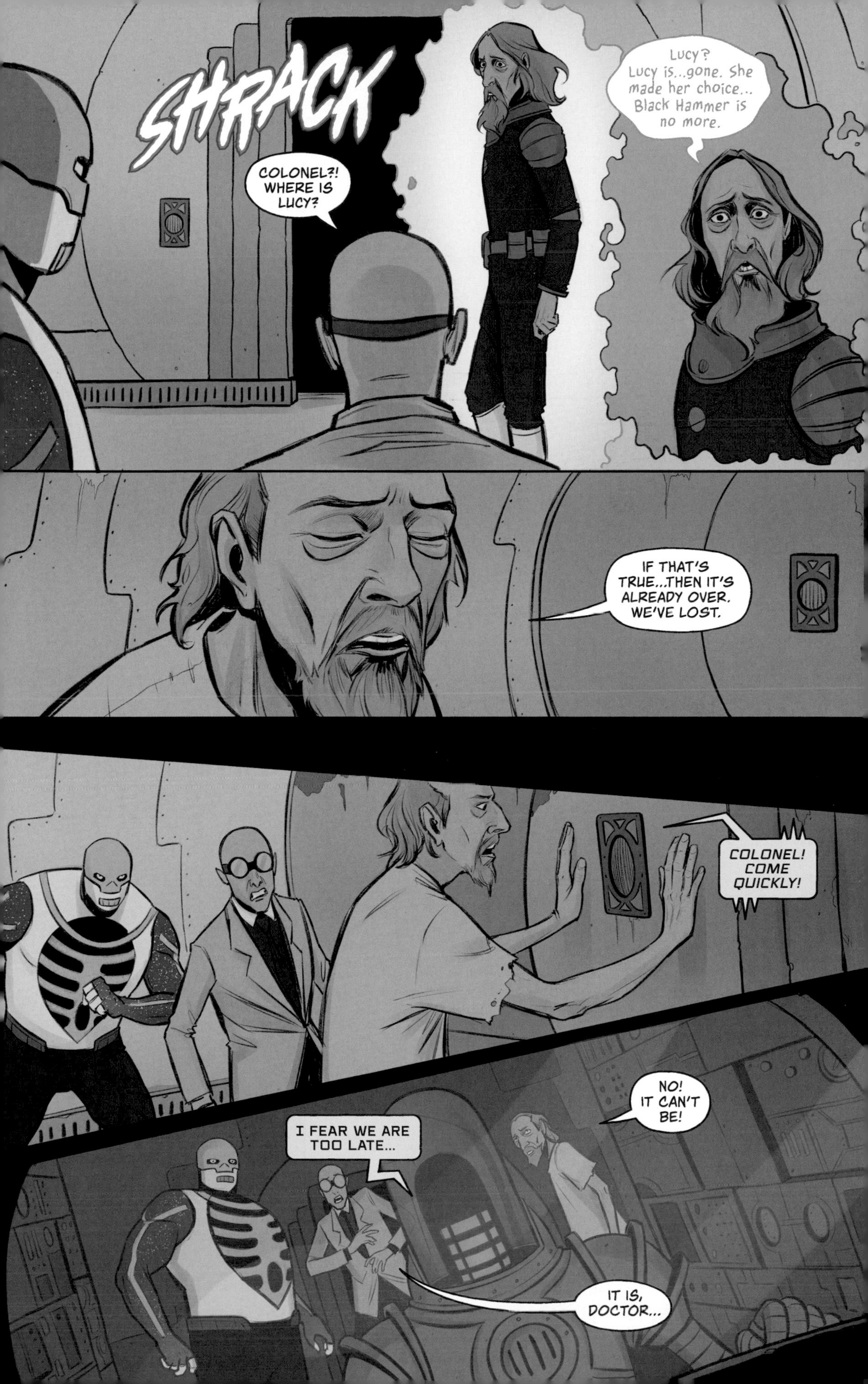
SHRACK
COLONEL?! WHERE IS LUCY?
Lucy? Lucy is...gone. She made her choice... Black Hammer is no more.
IF THAT'S TRUE...THEN IT'S ALREADY OVER. WE'VE LOST.
COLONEL! COME QUICKLY!
I FEAR WE ARE TOO LATE...
NO! IT CAN'T BE!
IT IS, DOCTOR...

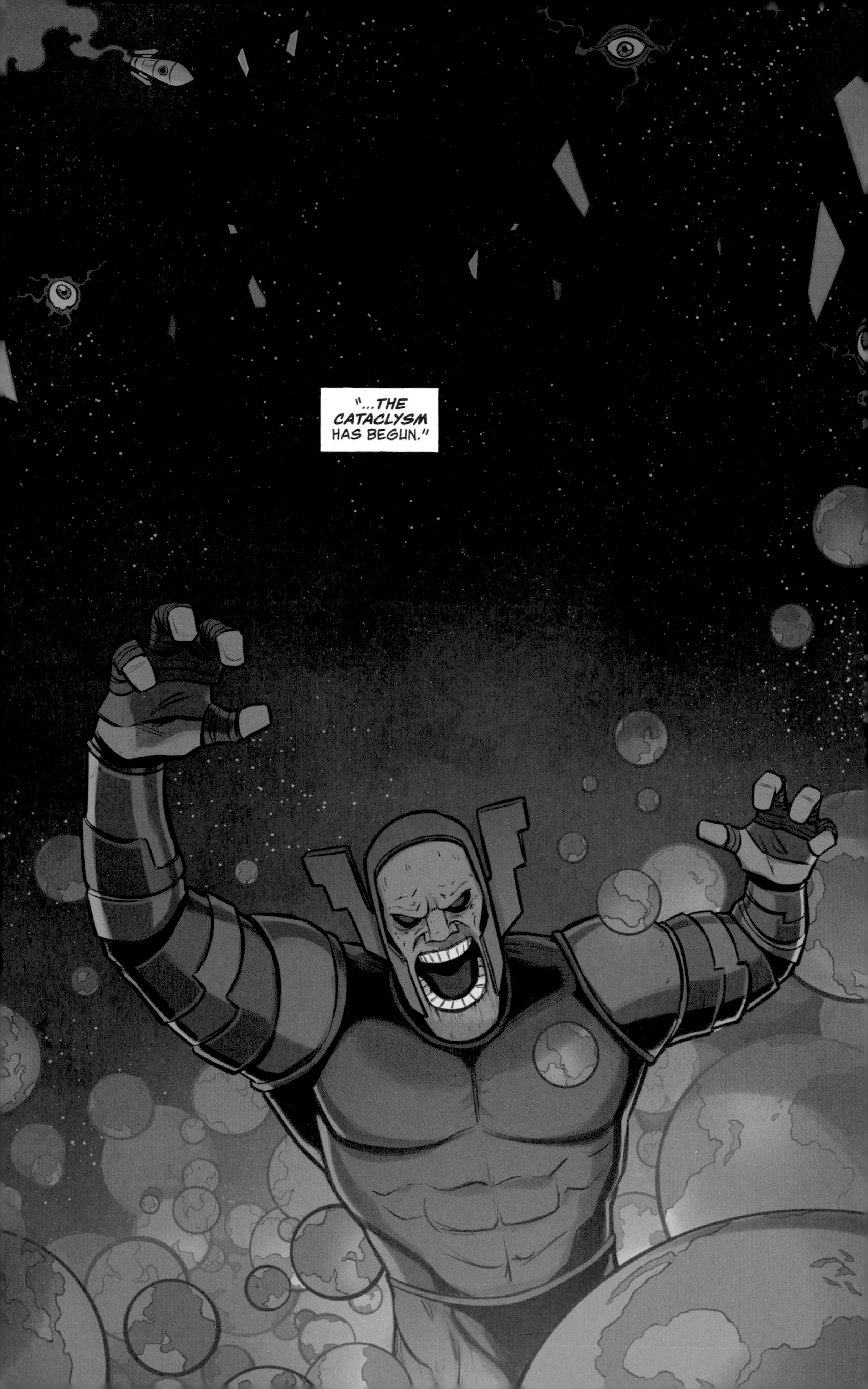
"...THE CATACLYSM HAS BEGUN."

BLACK HAMMER REBORN SKETCHBOOK

NOTES BY CAITLIN YARSKY

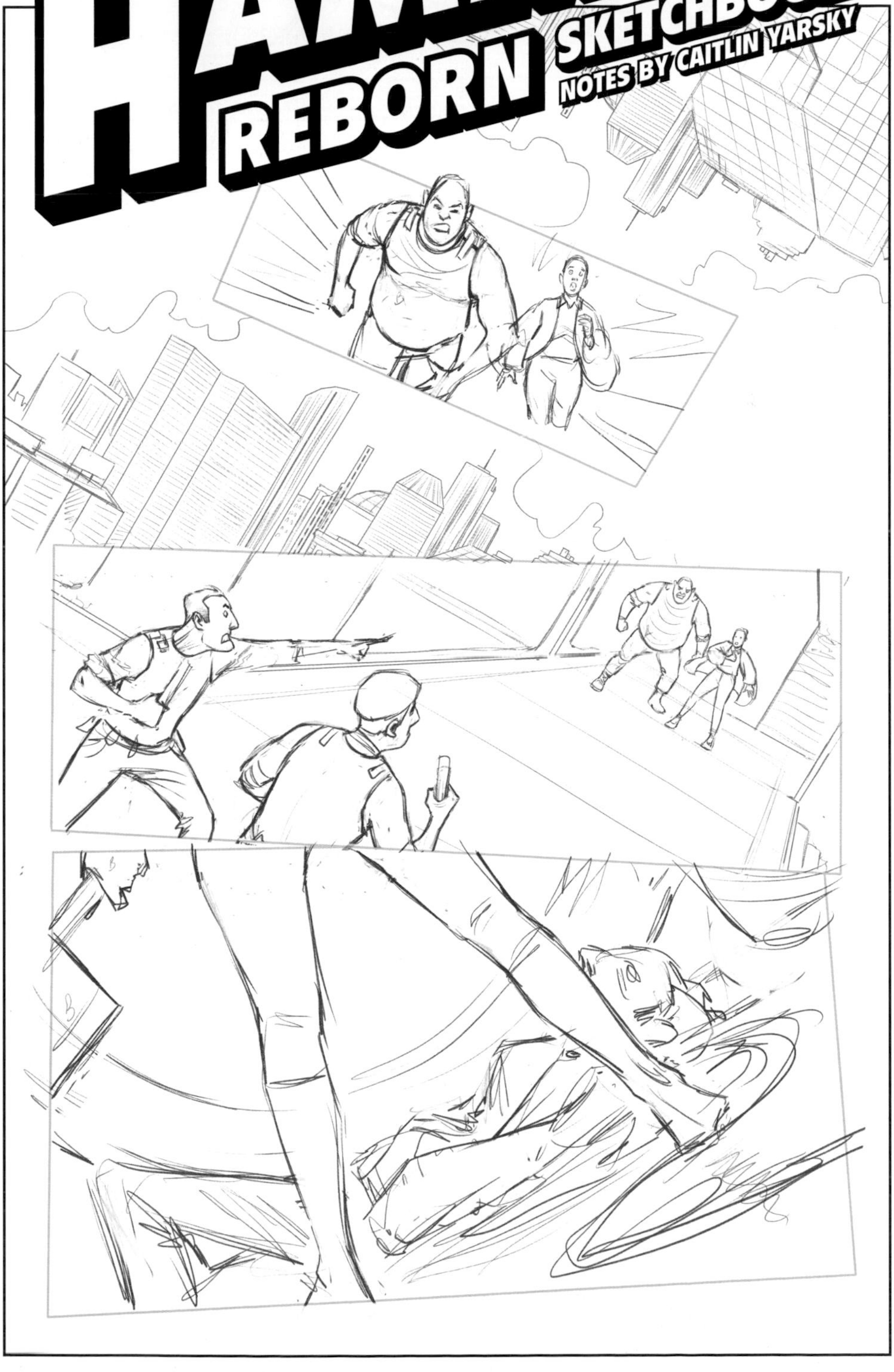

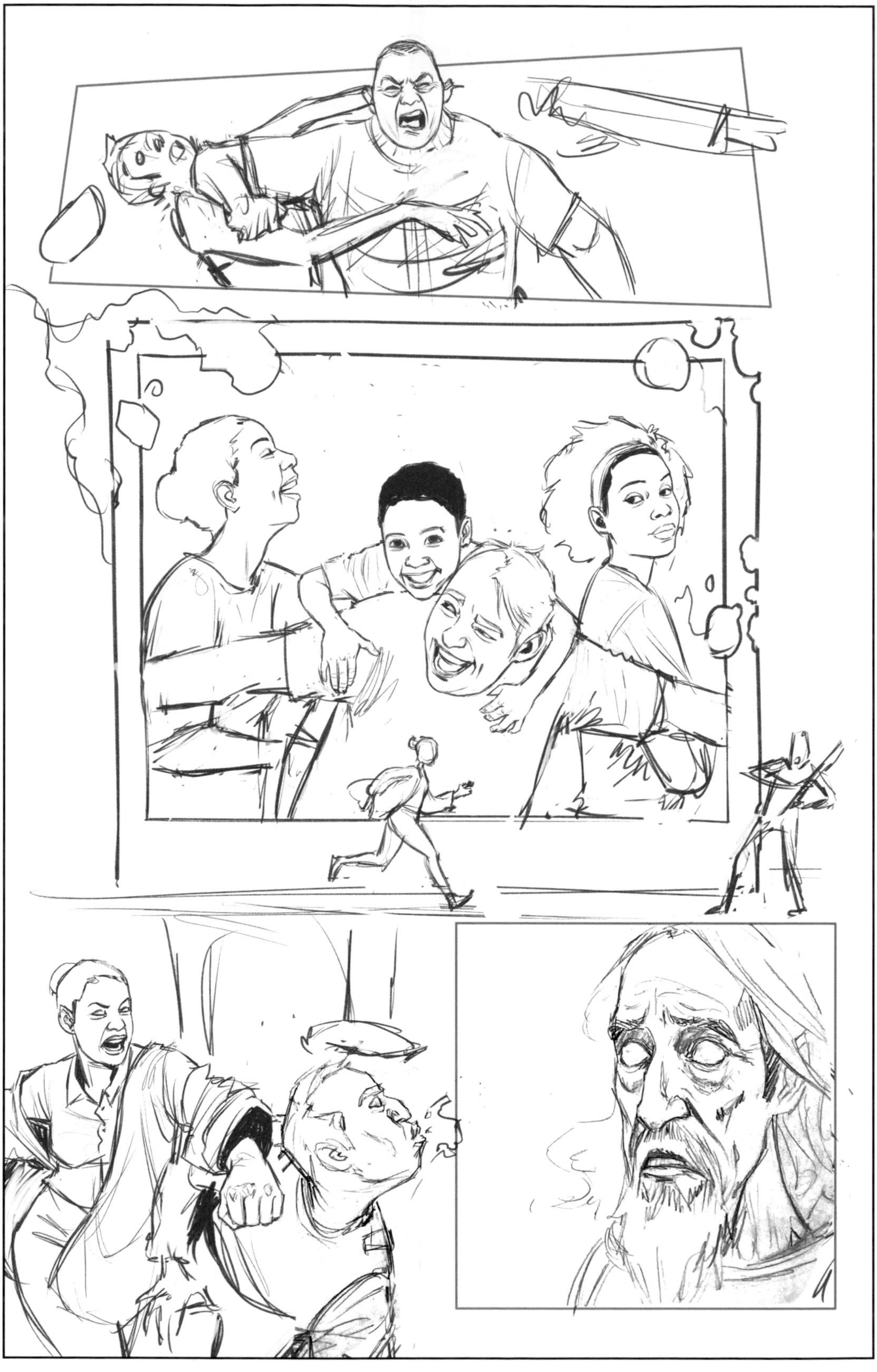

The panel with the Polaroid reminds you what is fueling Lucy's rage. Although there are other things to think about, this all-encompassing grief is what's sending her back into superhero mode.

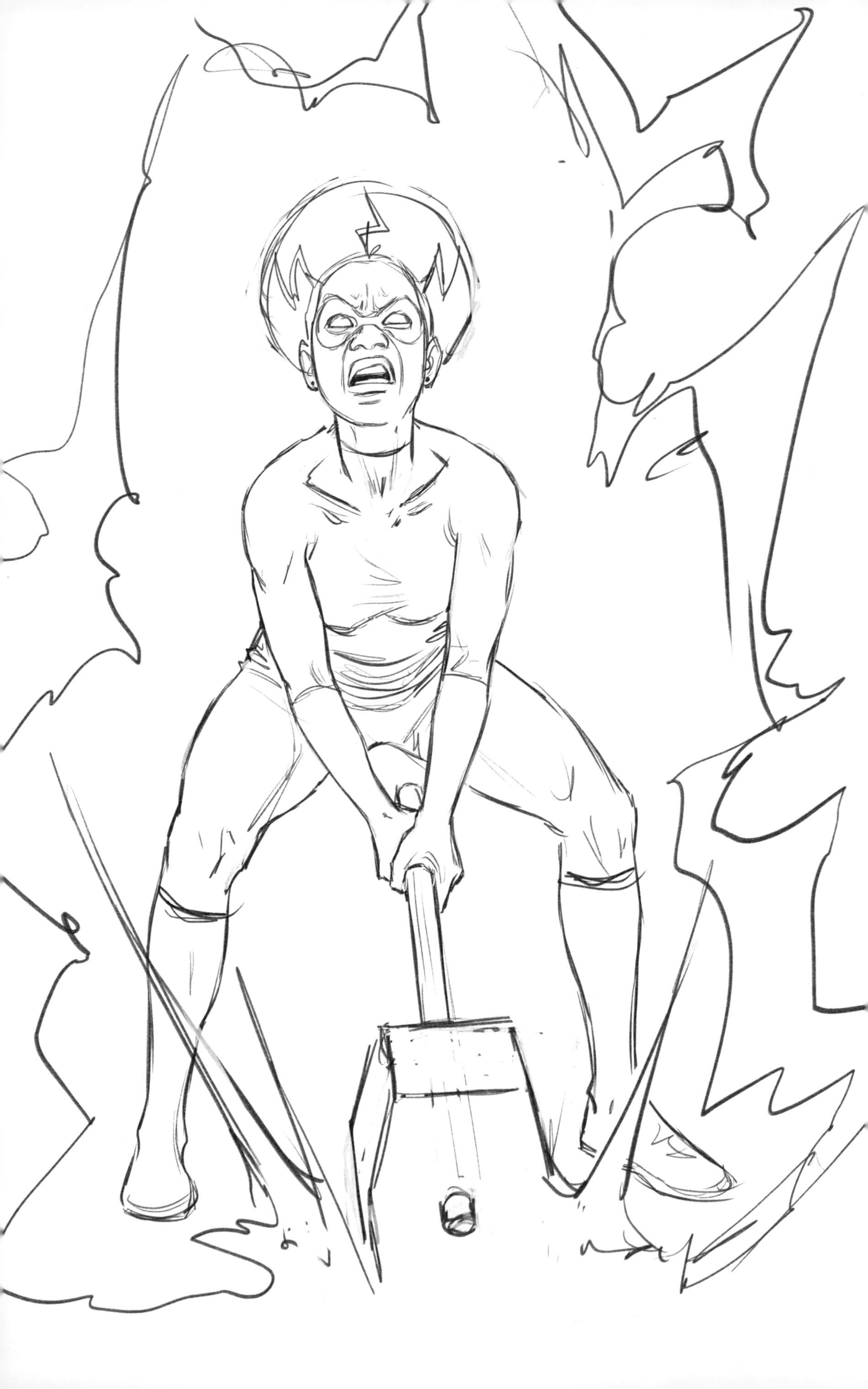

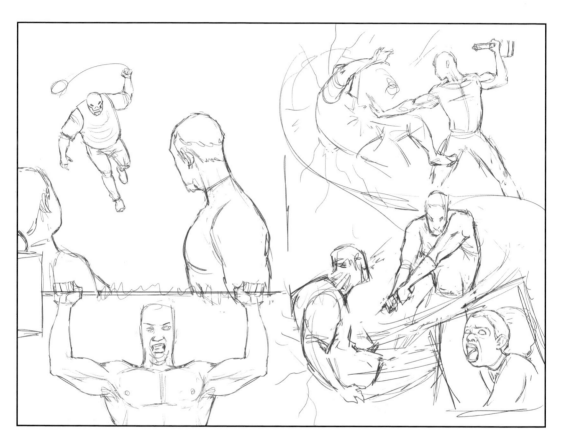

Action never felt like my strong suit, so I've been trying to push myself with it—and it turned out to be really fun, exaggerating Skulldigger's pose to emphasize how hard he was hit. It feels a little like doing key frames for animation, which also tend to exaggerate action.

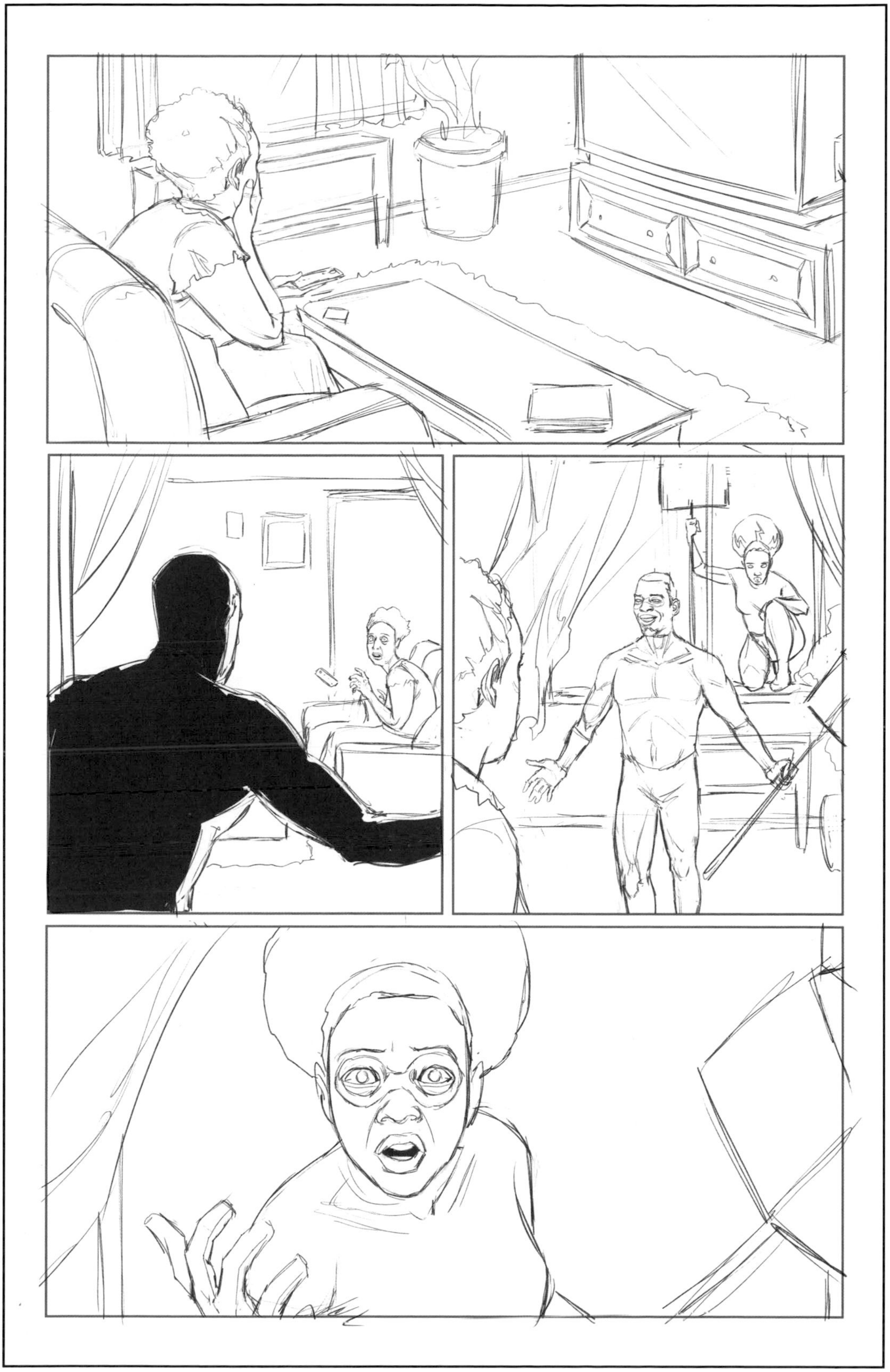

I wanted to give Lucy's mom some personality quirks—in the inks I added some stuff around her to indicate an obsession with birds.

Insector was so much fun to draw, and this scene was really wild and surreal.

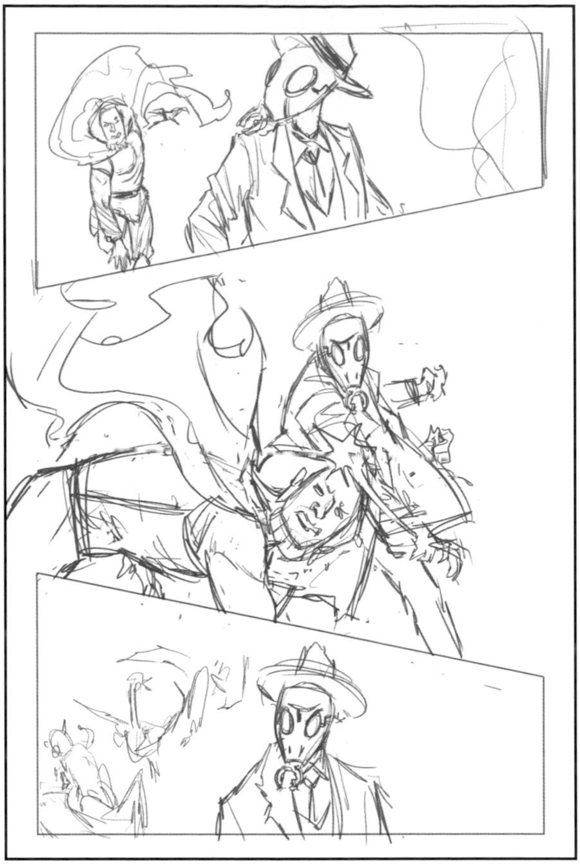

I love trying to nail down emotions, so the panel with the closeup of Doc and Skulldigger was a fun challenge. I really enjoyed their relationship in this series.

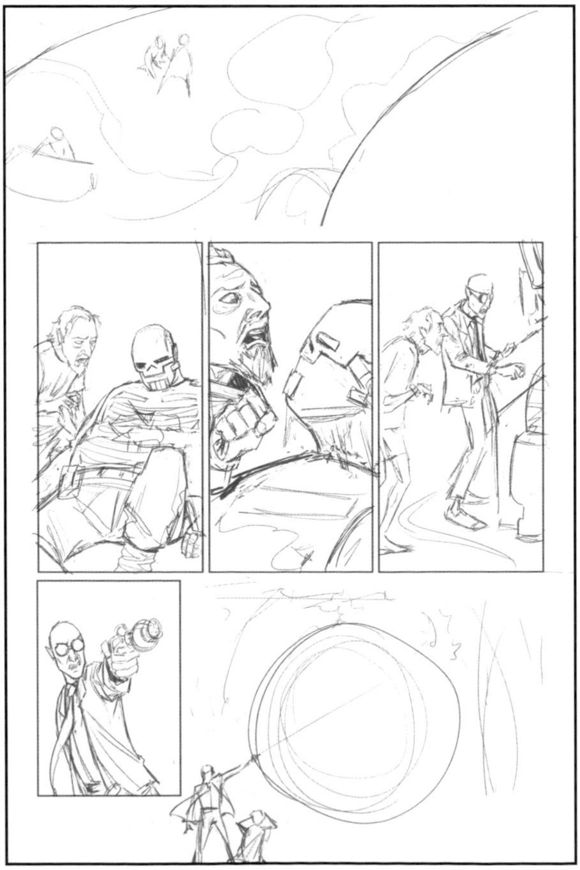

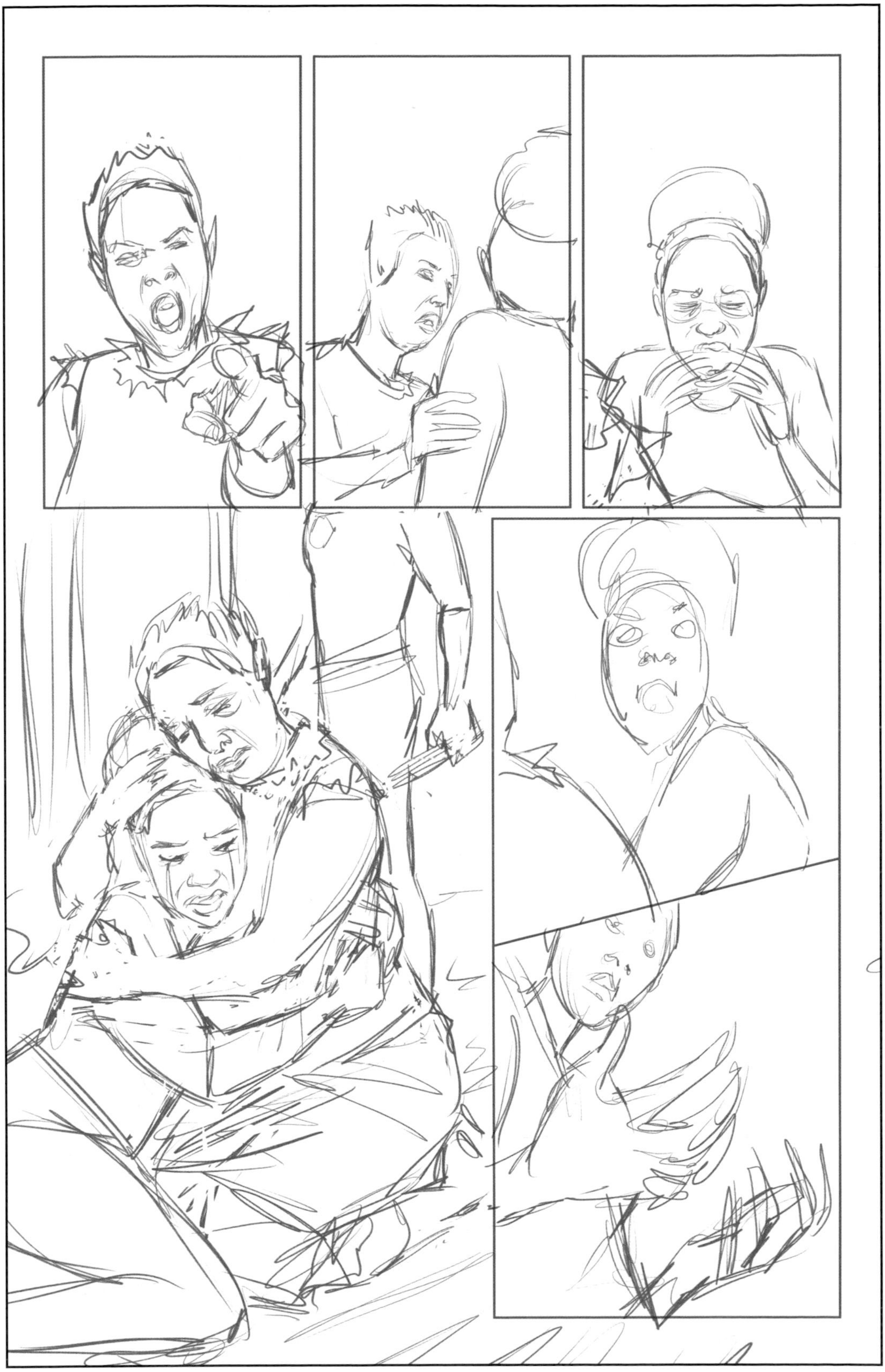

I wanted to show an embrace on this page between Lucy and her mom that only happens between people who know each other better than anyone else does.

Lucy sending her dad flying was a really fun panel. Also, I did the dreaded repeating panel bit for the dirt road scene, but hey, it can be real effective!

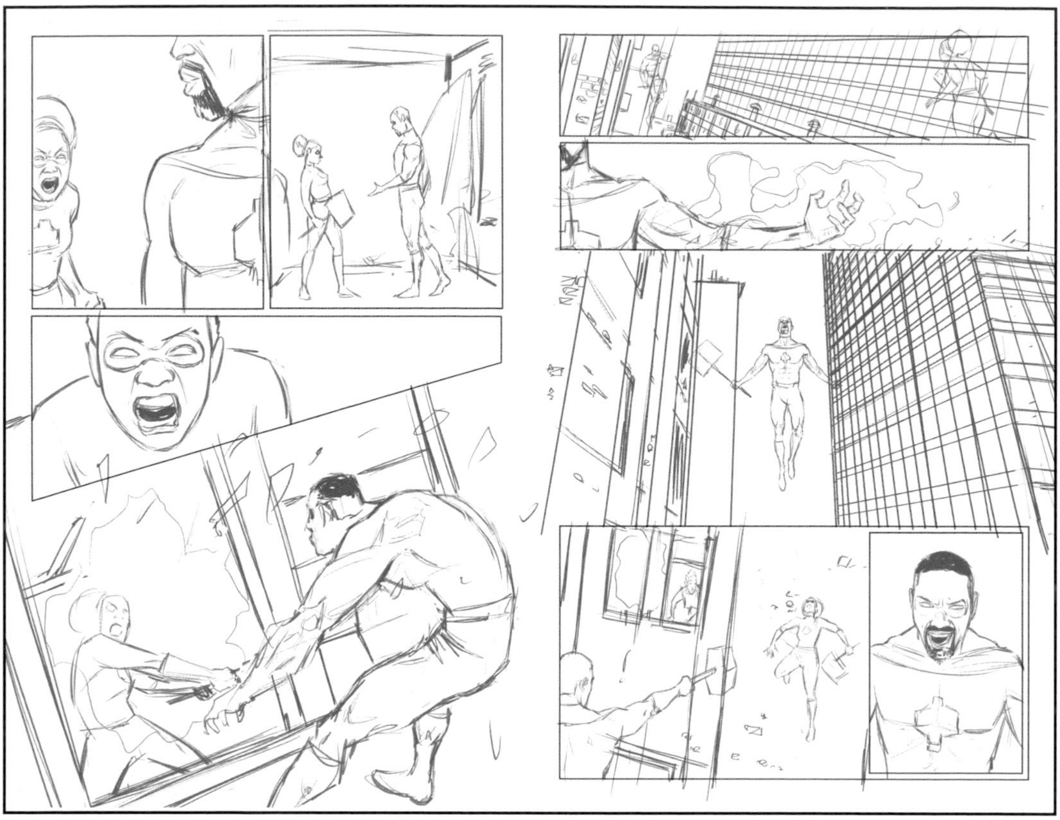

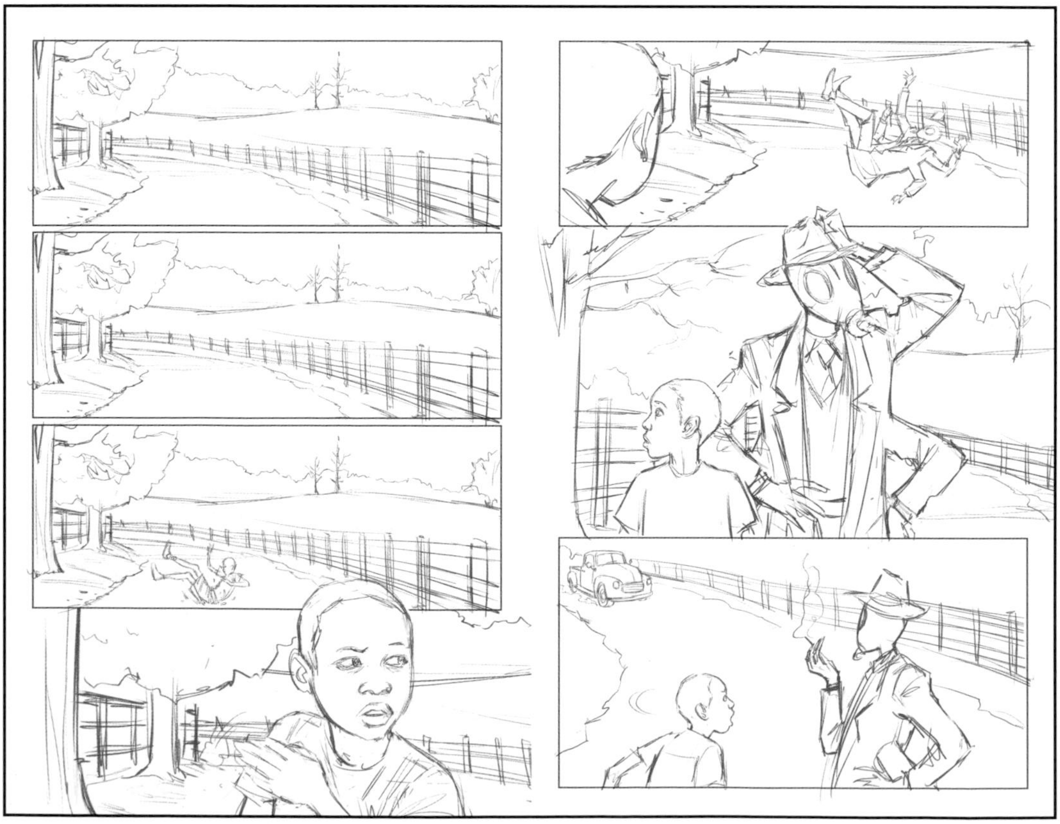

This was a particularly difficult (and dark) spread and took me longer than I care to admit. That said, I do love how the story broke into our world.

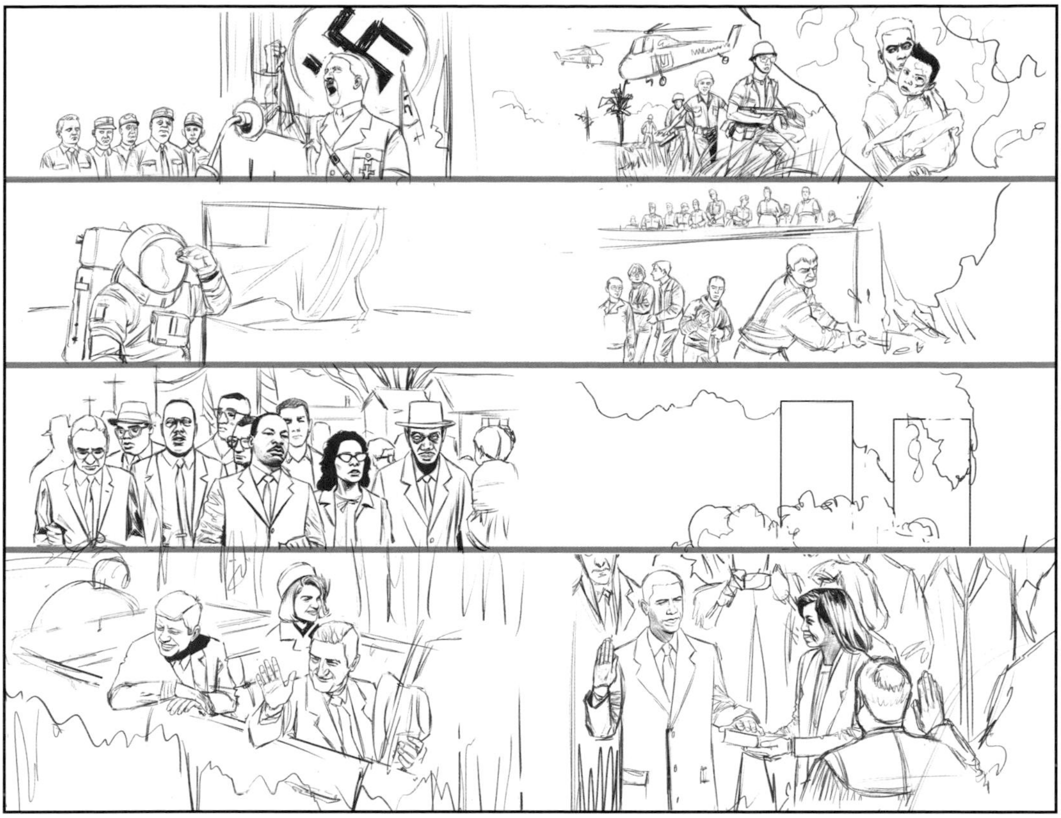

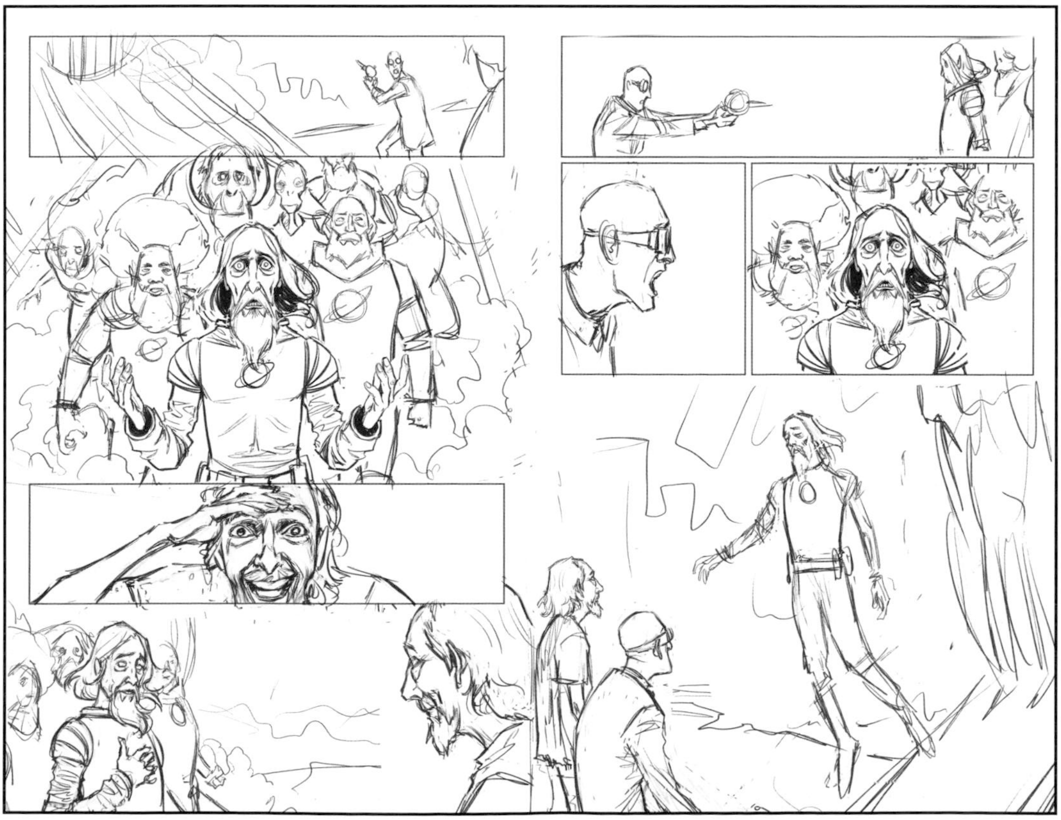

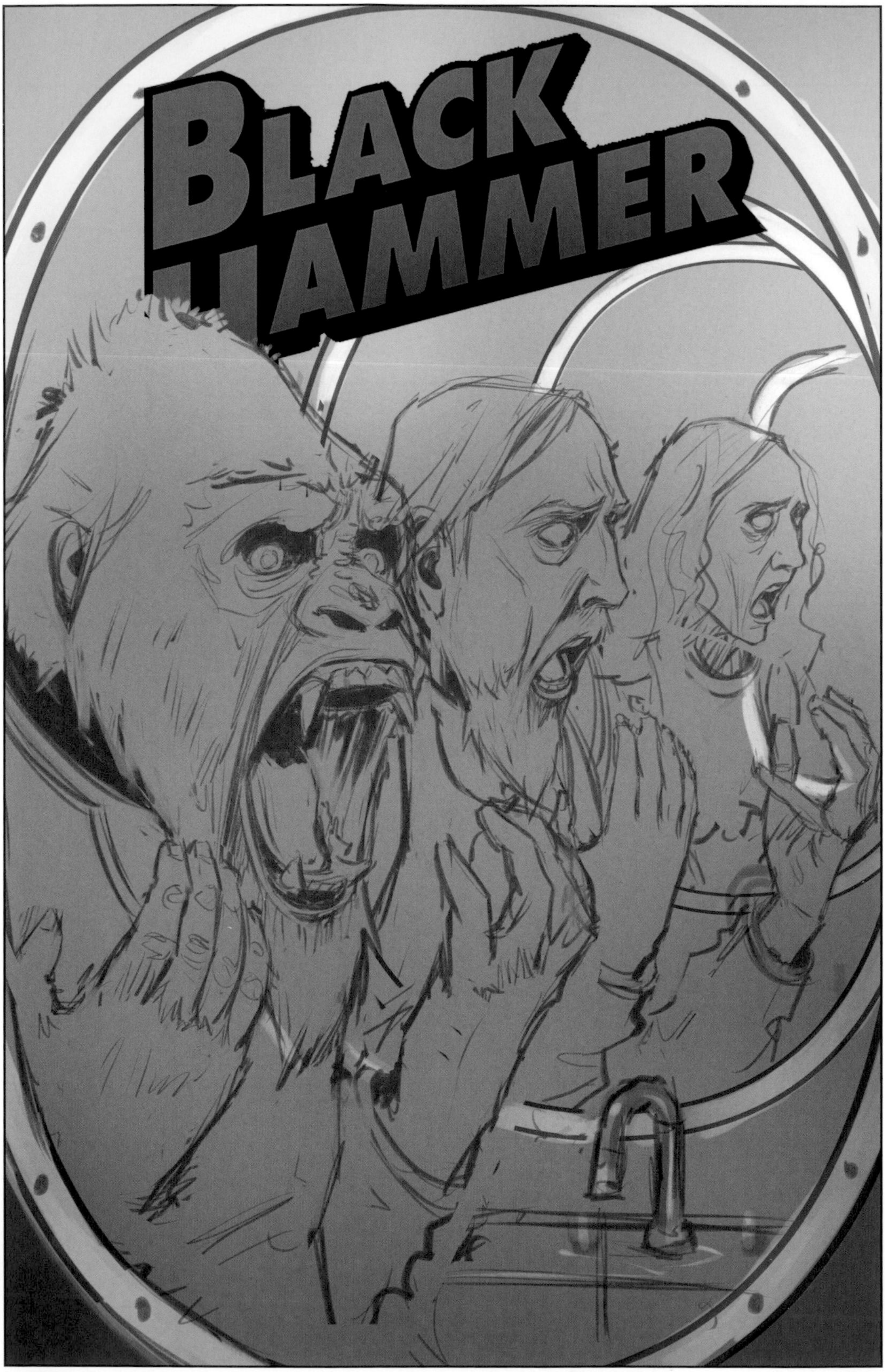
BLACK HAMMER

I had a blast drawing different multiverse versions of Weird, and I used his bathroom mirror to indicate endless possibilities.

BLACK HAMMER
RECOMMENDED READING ORDER

TRADES

1 **BLACK HAMMER VOL. 1: SECRET ORIGINS TPB**
Collects *Black Hammer* #1–#6
ISBN 978-1-61655-786-7 | $14.99

2 **BLACK HAMMER VOL. 2: THE EVENT TPB**
Collects *Black Hammer* #7–#11, #13
ISBN 978-1-50670-198-1 | $19.99

3 **SHERLOCK FRANKENSTEIN AND THE LEGION OF EVIL TPB**
Collects *Black Hammer* #12 and *Sherlock Frankenstein and the Legion of Evil* #1–#4
ISBN 978-1-50670-526-2 | $17.99

4 **DOCTOR ANDROMEDA AND THE KINGDOM OF LOST TOMORROWS TPB**
ISBN 978-1-50672-329-7 | $19.99

5 **BLACK HAMMER VOL. 3: AGE OF DOOM PART 1 TPB**
Collects *Black Hammer: Age of Doom* #1–#5
ISBN 978-1-50670-389-3 | $19.99

6 **BLACK HAMMER VOL. 4: AGE OF DOOM PART 2 TPB**
Collects *Black Hammer: Age of Doom* #6–#12
ISBN 978-1-50670-816-4 | $19.99

7 **THE QUANTUM AGE TPB**
Collects "The Quantum Age" from *Free Comic Book Day 2018* and *The Quantum Age* #1–#6
ISBN 978-1-50670-841-6 | $19.99

8 **BLACK HAMMER '45 TPB**
Collects *Black Hammer '45* #1–#4
ISBN 978-1-50670-850-8 | $17.99

9 **BLACK HAMMER: STREETS OF SPIRAL TPB**
Collects *Black Hammer: Giant-Sized Annual*, *Black Hammer: Cthu-Louise*, *The World of Black Hammer Encyclopedia*, and "Horrors to Come" from *Free Comic Book Day 2019*
ISBN 978-1-50670-941-3 | $19.99

10 **BLACK HAMMER/ JUSTICE LEAGUE HC**
Collects *Black Hammer/Justice League: Hammer of Justice!* #1–#5
ISBN 978-1-50671-099-0 | $19.99

11 **SKULLDIGGER AND SKELETON BOY TPB**
Collects *Skulldigger and Skeleton Boy* #1–#6
ISBN 978-1-50671-033-4 | $19.99

12 **COLONEL WEIRD: COSMAGOG TPB**
Collects *Colonel Weird: Cosmagog* #1–#4
ISBN 978-1-50671-516-2 | $19.99

13 **BARBALIEN: RED PLANET TPB**
Collects *Barbalien: Red Planet* #1–#5
ISBN 978-1-50671-580-3 | $19.99

14 **BLACK HAMMER VOLUME 5: REBORN PART ONE TPB**
Collects *Black Hammer Reborn* #1–#4
ISBN 978-1-50671-426-4 | $19.99

15 **BLACK HAMMER VOLUME 6: REBORN PART TWO TPB**
Collects *Black Hammer Reborn* #5–#8
ISBN 978-1-50671-515-5 | $19.99

16 **BLACK HAMMER VOLUME 7: REBORN PART THREE TPB**
Collects *Black Hammer Reborn* #9–#12
ISBN 978-1-50672-015-9 | $19.99

17 **THE UNBELIEVABLE UNTEENS TPB**
Collects *The Unbelievable Unteens* #1–#4
ISBN 978-1-50672-436-2 | $19.99

LIBRARY EDITIONS

1 **BLACK HAMMER LIBRARY EDITION VOL. 1**
Collects *Black Hammer* #1–#13 and *Black Hammer: Giant-Sized Annual*
ISBN 978-1-50671-073-0 | $49.99

2 **THE WORLD OF BLACK HAMMER LIBRARY EDITION VOL. 1**
Collects *Sherlock Frankenstein and the Legion of Evil* and *Doctor Andromeda and the Kingdom of Lost Tomorrows*
ISBN 978-1-50671-995-5 | $49.99

3 **BLACK HAMMER LIBRARY EDITION VOL. 2**
Collects *Black Hammer: Age of Doom* #1–#12, *Black Hammer: Cthu-Louise*, and *The World of Black Hammer Encyclopedia*
ISBN 978-1-50671-185-0 | $49.99

4 **THE WORLD OF BLACK HAMMER LIBRARY EDITION VOL. 2**
Collects *The Quantum Age* and *Black Hammer '45*
ISBN 978-1-50671-996-2 | $49.99

5 **THE WORLD OF BLACK HAMMER LIBRARY EDITION VOLUME 3 HC**
Collects *Colonel Weird: Cosmagog* and *Barbalien: Red Planet*
ISBN 978-1-50671-997-9 | $49.99

6 **THE WORLD OF BLACK HAMMER LIBRARY EDITION VOLUME 4 HC**
Collects *Skulldigger and Skeleton Boy* and *The Unbelievable Unteens*
ISBN 978-1-50672-601-4 | $49.99

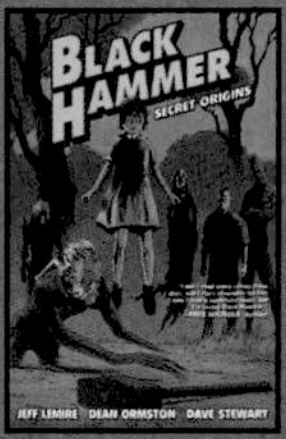
BLACK HAMMER
SECRET ORIGINS
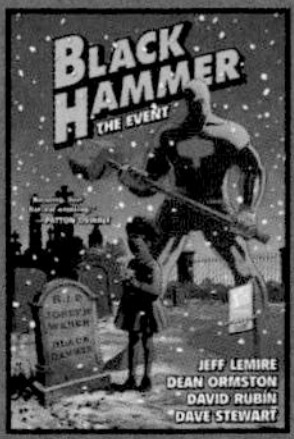
BLACK HAMMER
THE EVENT
JEFF LEMIRE
DEAN ORMSTON
DAVID RUBIN
DAVE STEWART
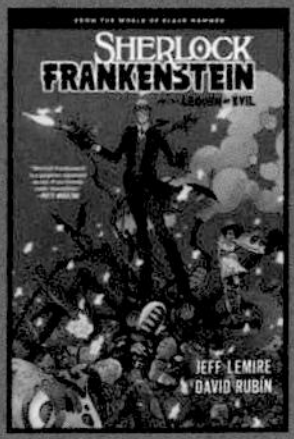
SHERLOCK FRANKENSTEIN
JEFF LEMIRE
DAVID RUBIN
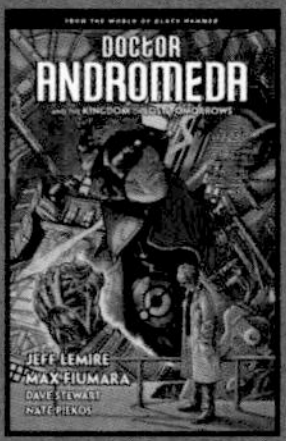
DOCTOR ANDROMEDA
JEFF LEMIRE
MAX FIUMARA
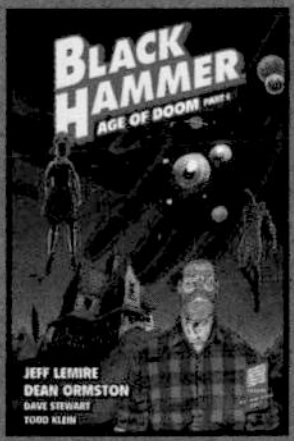
BLACK HAMMER
AGE OF DOOM
JEFF LEMIRE
DEAN ORMSTON
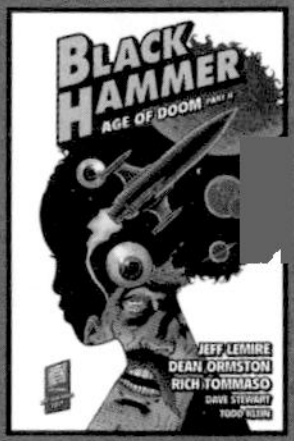
BLACK HAMMER
AGE OF DOOM
JEFF LEMIRE
DEAN ORMSTON
RICH TOMMASO
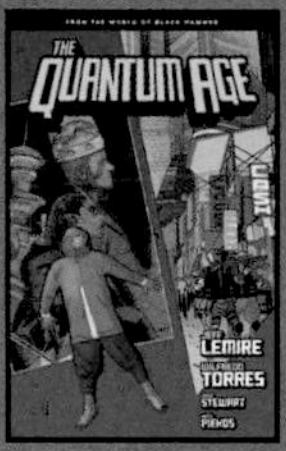
THE QUANTUM AGE
LEMIRE
TORRES
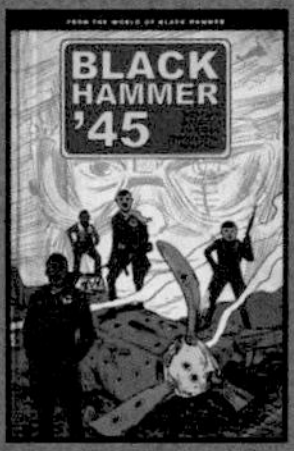
BLACK HAMMER
'45
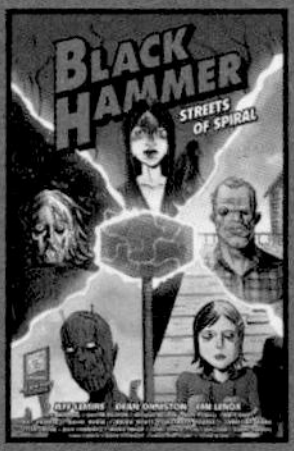
BLACK HAMMER
STREETS OF SPIRAL
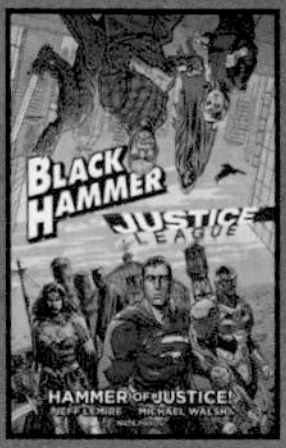
BLACK HAMMER
JUSTICE LEAGUE
HAMMER OF JUSTICE!
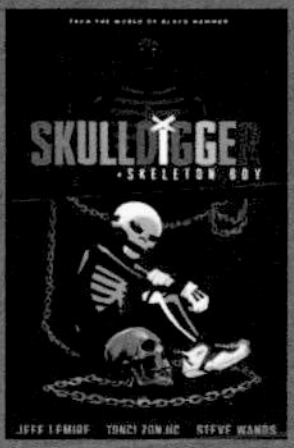
SKULLDIGGER
+ SKELETON BOY
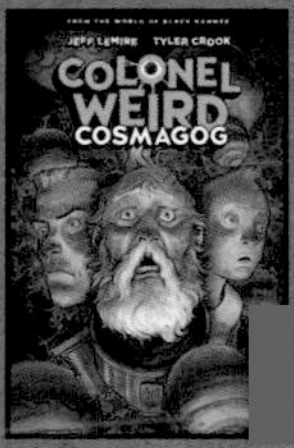
JEFF LEMIRE
TYLER CROOK
COLONEL WEIRD
COSMAGOG
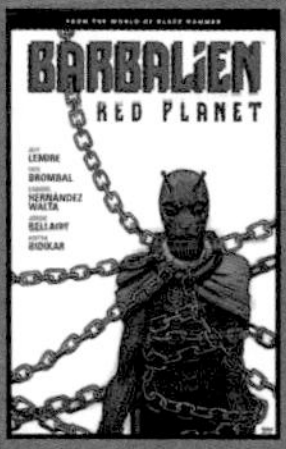
BARBALIEN
RED PLANET
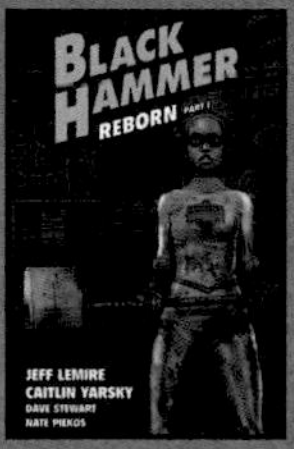
BLACK HAMMER
REBORN
JEFF LEMIRE
CAITLIN YARSKY
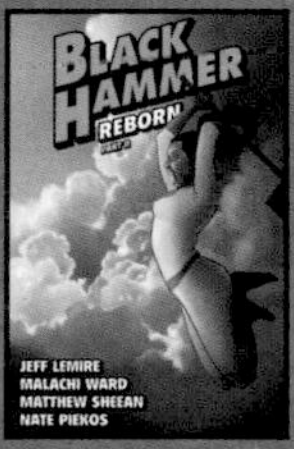
BLACK HAMMER
REBORN
JEFF LEMIRE
MALACHI WARD
MATTHEW SHEEAN
NATE PIEKOS
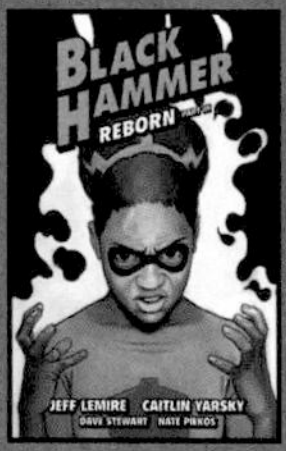
BLACK HAMMER
REBORN
JEFF LEMIRE
CAITLIN YARSKY
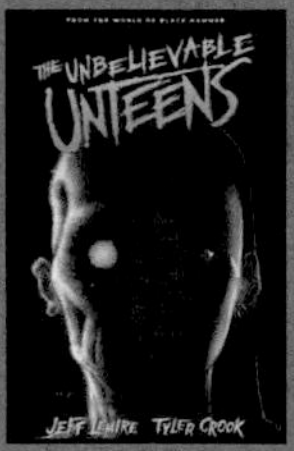
THE UNBELIEVABLE UNTEENS
JEFF LEMIRE
TYLER CROOK
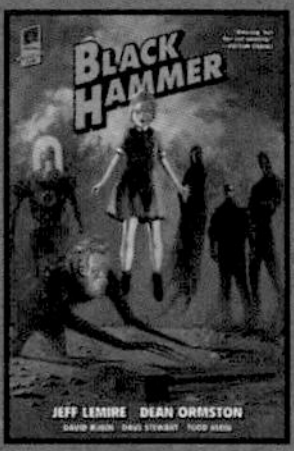
BLACK HAMMER
JEFF LEMIRE
DEAN ORMSTON
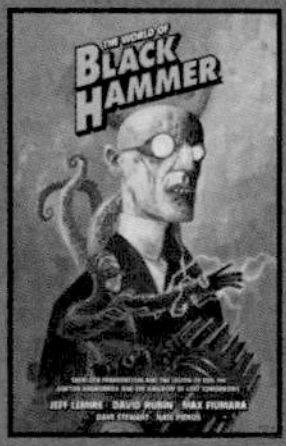
THE WORLD OF BLACK HAMMER
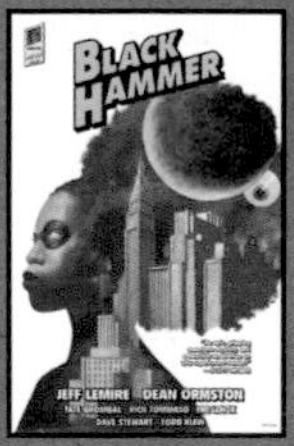
BLACK HAMMER
JEFF LEMIRE
DEAN ORMSTON
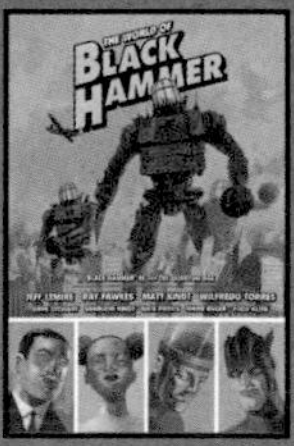
THE WORLD OF BLACK HAMMER
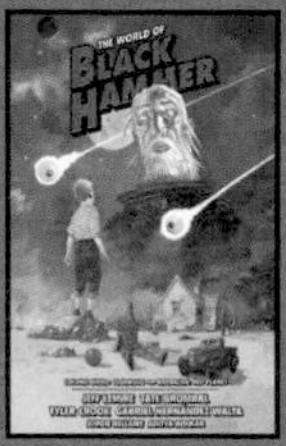
THE WORLD OF BLACK HAMMER
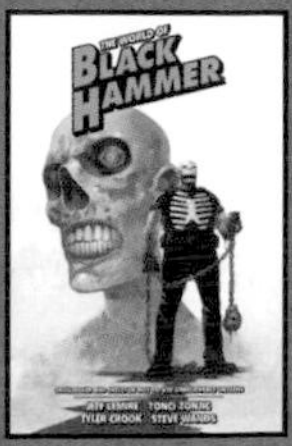
THE WORLD OF BLACK HAMMER

BLACK HAMMER

ONCE THEY WERE HEROES, but the age of heroes has long since passed. Banished from existence by a multiversal crisis, the old champions of Spiral City—Abraham Slam, Golden Gail, Colonel Weird, Madame Dragonfly, and Barbalien—now lead simple lives in an idyllic, timeless farming village from which there is no escape! And yet, the universe isn't done with them—it's time for one last grand adventure.

BLACK HAMMER
Written by Jeff Lemire • Art by Dean Ormston

LIBRARY EDITION VOLUME 1
978-1-50671-073-0 • $49.99

LIBRARY EDITION VOLUME 2
978-1-50671-185-0 • $49.99

THE WORLD OF BLACK HAMMER
LIBRARY EDITION VOLUME 1
978-1-50671-995-5 • $49.99

LIBRARY EDITION VOLUME 2
978-1-50671-996-2 • $49.99

VOLUME 1: SECRET ORIGINS
978-1-61655-786-7 • $14.99

VOLUME 2: THE EVENT
978-1-50670-198-1 • $19.99

VOLUME 3: AGE OF DOOM
PART ONE
978-1-50670-389-3 • $19.99

VOLUME 4: AGE OF DOOM
PART TWO
978-1-50670-816-4 • $19.99

VOLUME 5:
BLACK HAMMER REBORN
PART ONE
Art by Caitlin Yarsky
978-1-50671-426-4 • $19.99

VOLUME 6:
BLACK HAMMER REBORN
PART TWO
Written by Jeff Lemire
Art by Malachi Ward
and Matthew Sheean
978-1-50671-515-5 • $19.99

SHERLOCK FRANKENSTEIN & THE LEGION OF EVIL
Written by Jeff Lemire
Art by David Rubín
978-1-50670-526-2 • $17.99

DOCTOR ANDROMEDA & THE KINGDOM OF LOST TOMORROWS
Written by Jeff Lemire
Art by Max Fiumara
978-1-50672-329-7 • $19.99

THE UNBELIEVABLE UNTEENS: FROM THE WORLD OF BLACK HAMMER
VOLUME 1
Written by Jeff Lemire
Art by Tyler Crook, Tonci Zonjic, Ray Fawkes, and others
978-1-50672-436-2 • $19.99

THE QUANTUM AGE: FROM THE WORLD OF BLACK HAMMER
VOLUME 1
Written by Jeff Lemire
Art by Wilfredo Torres
978-1-50670-841-6 • $19.99

BLACK HAMMER '45: FROM THE WORLD OF BLACK HAMMER
Written by Jeff Lemire and Ray Fawkes
Art by Matt Kindt and Sharlene Kindt
978-1-50670-850-8 • $17.99

COLONEL WEIRD— COSMAGOG: FROM THE WORLD OF BLACK HAMMER
Written by Jeff Lemire
Art by Tyler Crook
978-1-50671-516-2 • $19.99

BLACK HAMMER: STREETS OF SPIRAL
Written by Jeff Lemire, Tate Brombal, and Ray Fawkes
Art by Dean Ormston, Matt Kindt, Tyler Crook, and others
978-1-50670-941-3 • $19.99

BLACK HAMMER/ JUSTICE LEAGUE: HAMMER OF JUSTICE!
Written by Jeff Lemire
Art by Michael Walsh
978-1-50671-099-0 • $29.99

BARBALIEN: RED PLANET
Written by Jeff Lemire and Tate Brombal
Art by Gabriel Hernández Walta and Jordie Bellaire
978-1-50671-580-3 • $19.99

SKULLDIGGER AND SKELETON BOY
Written by Jeff Lemire
Art by Tonci Zonjic
978-1-50671-033-4 • $19.99

BLACK HAMMER VISIONS
VOLUME 1
Written by Patton Oswalt, Geoff Johns, Chip Zdarsky, and Mariko Tamaki
Art by Johnnie Christmas, Scott Kollins, and Diego Olortegui
978-1-50672-326-6 • $24.99

VOLUME 2
Written by Kelly Thompson, Scott Snyder, Cecil Castelluci, and Cullen Bunn
Art by David Rubín, Matthew Sheean, Melissa Duffy, and others
978-1-50672-551-2 • $24.99

DARK HORSE BOOKS